LOCAL CAMPAIGN BEHAVIOUR IN CANADIAN ELECTIONS

The Contours of Centralization

Local Campaign Behaviour in Canadian Elections investigates the relationship between the local and national components of Canadian political parties. Jacob Robbins-Kanter emphasizes the significance of local campaigns – often overlooked by scholars, voters, and the media – and examines when and why these campaigns deviate from national directives during federal elections.

Grounded in original data, the book explores the intricate dynamics between local campaigns and central party headquarters during Canadian elections, highlighting their cooperation, clashes, and divergences. It reveals the prevalence of undisciplined local campaign behaviour and the underestimated agency of local actors. The book argues that local campaigns retain meaningful agency to make critical decisions, influence election outcomes, and articulate local interests.

Drawing on nearly 100 interviews, primary source documents, and data collected as an embedded researcher during the 2019 federal election, Robbins-Kanter delves into the practice of undisciplined local campaign behaviour, which often challenges or diverges from central party directives. *Local Campaign Behaviour in Canadian Elections* presents a nuanced portrayal of local actors, positioning them as neither entirely autonomous nor merely instruments of a central party apparatus.

JACOB ROBBINS-KANTER is an assistant professor in the Department of Politics and International Studies at Bishop's University.

Local Campaign Behaviour in Canadian Elections

The Contours of Centralization

JACOB ROBBINS-KANTER

UNIVERSITY OF TORONTO PRESS

Toronto Buffalo London

© University of Toronto Press 2025
Toronto Buffalo London
utppublishing.com
Printed in Canada

ISBN 978-1-4875-6476-6 (cloth)   ISBN 978-1-4875-6479-7 (EPUB)
ISBN 978-1-4875-6477-3 (paper)   ISBN 978-1-4875-6478-0 (PDF)

Library and Archives Canada Cataloguing in Publication

Title: Local campaign behaviour in Canadian elections : the contours of
    centralization / Jacob Robbins-Kanter.
Names: Robbins-Kanter, Jacob, author.
Description: Includes bibliographical references and index.
Identifiers: Canadiana (print) 2025019886X | Canadiana (ebook)
    20250198886 | ISBN 9781487564766 (hardcover) | ISBN 9781487564773
    (softcover) | ISBN 9781487564797 (EPUB) | ISBN 9781487564780 (PDF)
Subjects: LCSH: Canada. Parliament – Elections, 2019. | LCSH: Local
    elections – Canada. | LCSH: Political campaigns – Canada. |
    LCSH: Campaign management – Canada. | LCSH: Political parties – Canada.
Classification: LCC JL193 .R57 2025 | DDC 324.971 – dc23

Cover design: Sebastian Frye

We wish to acknowledge the land on which the University of Toronto Press
operates. This land is the traditional territory of the Wendat, the Anishnaabeg,
the Haudenosaunee, the Métis, and the Mississaugas of the Credit First Nation.

This book has been published with the help of a grant from the Federation
for the Humanities and Social Sciences, through the Awards to Scholarly
Publications Program, using funds provided by the Social Sciences and
Humanities Research Council of Canada.

University of Toronto Press acknowledges the financial support of the
Government of Canada, the Canada Council for the Arts, and the Ontario Arts
Council, an agency of the Government of Ontario, for its publishing activities.

Canada Council   Conseil des Arts
for the Arts   du Canada

ONTARIO ARTS COUNCIL
CONSEIL DES ARTS DE L'ONTARIO
an Ontario government agency
un organisme du gouvernement de l'Ontario

Funded by the   Financé par le
Government   gouvernement
of Canada   du Canada

Canadä

MIX
Paper | Supporting
responsible forestry
FSC
www.fsc.org   FSC® C103423

Contents

Figures and Tables

Figures

Tables

Acknowledgments

This book would not have been possible without the many contributions of helpful and generous research participants. I cannot adequately thank the members of Parliament, political candidates, local activists, party strategists, and others who contributed substantial time and expertise. Along these lines, the book is dedicated to those who, despite the cynicism, adverse consequences, and often thankless experience, continue to step forward and run for office.

I would also like to thank my excellent academic mentors, Elizabeth Goodyear-Grant and Jonathan Rose, who were the best possible supervisors at Queen's. Among amazingly supportive colleagues and friends who helped make this research possible over the years, I must single out Dan Troup, Dan Westlake, Jean-François Daoust, Ben Lerer, Ben Hanff, Alexander Parsilidis, Amy Zhang, Ali Bhagat, Bryn Jones-Square, and Patricia Mockler. There's no way I would have completed this project without Amy Forsythe, whose love and support kept me sane during the height of the pandemic and beyond. I'm so glad we had Silver's cabin on Fourteen Mile Lake, even with the second-degree burns.

Thanks are also due to Raphaël Lauret and Sarah Despatie for excellent research assistance. Data collection and analysis for the project were generously funded by the Social Sciences and Humanities Research Council of Canada and by Queen's University. Likewise, I have much gratitude to University of Toronto Press for their invaluable assistance in the publication process and especially to Daniel Quinlan for his guidance and support throughout the various stages of this project.

Lastly, I must thank my parents, Karen and Michael, for modelling humility, generosity, compassion, and curiosity about the world, all of which provide inspiration. Your unconditional love, patience, and gentle encouragement are reminders of Pearl, Dave, Edie, and Ben. We miss them very much and will continue to remember their lives well lived.

LOCAL CAMPAIGN BEHAVIOUR IN CANADIAN ELECTIONS

Chapter 1

Introduction

On 21 October 2019, the Liberal Party of Canada won a narrow re-election victory. The following day, in a Quebec storefront serving as a local campaign office, large cardboard boxes of campaign flyers sat unopened. The flyers were sent from and paid for by party headquarters, but the local candidate refused to distribute them because they disliked their content and appearance. While largely inconsequential on its own, this waste of ink and paper demonstrates an underlying tension that is common within Canadian parties during an election campaign.

For the major parties, elections require substantial cooperation between local campaigns and central party headquarters. We might assume that this cooperation is built into the campaign apparatus. Local and national party officials are members of the same partisan team and hold shared political values, as well as sharing the overriding goal of winning an election. Cooperation may also be ensured by implicit or explicit threats. Indeed, parties have a reputation for strictly enforcing discipline and punishing local actors who defy their instructions. But in reality, ideas of obedient local campaigns are overly simplistic. There are complex dynamics of cooperation and conflict that play out within parties, amid the various actors, ideas, interests, and moving parts of a campaign machine. Understanding this reality begins with a recognition that many scholars, journalists, and citizens tend to overlook local campaigns, often barely considering them at all.

This book is about the behaviour of local campaign actors within the larger campaign ecosystem. Canada's federal parties have been described as stratarchical or multi-tiered organizations where authority is shared between the national and local levels. During elections, the central party and local organizations depend upon each other to execute a successful campaign. To be sure, they are not coequals, as the central party seeks to impose discipline on local campaigns, of which there are currently 338 per major party, in electoral districts spread across Canada. In the central party's view, discipline is essential for implementing an effective campaign strategy, as parties aim to emphasize their perceived electoral strengths and desired messages. As such, party headquarters must support and manage local campaigns, in addition to directing the national campaign and media strategy. For their part, local candidates are simultaneously pressured to conform with their political parties and respond to local conditions. In certain cases, they may even deviate from the central party in order to pursue their own interests (Carty and Eagles 2005, 2; Kam 2009, 154; Koop 2011, 9–10; Sayers 1999, 146; Stephenson et al. 2019, 71; Yates 2022, 296). While the central party may prefer to influence constituency campaigns as much as possible, they are ultimately controlled by nearly seven hundred individual candidates and campaign managers. Even when local political conditions are favourable to central party dictums and the national message, constituency campaigns may have distinct preferences for how to conduct their affairs.

Along these lines, this book seeks to better understand local-national party relations and local campaign discipline. It asks why and to what extent constituency campaigns behave in a disciplined manner during recent Canadian elections. Parties have increasingly centralized decision-making authority, yet there is limited and sometimes contradictory understanding of how this is reflected during election campaigns. Similarly, we still know relatively little about how local political actors think, behave, and contribute to democratic life (Cross 2016, 603; Marland and Giasson 2022). This book follows those who affirm the importance of constituency-level actors in understanding party strategy, campaign dynamics, representational outcomes, and the performance of democratic institutions (e.g., Carty and Eagles 2005; Cross 2016, 2018; Koop 2011). Those reasserting the importance of local actors do so at a time when the centralization of power around party leaders, a longstanding concern for observers of Canadian politics, has reached concerning heights and raised questions about the quality of Canadian democracy.

The primary research question of this book is the following: to what extent and why do constituency campaigns behave in a disciplined manner during Canadian federal elections? Given the current environment of centralized campaigning, message discipline, and digital technologies, this investigation consists of three sub-questions:

1) To what extent do local campaigns engage in undisciplined behaviour that contravenes central party preferences?
2) Why do some local campaigns behave in an undisciplined manner?
3) How is party cohesion maintained during a federal campaign period?

To answer these questions, this book draws principally from four original data sources:

1) Interviews with former (successful and unsuccessful) candidates for the Conservative, Liberal, and New Democratic parties (n=87)
2) Interviews with senior party strategists for the Conservative, Liberal, and New Democratic parties (n=8)
3) Publicly available party documents and newly obtained internal party documents
4) Field observation of ten constituency campaigns during the 2019 federal election

It can be challenging to study the internal practices of political parties, due to their understandable reluctance to disclose politically sensitive information. Nonetheless, the investigation of multiple data sources permits the triangulation of information to refine its inferential validity (Fielding 2012). For example, constituency campaign observation facilitates the validation of information obtained during interviews. Altogether, this evidence sheds light on the nature of local-national party relations and local campaign behaviour, as our understanding of these topics largely lacks firsthand data.

In brief, four major findings emerge from these data. First, undisciplined constituency campaign behaviour is greater than anticipated by existing research. This finding is derived from identifying indicators of undisciplined behaviour, the patterns of which are classified into a typology of constituency campaigns based on their degree of discipline. Second, insubordination, innovation, and incompetence are the primary forms of undisciplined behaviour by constituency campaigns. Third, the central party is constrained in its ability to enforce discipline during a campaign period, primarily due to limitations with digital technologies and logistical realities of campaigning across a vast country with finite resources. Fourth, constituency campaigns behave in a disciplined manner primarily because they practice self-discipline, rather than due to party authority or coercion. This leads to a further question of why local campaigns practice self-discipline. To answer this, the book draws from organizational behaviour theory to identify behavioural logics that serve as mechanisms underlying constituency campaign self-discipline.

Taken together, these findings suggest that party cohesion depends upon local compliance and constituency campaign decision-making. Despite increased campaign centralization, there are limits to what the central office can manage or accomplish during a dynamic and demanding election period. Nonetheless, constituency campaigns often use their agency and discretion to act in accordance with central party preferences.

Party Organization

Katz and Mair (1993) contend that political parties in Western democracies can be viewed as composed of distinct elements (faces) rather than as unitary actors. The authors emphasize the stratarchical nature of modern parties, meaning authority is distributed across various levels or organizations. They distinguish between the party in public office, the party on the ground, and the party central office.[1] Mair (1994) further observes a trend within major parties towards mutual autonomy between the three faces.

In the Canadian context, Carty's influential analogy (2002, 2004) contends that Canada's federal parties have developed a franchise-style organizational structure. As with a corporate franchise model, parties benefit from a standardized product, created at their central headquarters, along with specialized delivery of the product within local franchises (Carty 2002, 731). Carty outlines the division of labour during an election campaign, as parties maintain organizational coherence with pan-national campaign messages and themes, an electoral platform, and an overarching brand.[2] For their part, constituency-level franchises build a volunteer base, nominate candidates, and manage the ground campaign (Carty and Cross 2006). Carty (2002, 733) contends that this arrangement is underpinned by a core bargain, where franchises agree to trade "national discipline for local autonomy." In other words, they support the party's policies and strategic objectives determined by the centre in exchange for autonomy over their local functions, namely candidate selection and authority over the ground campaign.

Carty's model provides a theoretical lens through which to analyse the interaction of local and national party organizations. This book builds on Carty's work by examining how this core franchise bargain is maintained and enforced, in terms of campaign discipline, as well as the extent to which such a bargain persists in a contemporary era of intensified message discipline and centralization of party authority. In examining constituency campaign discipline and local-national party relations, the book interrogates the franchise model with the use of original data, including evidence from an active campaign setting. This allows an assessment, decades after the original work, of whether the power-sharing dynamic comprised by Carty's franchise bargain accurately explains recent campaigns or if it has been replaced by something else altogether.

Shared authority rather than hierarchy was an initial assumption regarding Canadian party organization (Carty 2002; 2004; 2015, 63; Carty and Cross 2006). But recent technological and organizational changes suggest greater centralization and a diminished local role. In particular, top-down message discipline enabled by instantaneous digital communications (Marland, Giasson, and Small 2014) and electronic data collection (Belfry Munroe and Munroe 2018) raise questions about the role, abilities, and importance of local actors.

Political marketing, or the use of marketing techniques and intelligence by political parties (Lees-Marshment 2014),[3] is a driving force behind campaign centralization. Party headquarters now routinely gathers sophisticated data on voter preferences and uses this information in the development of their offerings to voters. The central party can also sort citizens into precise audience segments and target them with specific messages (Marland and Giasson 2017). These practices require minimal local participation. Moreover, the fact that extensive market research and other data now inform party messages makes parties prone to demand message cohesion (Marland, Giasson, and Esselment 2017, 11). Increased central party control of local finances (Coletto, Jansen, and Young 2011; Currie-Wood 2020) and the leader-centric nature of campaigns (Bittner 2011; Cross, Katz, and Pruysers 2018) may also generate centralization. And the increased ability to bypass local actors certainly results in greater centralization of decision-making authority. Altogether, in Flanagan's (2014, 107) assessment, "Canadian campaigns remain highly disciplined and controlled from the centre."

The Local Context

Despite centralization, local actors remain relevant to party headquarters, which aspires to execute its preferred strategy with maximum local cooperation and assistance. Research shows that parties have relied on local actors to remain attuned to regional and local political dynamics and tailor messages based on their environment (Carty 2002; Cross 2004). Similarly, local campaigns and Electoral District Associations (EDAs) constitute a network of "brand ambassadors" to disseminate key messages across the country (Marland and Wagner 2020). They are also helpful in raising money and attracting regional or local media coverage. And local candidates with strong track records or name recognition can provide a credibility boost to parties (Coletto 2010). That said, from the headquarters' perspective, local interventions must be centrally approved, lest they undermine the national campaign strategy, squander media attention, and diminish political credibility (Marland 2020, 38). For these reasons, local actors remain important components of the campaign machine, while also presumably experiencing heightened central party control.

Crucially, constituency campaigns may not view their objectives and aspirations in the same manner as each other or the central office. Given the internal diversity in most large organizations, including Canada's big-tent political parties (Carty 2015, 63; Clarkson 2014), it would be surprising if they did. Constituency campaigns' perceptions of their roles and responsibilities, and their concrete attitudes and behaviours, are shaped by the nature of campaign discipline. From the local view, elections entail competing pressures for constituency campaigns and candidates. In essence, their parties demand cohesion, discipline, and deference, while their more immediate environment presents a variety of local and particularistic political incentives, alongside their personal strategic preferences. The single-member-plurality (SMP) electoral system ensures that the local electoral district is the relevant political unit and the salience of regional and ethnocultural differences (e.g., Gidengil et al. 2012; Henderson 2004;) incentivizes a locally tailored campaign strategy. Therefore, constituency campaigns may have motivations to resist the imposition of central party tactics and practices (Carty and Eagles 2005; Sayers 1999; Stephenson et al. 2019). They may also aim to preserve local control in resistance to a remote party headquarters. For these reasons, local campaigns may be reluctant to acquiesce to demands for discipline.

Most research on party discipline in Canada and elsewhere has focused on the behaviour of elected politicians rather than local candidates, campaign managers, or other actors (e.g., Godbout 2020; Kam 2009, 2014; Malloy 2003; Morden 2020; Sieberer 2006).[4] To borrow Katz and Mair's (1993) terminology, we have a strong understanding of party discipline when it involves the party in public office, but the party on the ground presents an additional challenge. Like elected legislators, local candidates and their constituency campaigns are dually accountable to their parties and to local electorates. But the disciplinary pressures faced by elected officials do not necessarily extend to local candidates and campaign actors. For example, Rathgeber (2014) argues that members of Parliament primarily behave in a disciplined manner for career advancement, as they seek to attain prominent portfolios in the House of Commons. Local candidates and their staff, many of whom are volunteers, do not face comparable career pressures. And unlike in a party caucus setting, a campaign environment is fleeting and dynamic. It is comparatively difficult for party staff to keep track of local actors and the various unwieldy components of a campaign operation. Related to this, media scrutiny and visibility of local candidates is typically low in most federal constituencies (Carty and Eagles 2005, Chapter 9).

In sum, since federal campaigns are fundamentally an aggregation of 338 local races, they require significant cohesion and cooperation between national parties and local branches. Nonetheless, local campaigns may prefer to act independently and sometimes disregard central party procedures. Despite apparent centralization, it is unwise to assume they are subservient or empty vessels of the central party. As Carty (2015, 63) suggests,

> [i]t is easy to think of political parties as essentially monolithic and hierarchical organizations ruthlessly dedicated to the pursuit of certain common goals. In fact, they are typically rather sloppy, complex organizations riven internally by a mix of contending ideas, interests, and ambitions, and held together by an unending series of internal compromises.

Carty evokes Katz (2002, 92), who declared that "in analysing the internal dynamics of party politics, it is necessary to take into account patterns of cooperation and competition between levels of the party (local v regional v national) as well as between faces."

Using Carty's (2002, 2004) frameworks to anchor its investigations, this book confronts the question of how dominant the central party has become, relative to constituency campaigns, given the potentially diminished role of the latter. It explores the extent of local compliance with party preferences, assessing the balance of powers within a franchise system. For example, what happens when the central campaign prefers one message and local campaigns prefer another? To what extent do local actors actually choose which messages to convey (Stephenson et al. 2019, 62)? By studying ground-level actors and events in recent federal campaigns, we can better appreciate how national directives interact with local realities and what this means for parties, elections, and representation.

Book Overview

The next chapter, Chapter 2, explains the book's conceptual focus on constituency activity in an era of campaign centralization and specifies the ways in which local-national party relations are a defining feature of Canadian elections. The chapter begins with definitional clarifications before assessing existing research that implies local campaigns are a relatively unimportant area of study. Chapter 2 challenges these assertions and highlights key reasons to study local campaigns. The chapter also traces the evolution of the franchise model since it was first outlined in 2002 and highlights conflicting scholarly perspectives on the model. It subsequently identifies potential implications of the tensions constituency campaigns face when they attempt to balance party pressures and local political incentives. Lastly, it introduces recent research on the personalization of local campaigns and argues this does not yet provide an adequate sense of local campaign autonomy.

Chapter 3 introduces the book's methods and data sources. Following this, it turns to addressing the main research questions surrounding campaign discipline by examining how closely constituency campaigns adhere to central party norms and preferences. The chapter identifies central office expectations for local campaigns primarily through analyses of party documents and interviews with party strategists and assesses discipline in terms of how closely constituency campaigns adhere to these preferences. The chapter establishes what undisciplined behaviour is, identifies what indicators can be used to detect it, and constructs a typology of campaigns based on degree of discipline. Thirteen per cent of constituency campaigns in the sample engage in openly defiant undisciplined behaviour, while 45 per cent engage in milder forms. The chapter further contends that undisciplined behaviour stems from innovation, insubordination, and incompetence within local campaigns.

Chapter 4 builds on these findings through in-depth examination of key responsibilities for constituency campaigns: voter canvassing and the development of campaign literature. This chapter seeks to demonstrate that these are two of the most politically important and resource-consuming responsibilities for local campaigns. The chapter establishes central party preferences for canvassing and the development of campaign literature and examines how closely constituency campaigns adhere to them. In examining the nature and prevalence of localized political branding, a sample of ninety-six pieces of campaign literature are coded based on their consistency with central party templates. The chapter's findings broadly demonstrate the central party's limitations in preventing undisciplined constituency campaign behaviour, as well as different areas of local resistance and acquiescence in the local implementation of national directives. In some cases, perceived interference with local autonomy and individuality produces a defiant response, such as refusing to distribute campaign leaflets provided by the central party. The chapter also identifies potential benefits stemming from undisciplined behaviour. For example, some constituency campaigns reach a more diverse group of electors because they refuse to follow canvassing directives that ask them to avoid citizens who are less likely to vote. Indeed, parties generally prefer canvassing to consist of brief data-focused interactions with likely supporters.

Chapter 5 builds on evidence from prior chapters of central party difficulties in knowing about and managing local campaign behaviour across 338 constituencies. In asking why the central party may fail to enforce campaign discipline, the chapter turns to intra-party communications channels as a critical factor. These channels are built to make central party directives widely known, but they show mixed effectiveness in achieving this. Local campaigns in 2015 and 2019 were unevenly incorporated within intra-party communications channels. Some remained insular from the central campaign despite potentially connecting with other local campaigns. Digital campaign tools cannot overcome communications barriers when logistical and resource constraints leave few options for the centre to deal with local actors who intentionally or unintentionally ignore them. The chapter focuses on the frequency and closeness of interactions between constituency campaigns and their parties, whether these interactions occur through formal or informal channels, and the role and authority of regional party offices. This provides an overall assessment of the effectiveness of internal communications in advancing party norms and expectations.

Chapter 6 turns to theorizing the sources of constituency campaign discipline. Although previous chapters identify and explain undisciplined campaign behaviour, most local campaigns still act in accordance with party preferences. This chapter focuses on explaining the behaviour of local actors that *do* act in a disciplined manner. The chapter first critiques the view that discipline is a result of central party authority and coercion. This chapter argues that self-discipline is a more compelling explanation for campaign cohesion than party coercion. Overall, constituency campaigns are less disciplined than anticipated, and when they are disciplined, it is not for the reasons we might expect. The chapter seeks to determine the balance of party-centered factors and local agency in explaining the mechanisms of local campaign self-discipline. It offers four different explanations for their self-discipline, derived from scholarly research on decision-making within large institutions, as well as the book's original data sources. Although party structures are important influences in explaining local campaign behaviour, they operate in nuanced ways that can be difficult to outwardly detect. Notably, some campaigns internalize party norms and self-police their behaviour according to a logic of appropriateness. Despite this, the central office's pervasive presence does not preclude the exercise of meaningful local agency. Local campaign behaviour continues to be determined by local actors, and their decision-making can only be explained in terms of their agency. Finally, Chapter 7 summarizes the book's findings and gathers broader conclusions for our understanding of Canadian electoral politics, party organization, and grassroots democracy.

Chapter 2

Local-National Party Relations

Canada's single-member-plurality electoral system awards legislative seats based on constituency-level elections. Accordingly, each federal election is truly a series of simultaneous local contests that demand collaboration between parties' national headquarters and constituency campaigns. This relationship may be analysed from two different viewpoints. First, constituency campaigns seek to accommodate local preferences under the disciplinary oversight of a central party. Second, from the central party's perspective, they must maintain campaign cohesion despite substantial organizational diversity. Both perspectives underlie the motivations and design of this research. They present a difference in emphasis rather than in fundamental significance. Each viewpoint is relevant in asking to what extent and why do constituency campaigns behave in a disciplined manner during federal elections.

This chapter argues that existing research implies conflicting expectations for party discipline and the status of constituency campaigns. Some research on federal campaign dynamics emphasizes strong party discipline enforced by a dominant central party, while other work highlights local autonomy and campaign diversity. The evidence thus far presents a gap that can be addressed through deeper scrutiny of local campaign behaviour and national-local party relations more generally.

This chapter has four main ambitions. First, it will synthesize existing research on local campaign behaviour and defend an empirical focus on local campaigns by challenging assertions that they are politically insignificant. Second, the chapter will trace the evolution of Carty's franchise model and assess its utility as a framework for understanding local-national party relations. Recent evidence may lead us to question whether the franchise model has lost relevance due to heightened centralization in federal party organizations. Third, the chapter will argue that existing research on intra-party campaign dynamics reveals ambiguous expectations for campaign cohesion and discipline. Lastly, the chapter identifies local campaign discipline as a means of assessing centralization and intra-party relations more broadly.

Definitional Parameters

Constituency Campaigns versus Constituency Associations

Before addressing the function of constituency campaigns, it is important to define them. Constituency campaigns are one component of local party organizations. As Koop (2011, 9) explains, they can be distinguished from the broader Electoral District Association (EDA), also known as a constituency or riding association. This refers to the organizational structure that exists in each constituency to fulfil local party functions such as selecting candidates, recruiting volunteers, and raising money. EDAs are composed of local party members and are directed by an executive committee (Sayers 1999).[1] Their membership size and resources vary considerably (Carty 2002). For their part, constituency campaigns are formed during the lead-up to an election (Carty and Eagles 2005). They feature a distinct organizational structure with a campaign manager, official agent, and so forth.[2] Constituency campaigns disband after an election, with staff dispersing to various party positions and non-political jobs. The EDA remains in place to conduct the affairs of maintaining a local party base, albeit with diminished intensity.

A substantial body of research (e.g., Cross and Pruysers 2019; Cross and Young 2013; Farney and Koop 2018; Koop and Bittner 2011; Pruysers and Cross 2016) has examined the work of EDAs, especially as it pertains to candidate nominations. For its part, this book focuses on the campaign period and the activities of constituency campaigns. Along these lines, constituency campaigns must be understood in terms of their position in a broader partisan organization (Belfry Munroe and Munroe 2018, 136). As Carty (2002, 730; 2004, 10) argues, their relationship to the central party is one of mutual interdependence. Constituency campaigns interact continuously with party headquarters through campaign training, fundraising, strategy, voter contact, event planning, and sending supporters to the polls on election day.

Major Functions of Constituency Campaigns

Research on constituency campaigns differentiates between their electoral and representational functions.[3] The overriding goal for constituency campaigns is to maximize their candidate's vote share. To do this, they engage in a variety of communications activities, such as voter canvassing, creating advertisements, erecting signs, distributing leaflets, and participating in public events.

As Carty and Eagles (2005) explain, constituency campaigns perform these functions with varying levels of resources and organizational strength. Some are intense sites of partisan competition while others are scarcely active. In another sense, these campaigns are constituent elements of the overall campaign and help represent the face of the party on the ground (Carty and Cross 2006; Katz and Mair 1993).

Constituency campaigns also serve a democratic and representational purpose by nominating candidates and therefore providing a supply of potential legislators (e.g., Pruysers and Blais 2018). They also provide a training ground for party activists, including those who advance to organizational leadership positions or seek elected office themselves (Docherty 2005; Pow 2018, 636). In addition, organizationally robust local campaigns confer legitimacy upon parties as national entities, when they maintain a competitive presence across the country (Bakvis and Tanguay 2020). Visibility and credibility across various regions may also provide indirect electoral benefits to parties.

Do Local Campaigns Matter?

Unfortunately, we lack understanding of what local campaigns actually do, as well as the nuances of their behaviour. This stems in part from scholarly, media, and public biases that view local campaigns as unimportant to Canadian politics. Indeed, there are two commonly offered and related reasons why local campaigns are labelled as unimportant by some scholars (and by implication, not worthy of study). First, they have minimal influence on vote choice, as most citizens cast their ballot based on party labels and leaders. Second, voters may be relatively unaware of constituency candidates and campaigns, compared to the more prominent national campaign. There is also a third aspect or critique that is implicitly raised by recent scholarship on the centralization of campaign authority. Some suggest that local campaigns lack meaningful autonomy and have become instruments of the central party. This is particularly relevant for the study of campaign centralization and the organizational status of constituency campaigns. This chapter contends that these critiques can be appreciated without dismissing the study of local campaigns.

Scholars have previously suggested that local campaigns are relatively unimportant to election outcomes. Indeed, evidence shows that most voters cast their ballots based on their preferred party or leader, rather than local candidates. Research based on Canada Election Study (CES) data tends to find that local candidates are a decisive electoral consideration for approximately 5 per cent of voters. For example, Blais et al.'s (2003) work with 2000 CES data finds that roughly 5 per cent of voters changed their vote from the party they would have otherwise supported based on the local candidate. Despite this modest number, Blais et al. suggest that "their impact was certainly not negligible" (663). This is because 5 per cent can be sufficient to change the local outcome in a close race. Sevi, Mendoza, and Blais (2022) subsequently extend Blais et al.'s analysis with CES data spanning from 2000 to 2008 and similarly find that local candidates are decisive for roughly 5 per cent of voters. These seemingly small changes in local vote totals can have major effects on party seat counts, and therefore on the national election result (Coletto 2010, 191; Koop 2011, 9).

Similarly, drawing from Local Parliament Project survey data (n= 20,115), Stevens et al. (2019) find that only 4 per cent of voters in the 2015 federal election made their selection based on the local candidate. Again, this impact is magnified when it comes to the election result, as it changed the outcome in roughly 10 per cent of ridings. The authors demonstrate that one out of ten voters preferred a candidate from a party other than their preferred party and roughly 40 per cent of these voters chose the candidate over the party.

The limitations of survey data also bear noting. It may be difficult to accurately assess the factors that inform individual vote choice based on large-scale survey responses. Existing research provides ample evidence of gaps between survey responses and real-world behaviours (e.g., Ansolabehere and Hersh 2017; Krosnick 1999; Loosveldt and Storms 2008; Stockemer and Sundstrom 2023; Warburton and Warburton 2004; Westwood et al. 2022).[4] This is because respondents may be torn between different response options, misunderstand questions, overestimate or underestimate the effects of various factors on their behaviour, or provide what they see as socially desirable responses.

Relying instead on an experimental research design, Roy and Alcantara (2015) ask online research participants to choose between fictitious local candidates of varying quality. The results suggest that a strong local candidate can boost vote shares by an average of 10 per cent. Roy and Alcantara refine these findings by specifying individual-level factors which mediate the impact of candidate quality. Those with greater political awareness and those with weaker partisan ties are more susceptible to local candidate effects.[5]

Local candidates may have a wider-reaching impact on vote shares than is typically captured by large-scale survey data. Since elections are typically won by the party with the most seats, target ridings occupy substantial party attention (Flanagan 2010). As mentioned above, even marginal candidate effects can be sufficient to change riding-level outcomes. High-profile candidates, who are able to shift higher percentages of the vote, are vigorously courted by federal parties (Carty and Eagles 2005). Such candidates can also provide a credibility boost to their parties. For example, the NDP's initial recruitment of Thomas Mulcair, a prominent former Quebec Liberal Party cabinet minister, was seen to lift the electoral fortunes of the party's Quebec-based candidates (Castonguay 2011).

Indeed, local candidates can also indirectly affect party performance (Coletto 2010, 20). These indirect effects include their ability to raise money and recruit volunteers (23). Along these lines, Milligan and Rekkas (2008) investigate the effects of local campaign spending and find that higher spending limits tend to shut out smaller parties and significantly increase victory margins for the winning candidate in Canadian federal elections. Incumbency constitutes a further advantage, as Kendall and Rekkas (2012) find that incumbents in Canadian elections are roughly 10 per cent more likely to be (re-)elected. Similarly, comparative research (Tavits 2009) has shown that candidates' prior local-level political experience tends to boost their vote shares. Moreover, EDA resources and organizational capacities may help to explain electoral outcomes. In this regard, Cross (2016) argues that EDA vitality and local campaign resources were important and understated components of the Liberal Party's convincing victory in the 2015 federal election.[6] Additionally, local issues are known to affect party performance. As Cutler (2002, 371) demonstrates, local economic conditions affect vote choice, regardless of voters' personal finances and political knowledge. For these reasons, local campaigns should not be considered insignificant to electoral outcomes.

Low public awareness of constituency campaigns constitutes another reason for their apparent insignificance. One of the earliest systematic studies of Canadian constituency campaigns was conducted by Bell and Fletcher (1991). The authors contend that local campaigns approximate "miniature replicas of the national race" (185). In this view, constituency campaigns lack distinguishing characteristics and pass without attention as voters follow the national campaign. Indeed, despite the local context and multilevel nature of federal campaigns, the national party organization tends to occupy most media, public, and scholarly attention (e.g., Gidengil et al. 2012, 103). Media coverage is understood to be horse race–driven, in other words, focused on national polls and party leader performances (e.g., Soroka et al. 2009). Overall, as Carty and Eagles explain (2005, 136), "[t]his pattern of coverage leaves little room for individual constituency contests, local issues, local candidates, or local conditions." Nearly 80 per cent of Canadians live in large cities, which tend to feature minimal coverage of local candidates, while candidates in rural areas tend to receive greater coverage, but from local media (Carty and Eagles 2005, Chapter 9).

As a result, voters may be minimally aware of local campaigns. While the Canadian electorate lacks general political knowledge, this tendency is especially pronounced in terms of local political awareness (Blais and Bodet 2006, 489; Tessier and Blanchet 2018, 83). For example, voters who cannot correctly identify major party ideologies or leaders are even less likely to have knowledge of their local candidates. As Tessier and Blanchet note (2018, 86), "[m]ost voters are unlikely to possess meaningful knowledge about the issue positions of most candidates, and in some instance, voters may not really hold any relevant information about candidates besides their affiliated party." That said, as political knowledge increases, voters also become more likely to consider their local electoral context when deciding how to vote (Blais and Bodet 2006). More specifically, voters will rely on previous constituency-level results to gauge the electoral strength of various parties.

Regardless, the extent of media or public attention paid to local campaigns is an incomplete barometer for their importance. Federal parties pay significant attention to constituency campaigns and shape their strategy to riding-level characteristics (Carty and Eagles 2005, 7–10; Flanagan 2010; Gidengil et al. 2012, 117–30). They continue to operate geographically differentiated strategies from their central headquarters (Stephenson et al. 2019) and campaigns on the ground tend to reflect distinctive features of their communities (Carty and Eagles 2005; Sayers 1999). Since voters ultimately cast ballots within their local constituency, the so-called ground game of federal parties, identifying supporters and turning them out to vote, occupies an essential component of election strategy (Carty et al. 2000, 154–77). These local races matter significantly for the candidates who are deeply invested in them. Serious candidates dedicate substantial time, effort, and money to the campaign, often sacrificing other professional opportunities. They raise and spend tens of thousands of dollars, travel large distances, subject themselves to public scrutiny, manage a strenuous campaign schedule, engage with hostile or indifferent citizens, appear in local and regional media, and produce a variety of campaign materials and advertising (Carty and Eagles 2005, 119; Thompson 2016).

Along these lines, scholars have begun to take an interest in previously neglected aspects of local party activity (Bodet 2013, 575–6). Blais and Daoust (2017, 1103) note that "what happens at the district level is still understudied compared to the national level ... For a better understanding of Canadian electoral politics, we must take into account the multilevel nature of campaigns and not only focus on the national level." Still others highlight constituency-level political dynamics as both electorally consequential (Coletto 2010; Cross 2016b; Eagles and Hagley 2010) and intrinsically important for understanding Canadian elections (Blidook 2012; Carty and Eagles 2005; Carty and Young 2012; Koop 2011). Ultimately, there is minimal justification for adhering to a view of local campaigns as minimally relevant for understanding federal elections. Public awareness and the statistical impact of local campaigns provide a narrow picture of their significance. Recent scholarship on local campaigns has improved our understanding of Canadian electoral politics, voting behaviour, and political representation.

Despite growing scholarly recognition of their political significance, constituency campaigns face an additional challenge to their relevance through changing intra-party campaign dynamics. Research suggests (e.g., Marland, Giasson, and Esselment 2017; Marland and Wagner 2020; Savoie 2019, 160, 174; Yates 2022, 287) that local campaigns tend to be heavily directed or controlled by parties' central offices. Distinct from Bell and Fletcher's (1991) view of miniature replica constituency campaigns, this research also implicitly minimizes their importance. Whether or not they resemble the national campaign as "replicas," constituency campaigns may be entirely subordinate to the centre. Yet there are reasons to anticipate that constituency campaigns might not willingly accept encroachments on their authority (Carty and Cross 2006). These concerns speak to a central issue of this book: do constituency campaigns strictly implement party directives, or can they reimagine and even contravene them?

The Franchise Model and Its Evolution

Single-member-plurality electoral rules have led federal parties to develop geographically defined organizational units.[7] Carty's (2002, 2004) seminal analyses of the organizational structure of Canadian parties explains how they confront the challenge of connecting diverse communities across a large territory in two official languages. Carty states (2002, 729) that "we need to ask: what kind of organization do they use to connect Tecumseh Corners with the House of Commons in Ottawa? How do such parties work? What are the consequences of the particular organizational model for our political life?" Carty perceives a similar organizational logic to corporate franchises, with a division of labour between the central party and riding-level units.

Parties retain overarching national coherence through a national office which sets the party brand, electoral platform, and pan-national themes. Meanwhile, the constituency franchise maintains a volunteer base, nominates candidates, and supports their campaigns with a ground organization and tailored political messages. This model combines efficiencies of scale and standardization with the benefits of participation from local units "more attuned to the immediate community's perspectives, practices and demands than those in a remote headquarters, an advantage in attracting support in a volatile and competitive environment" (731).

The model consists of two organizational strata with distinct roles and responsibilities. In terms of the relationship between the central party and local units, Carty highlights a core bargain, where franchises agree to trade national discipline for local autonomy (733). The riding-level franchises agree to support the policy and strategic objectives determined by the centre in exchange for autonomy over their local functions, namely candidate selection. Carty contends that local units have minimal influence on questions of leadership and party policy. In terms of campaign organization, the centre-periphery relationship assumes the following division of labour: the national office determines the party platform, pan-national campaign themes, and branding decisions, while constituency-level actors select candidates and organize the ground campaign. Carty states that this approach combines efficiencies of scale and standardization with benefits of participation from those immersed in local political life. Parties can maintain national coherence while adapting their electoral product to local preferences and realities.

Carty provides a mixed assessment of the model's national unity and democratic implications. The franchise structure entrenches a local representation and responsiveness. It reflects Canada's social pluralism, while also "perpetuating [divides] and reinforcing the peculiarities of party life and organization in the more than 300 constituencies of the country" (736). But the model is also unstable and prone to personal factionalism. Carty contends that the lack of meaningful local policy influence[8] can frustrate members, at times leading them to exit their party or militate for leadership change.[9] This entails shifting activist cohorts with allegiances to particular leaders or other party figures, which are eventually displaced when new leadership teams materialize.

Recent evidence suggests that the franchise bargain may be waning due to heightened centralization. Despite their apparent mutual autonomy and interdependence, national and local party organizations have never shared coequal status (Carty 2015, 68–71). While Carty (2002) argues that local autonomy consists primarily of control over candidate selection and the ground campaign (see also Carty and Cross 2010, 204), the nature and persistence of this autonomy is unclear. The central party currently intervenes to influence nomination outcomes (Pruysers and Cross 2016), dictates preferred campaign activities (Belfry Munroe and Munroe 2018), and implores local campaigns to repeat national talking points (Marland 2016). The party has also taken increased control over local finances (Coletto, Jansen, and Young 2011). By implication, it may appear that the central party can freely dictate orders that overwhelm or ignore local preferences. According to these accounts, the model may assume too much cooperation, if it is presently driven by fear, rather than mutual interdependence or power-sharing. The demise of the core franchise bargain carries democratic and representational consequences for the roles parties perform.[10] Before assessing evidence of the franchise model's decline, it is important to note elements of a political franchise arrangement that favour decentralized organization.

The Distinctiveness of Political Franchises

Below, I briefly explore three key aspects of a political franchise model, which distinguish it from a corporate franchise arrangement. These features complement rather than contradict Carty's analyses. First, corporate franchises are predicated on consistency and recognizability, as they offer an identical product across geographic space (Omar, Williams, and Lingelbach 2009, 178; Veloutsou and Moutinho 2009, 315). Customers can enjoy the same fast food or electronics to which they are accustomed, regardless of their location. In other words, homogeneity and familiarity attract most consumers. Although Canadian parties feature broad ideological underpinnings, essential themes, and consistent political aspirations, they also enjoy considerable programmatic flexibility (Carty and Cross 2010; Merolla, Stephenson, and Zechmeister 2008). This flexibility entails continuous political adaptation and reinvention, especially following leadership changes. There are also significant horizontal differences between franchises, evidenced in the tailoring of local messaging and strategy. Corporate franchises do not generally feature such manoeuvrability and must maintain a more consistent and recognizable product.[11] Conversely, the success of Canada's political franchises depends to a greater extent upon their adaptability, regional responsiveness, and local character. Managed by entrepreneurial local candidates and volunteers, political franchises can judiciously tailor their product and strategy for a limited audience. This entails diverse local management styles, strategic choices, and franchise capabilities.

A second difference concerns the role and visibility of the franchisee. The owner of a business franchise is typically an invisible figure. Their role consists primarily of management, logistical operations, and accounting (e.g., Davies et al. 2011). By contrast, political franchisees put themselves forward as ambassadors and brand extensions of their parties (Marland 2016, 10; Marland and Wagner 2020). Their role consists primarily of communications and image management. As this study will show, many candidates are concerned with their image and reputation in their communities, apart from their party or campaign commitment.

Third, most corporate franchises produce a tangible product. Conversely, political franchises offer no product in the traditional sense, and their most vital task consists of communications itself (Lees-Marshment 2014). An intangible communications- or information-based product arguably invites greater tailoring than a tangible mass-produced, locally distributed product such as a hammer or a hamburger. Regional and linguistic difference may invite further tailoring of local campaign strategy and political messages (Stephenson et al. 2019, 62). Accordingly, the distinctiveness of a political, rather than a traditional corporate franchise, invokes an appreciation of the difficulty of imposing centralized campaign operations.

Centripetal and Centrifugal Pressures in Canadian Parties

Local campaign behaviour can be understood in terms of the navigation of centripetal pressures from the central party alongside centrifugal pressures from local environments. Centripetal pressures exert centralizing effects and refer to the influences of party structures that enforce conformity. For decades, leader-centric politics (e.g., Bittner 2011; Carty 2015, 68; Gidengil et al. 2012, 103; Savoie 2019, 160) and the growth and influence of professional consultants (Craft 2017; Esselment and Wilson 2017) have in some ways led to centralization of decision-making authority. In Carty's (2015, 68) view, party intrusions in local operations have long arisen due to the "nationalization of political life and communication." Similarly, Cross (2018, 215) contends that the franchise bargain "has always been rather high level and theoretical."

There are also more recent pressures, most notably the rise of political marketing and digital technologies. The former refers to using business marketing techniques to inform party policy, strategy, and communications, with the goal of identifying and responding to demands of the electoral marketplace (Cwalina, Falkowski, and Newman 2011, 17; Lees-Marshment 2014; Marland, Giasson, and Esselment 2017, 231;

Marland, Giasson, and Lees-Marshment 2012a, 262). Although this logic is not new, the propensity for parties to be market-oriented has increased, meaning parties now continuously gather precise voter preferences using tools such as polling, focus groups, consumer research, and resonance testing, and use this information in the development of party policy (Delacourt 2016; Marland 2016; Marland, Giasson, and Lees-Marshment 2012a). This can be done because parties with sufficient resources can access reliable, precise, and up-to-date voter data. These practices are centralizing because they allow parties to bypass local actors and spend large sums fine-tuning messages they feel will resonate with target voters. Notably, the work of Marland and colleagues (e.g., Marland 2016, 10; Marland and Wagner 2020) demonstrates how a branding lens colours party decision-making, including regulation of local actors from the centre.

Related digital technologies, such as party software[12] and social media, also have centralizing implications (Stephenson et al. 2019, 171). Campaign software enables parties to store large amounts of voter data and to oversee local campaign activities with ease and precision (Belfry Munroe and Munroe 2018; Patten 2017). In theory, social media may appear to be decentralizing, in offering candidate-centered outlets for political communication. However, social media's disruptive potential may accentuate centralizing and disciplinary pressures, as it provides venues for potential communications errors, which are carefully monitored by party staff (Marland, Giasson, and Small 2014).

There is evidence these centralizing trends have affected all three major parties: the Conservative Party (Farney and Koop 2017; Flanagan 2013, 90), Liberal Party (Carty 2015; Jeffrey 2017), and New Democratic Party (McGrane 2019; McLean 2012).[13] Each operates in a constant heightened state of election readiness, referred to as the permanent campaign (Marland, Giasson, and Esselment 2017). Local actors are implored to behave in a disciplined and predictable matter. There is a clear expectation of deference to the centre and heightened vigilance with respect to deviation from party expectations. Central offices and election war rooms increasingly command resources and influence, relative to local or regional offices.

In this view, local campaigns may be viewed as high risk, low reward sources of potential distraction rather than component parts of federal parties or complementary electoral organizations. Accordingly, since the time of Carty's initial (2002) writing, the franchise dynamic appears to have evolved towards a diminished role for local party organizations. This suggests that contemporary parties can micromanage significant aspects of local campaign operations. Applying these findings to this book's research questions would suggest central party dominance evidenced through one-way communications from the centre, an absence of local influence of the central campaign, minimal undisciplined behaviour, party mechanisms to monitor and ensure local compliance, and substantial intra-party cohesion. Yet concrete evidence from local campaigns is needed to better understand national-local party relations and detectable effects of centralization on local behaviour.

These apparent tendencies are consistent with a legacy of strong party discipline and centralization of power in Canada's federal parties. Scholars have documented an apparent increase in party discipline, diminished threshold for intra-party dissent, and heavy-handedness of party leaders, linking these trends to Canada's so-called democratic deficit (e.g., Godbout 2020; Savoie 2019; Smith 2007; White 2012).[14] Although such concerns are commonly associated with elected legislators, another dimension of centralization and leader-centric politics concerns how they extend to the campaign period. In contrast to the legislative realm, there is relatively little empirical evidence concerning the nature of central authority during a campaign period when legislators are candidates rather than MPs.[15] Thus, while there are numerous instances of central party intrusions into local areas of campaign jurisdiction, it remains to be seen whether constituency candidates retain meaningful autonomy in the current era of message discipline and the permanent campaign.

To recall, the franchise bargain consists of "national discipline for local autonomy" (Carty 2002, 733). We know that the central party frequently interferes with local autonomy, namely in candidate selection (Cross, Pruysers, and Currie-Wood 2022). But this bargain can also be breached by local actors if they fail to respect disciplinary norms. This remains possible, given the duelling incentives faced by local campaigns and their abilities to manage the ground campaign. The central party benefits from shared values and policy goals with its local branches, which contribute to party loyalty and cohesion. Nonetheless, candidates and party supporters may experience disappointment with their parties, differences of opinion, personal disputes, or changing career incentives (e.g., Chong, Simms, and Stewart 2017).

In assessing centrifugal pressures, it bears noting that local campaigns possess meaningful autonomy and can adopt their desired campaign strategies (Carty and Eagles 2005, 175; Koop 2011). Sayers (1999) underlines the institutional entrenchment of local independence, arguing that "national parties do not have available a strong, hierarchical management structure to enforce the central party's will at the local level" (4). Sayers attributes this to a lack of career incentives to motivate local compliance and ensure party directives are respected (5). Even those ridings targeted for special attention from the central party can in some cases "ignore national advice and the resources that might come with it, and head off in their own strategic direction" (10). There are substantial reasons to expect that constituency campaigns may not always share national priorities or comply with the central party. This chapter highlights tensions in reconciling these realities with parties' increased demands for discipline and cohesion. Centrifugal pressures largely stem from electoral rules and the substantial regional and sociocultural diversity encompassed in federal constituencies.

Parties play a significant gatekeeping role in determining who can become a politically viable candidate (Cross 2004). However, SMP systems incentivize greater attention to local conditions, relative to party demands, as the local electorate directly elects candidates (Carey 2007; Sieberer 2006, 155, 163). Fox (2018) contends that proportional electoral systems tend to produce nationally focused elections, while majoritarian rules such as SMP increase the salience of local campaigns and candidates. Similarly, Tavits (2009) asserts that legislators with local ties are more susceptible to maverick behaviour. These local ties provide the incentives and support for legislators to break with their parties.

For federal candidates, their constituency is the relevant political unit. Each district captures a unique blend of geographic and demographic ingredients. As Carty and Eagles (2005, 4) argue, it is the constituencies that define the "footprint of the political system. Each federal constituency represents a small world unto itself … The vitality of party organizations, the stability of partisan support, the levels of voter participation and financial commitment, the character of communications networks, and the impact of personality all vary from riding to riding." To understand constituency campaign behaviour and discipline, we must consider the local context of federal campaigns. These centrifugal pressures underline the merit of a decentralized analysis of federal parties.

Regional and sociocultural divides can also incentivize dissonant local campaign behaviour. Indeed, the organization of Canada's federal parties cannot be understood without reference to regionalism (see for example, Cross 2002).[16] Regional cleavages structure Canadian voting behaviour to a greater extent than most other social cleavages (Gidengil et al. 1999). As noted by Gidengil et al. (2012), voters sharing the same social background characteristics vote differently by region. Regional differences reflect tensions between divergent economic interests, political cultures, policy preferences, demographic and settlement patterns, and centre-periphery relations (46).

Writing in 2000, Carty, Cross, and Young argue that following the 1993 electoral realignment and attendant regional tensions, parties have ceased to conduct pan-national campaigns and instead wage concurrent regional campaigns. This finding is reaffirmed by Stephenson et al. (2019).[17] Despite the nationalization of electoral politics, regional and local differences continue to structure party organization, campaign strategy, and voting behaviour. Stark regional differences in party support were evident in the 2019 federal election, which saw the victorious Liberal Party win only fifteen seats west of Ontario, with similar results seen in the 2021 election. Parties continually consider territorial cleavages in their campaign strategies (Carty and Eagles 2005, 7–10; Gerber 2006; Gidengil et al. 2012, 117–30). This all suggests potential tensions between local campaigns and the central party, since party policies and messages are likely to vary in popularity by region (Stephenson et al. 2019). These conflicting regional demands may in turn compel campaign dissonance between constituency campaigns and the national party (Robbins-Kanter 2022a).[18]

This is all to say that there is an understated tension, faced by constituency campaigns, between accommodating party imperatives and local forces. Put differently, the literature on local-national party relations implicitly identifies campaigns to be a site of countervailing localizing and nationalizing pressures. But it only provides a partial understanding of how these contradictions are reflected in campaign behaviour.

Campaign Personalism and Local Autonomy

Local campaigns may aspire to make their own strategic decisions, but can they actually do this within a modern campaign organization? An emergent literature on campaign personalism sheds light on this question. Decentralized campaign personalism refers to candidates' abilities to emphasize their personal characteristics at the expense of their parties (Balmas et al. 2012).[19] These candidates rely on personal reputations, locally tailored messages, and even distance themselves from the central campaign and party leader. Scholars have examined the prevalence of decentralized personalism for elections in Israel (Balmas et al. 2012), in Romania (Chiru 2018), and in the European Parliament (Bøggild and Pedersen 2018). Unlike these cases, Canada employs a single-member-plurality electoral system, with substantial incentive for candidates to personalize their campaigns (Zittel 2015). Cross and Young (2015) find a high overall level of decentralized personalism among candidates in the 2008 Canadian election. This is consistent with Koop's (2011, 105) view that "local candidates enjoy significant freedom to organize their campaigns in ways that most closely adapt to the conditions of their individual ridings."

To understand and measure decentralized personalism, existing research has often drawn from Zittel and Gschwend's (2008, 989) conception of personalization in terms of campaign means, agendas, and organization. Cross and Young (2015) classify personalism as locally produced campaign messages (means of communication), distinct campaign issues (agendas), and campaign volunteers drawn from the personal networks of the candidate and core campaign staff (organization). Pruysers and Cross (2018, 73) define decentralized personalism as covering issues not raised by the central campaign and creating personalized radio or television advertisements. Similarly, Cross, Currie-Wood, and Pruysers (2020, 5) rely on survey responses where former candidates are asked to assess the extent to which they emphasized their parties versus themselves as candidates and the extent to which their campaign communications were produced independently from their parties.

But decentralized campaign personalism has limited use for understanding local discipline and autonomy. This is because tactics such as highlighting local concerns and candidate attributes can be orchestrated by party headquarters. Parties may benefit from the ability to downplay an unpopular leader, policy position, or party brand while benefiting from locally conscious strategy and perceived strengths of the local candidate. For these reasons, parties may expect or demand a degree of local campaign personalism (Koop 2011, 9). As Cross and Young (2015, 308) explain, "We do not find 'disloyal' local candidates in the Canadian context; rather, personalization is expressed through subtle emphases on local issues, an implicit downplaying of the national platform and organizational reliance on the resources and skills of the individual candidate." While decentralized personalism reflects the coexistence of local and national campaign elements, it cannot explain intra-party conflict and whether local actors contravene party preferences. To address this, campaign personalism can inspire reflection on a wider scope of local campaign behaviour, including more entrepreneurial or subversive acts.

In sum, constituency campaigns simultaneously face centripetal pressures towards party conformity and centrifugal pressures from more proximate regional or constituency-level forces. In addition, technical and logistical tensions may arise from organizational distance in a large federal campaign operation. Despite compelling accounts of central party dominance, there are competing perspectives on the extent to which constituency campaigns are instruments of a central party apparatus. The strength of centripetal campaign forces would suggest a limited scope for undisciplined constituency campaign behaviour, while the existence of centrifugal pressures offers a counterpoint. Accordingly, we should not assume effective discipline and cohesion within federal parties. Nor can we anticipate the fluid transmission and translation of party directives through an organizational chain of command. Instead, conflicting incentives produce ambiguous expectations for campaign discipline. Can parties effectively use their disciplinary authority to maintain party cohesion? To what extent do constituency campaigns capitalize on their apparent autonomy and incentives for dissonant behaviour?

This chapter has emphasized four major insights. First, constituency campaigns remain important actors in federal politics and the topic of constituency campaign behaviour merits further investigation to improve our understanding of Canadian parties, elections, political communication, and representation. This viewpoint is shared by scholars currently advancing an emerging research focus centred on local party activity. This chapter has confronted general disinterest in local campaigns due to their relatively small electoral impact, the nationalization of campaign discourse, and low public awareness. While the aforementioned critiques are unconvincing reasons to neglect local campaigns, the potential domination of local campaigns by the central party is an emerging challenge to their abilities and significance.

Second, the chapter has explained the importance of Carty's franchise model as the primary framework for understanding local-national party relations, as well as the model's limitations. Despite the model's virtues, it leaves gaps in terms of providing a limited conception of local autonomy, local campaign behaviour, and certain distinctive features of Canada's political franchises. To apply Carty's language, the franchisees that manage local campaigns are best understood as entrepreneurs rather than employees. It is important to assess how the franchise model's core bargain of local autonomy for national discipline has fared in the current era of heightened campaign centralization. Third, the chapter contends that existing research sets clear but implicitly conflicting expectations regarding the extent of local autonomy and central party authority. There are understated tensions between scholarship that implies parties maintain strong campaign oversight and other research that emphasizes politically and organizationally distinctive constituency campaigns. Fourth, while the concept of campaign personalism helps to understand the coexistence of centralized and decentralized campaign logics, it is not applicable to instances where local and national objectives are at odds. To help fill these gaps, the next chapter turns to addressing the book's major research questions on the extent of central party authority and local campaign discipline.

Chapter 3

Constituency Campaign Discipline

Four weeks before the 2019 election, a party official enters a Toronto-area local campaign office and asks to speak with the campaign manager. The visitor has travelled from the party's regional headquarters to monitor this closely contested riding. As their discussion moves to a more private section of the office, the visitor asks about the general state of the campaign and what is needed from the central party. Shortly after, the campaign manager shows them[1] a promotional video they are preparing to publish on the candidate's website and social media pages. Following this, a lengthy and technical discussion revolves around the key campaign practice of identifying and canvassing supporters. Local campaigns rank their electors by most to least likely supporters. The party official and local campaign manager disagree on which categories of voters should be canvassed: the party wants likely supporters to be canvassed, while the campaign manager politely disagrees and prefers a broader canvass that includes weaker tiers. The party official leaves with some adamant quiet instructions.

Afterwards, I ask the campaign manager if they will follow this directive. They reply, "definitely not," and explain the central party's concern is that canvassing voters in less promising tiers is inefficient and risks mobilizing the supporters of opposing parties. Central party data show that the top three tiers of likely supporters in this constituency yield a 60 per cent positive response rate, versus a less than 20 per cent positive response rate for the next tier. In their view, canvassing lower tiers may even cost them the election when iterated across thousands of upcoming voter interactions.[2] However, the campaign manager explains, "that data doesn't tell you everything. They think we're poking the bear each time, but our [weaker tiers] are mostly going to vote anyways. Turnout is very high here and having our canvassers be as visible as possible [to all tiers of voters] is [beneficial]. It frames the race in our favour."

In addition, the central party is reportedly concerned with canvasser morale. Canvassing favourable tiers typically results in an efficient and generally positive experience for volunteers. Conversely, canvassing other tiers means volunteers are more likely to encounter hostility and indifference. Such experiences make valuable volunteers reluctant to return. But the campaign manager maintains that "For our volunteers, that's just not true. They can get yelled at or worse, whatever happens ... [Those numbers] are for the median riding." Lastly, I ask what the party official thought of the local campaign team's video: "it doesn't matter because that version's going to be changed, but I didn't tell [them]. I showed [them] something they'll be happy with. That avoids a headache we don't need right now ... Beg for forgiveness, not permission."

This twenty-minute interaction between a local campaign manager and central party official illustrates four recurring issues in local-national relations. First and foremost, constituency campaign discipline should not be taken for granted, as local actors may hold conflicting preferences from their parties and be willing to act on them. Second, the central party typically holds firm to its data-driven analysis, while local campaigns are sceptical of applying these tendencies to their particular situation. Third, the concept of asking forgiveness for contentious actions, rather than prior permission, is a recurring idea in many campaign offices. Local campaigns are sometimes unwilling to wait for permission when they prefer timely action. And during a dynamic campaign period, the centre may have difficulty keeping track of local actions. Fourth, local campaigns are populated by staff and volunteers who often view their primary allegiance to the candidate, rather than the party. Many are personal friends of the candidate. As a 2019 Conservative campaign manager explains: "If I can do something that helps my candidate and helps the party, that's great, but if it's something that really helps my candidate but could hurt the party, I'd do that too."

This chapter considers each of these four issues in local-national party relations.[3] It examines the extent to which campaigns behave in a disciplined manner in relation to the central party. The chapter identifies essential party expectations for local campaigns and assesses discipline in terms of how closely campaigns adhere to them. Put differently, campaign discipline can be assessed as the extent to which local actors behave consistently with party preferences.

The chapter establishes a definition of undisciplined behaviour, presents indicators that can be used to detect it, and constructs a typology of campaigns based on their degree of discipline. Furthermore, it argues that undisciplined behaviour is a result of insubordination, innovation, and incompetence within local campaigns. The chapter's findings suggest that there is more undisciplined behaviour, and therefore less campaign discipline, than anticipated by existing research. While local campaigns are conventionally assumed to feature high discipline and low autonomy, these findings provide a more nuanced assessment.

Methods

The findings presented in this book are derived from three major data sources: interviews, field observation, and primary source documents.[4] The time period covered by this study includes the 2015 and 2019 federal elections. The first major data source is a series of interviews conducted with federal politicians and party strategists. The target population from which to sample consisted of former federal candidates for the three largest federal parties who stood for election in 2015, as well as party strategists employed in senior positions during the 2015 and/ or 2019 campaign periods. Eighty-seven former candidates and eight party strategists (three Conservatives, three Liberals, and two NDP) were interviewed. This includes roughly equal numbers of candidates from the Conservative, Liberal, and New Democratic parties. As former federal candidates, the target population included a mix of incumbent MPs, former MPs, and candidates who had never held office. All had stood for election in 2015, some planned to run again in 2019, and others were retired from politics at the time of their interview. The sample attributes are summarized in figures 3.1 and 3.2. The former displays politically relevant candidate traits and the latter displays riding-level attributes.

In-person interviews in participants' home ridings were preferred over telephone interviews When feasible, in-person interviews can be preferable to telephone interviews, as they tend to generate higher quality data (Holbrook, Green, and Krosnick 2003; Seitz 2016; Shuy 2002).[5] They permit greater nuance in tone and body language and facilitate a stronger rapport with the interviewee, which is especially important when discussing controversial or sensitive topics such as campaign discipline, local autonomy, and party cohesion.[6] Building trust is essential, given the nature of these interviews and the candour they require (Mikecz 2012). Conversely, telephone interviews tend to produce more guarded answers.

Additionally, in-person meetings allowed former candidates to provide concrete examples of campaign documents, which enriched these discussions, provided visual verification of certain statements, and provided access to primary source documents that would be otherwise inaccessible. Lastly, travelling to actual constituencies revealed

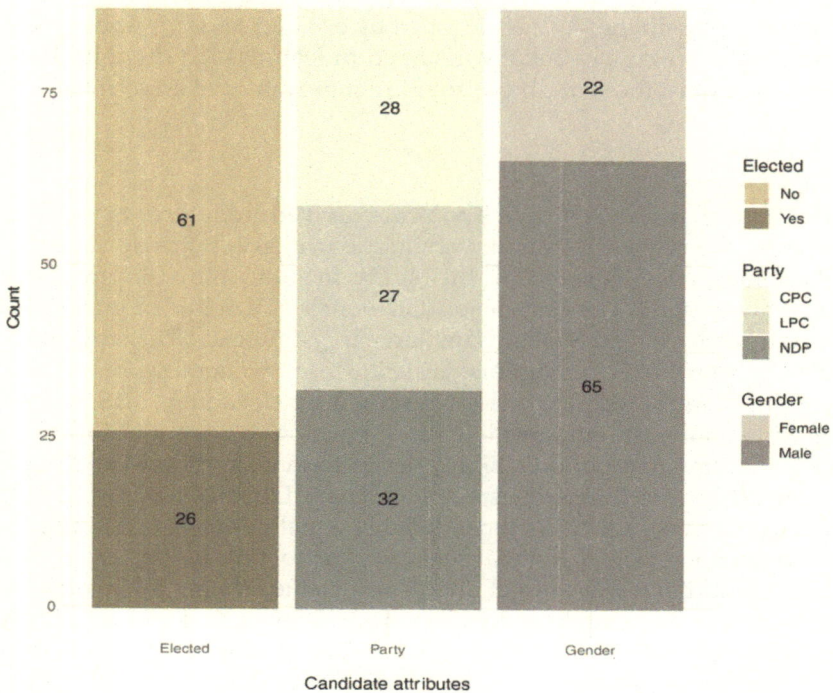

Figure 3.1 Sample Attributes, Candidate Traits

local political perspectives in a manner and context not captured when discussing by phone or videoconference from many kilometres away. Interview subjects were offered confidentiality in order to obtain reliable data while mitigating professional or social risks associated with the disclosure of politically sensitive information. Confidentiality guarantees were offered both in writing, on research consent forms, and verbally, at the start of interviews. Most participants chose to be identified only by their party and region.[7]

The second major data source consists of observational data derived from participant observation of local campaigns during the 2019 federal election. Participant observation allows researchers to make inferences about the activities of people and groups under study by participating in these activities and observing them in their natural setting (Kawulich 2005, 2). In this case, it entailed spending long periods of time immersed within local campaigns, while observing and participating in their

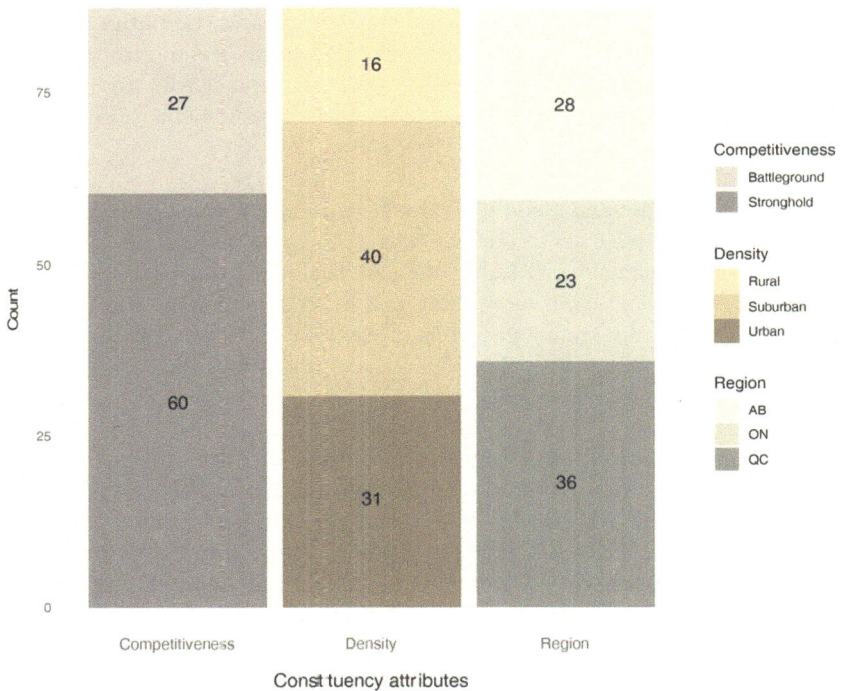

Figure 3.2 Sample Attributes, Constituency Characteristics

activities. In explaining the appeal of participant observation, Blidook and Koop (2019, 2) cite Fenno, who contends that the best way to "learn about politicians [is] by talking to them, watching them and following them around" (1990, 2).

Examples of this research in Canada include McLean's (2012) work as an embedded researcher in the NDP's 2006 federal campaign head-quarters and Koop, Bastedo, and Blidook's (2018) research on MPs' representational styles.

Observation in ten local campaign offices began at the official start of the campaign period on 11 September 2019 and continued until election day on 21 October. This included frequent observation inside constituency campaign offices,[3] as well as voter canvassing, meetings with community members, and various local events, including fundraisers. Notes were taken throughout the day and were organized at the end of each day.

The observation of real-life campaign dynamics is a compelling way to understand the behaviour of local campaigns and the national-local party relationship in Canada.[9] The method emphasizes the importance of firsthand experience with relevant concepts and actors and underscores the "humanness" of social science research. As Fenno (1998, 8–9) explains,

> it is, after all, flesh and blood individuals, real *people* we are talking about when we generalize about our politicians ... [T]here is something to be gained by occasionally unpacking our analytical categories and our measures to take a first-hand look at the real live human beings subsumed within ... [R]epresentative government has local roots and a bottom-up logic. And that is precisely the perspective of the observational research that is conducted on the campaign trail.

An important benefit of observational research is the ability to focus on the subjectivity or context of behaviour. An ability to incorporate participants' self-understanding or meaning-making is particularly helpful for studying local campaign behaviour.[10] Sayers (1999, 13) advocates such an approach, juxtaposing it against large-scale survey research, which can resemble "'a meat-grinder, tearing the individual from his social context and guaranteeing that nobody in the study interacts with anyone else in it'[11] ... [I]n studying elections, contextualization is best accomplished by interviewing candidates, campaigners, party strategists, and journalists." Similarly, Bevir and Rhodes (2003, 190) argue that we must not "neglect the differences in the beliefs of the individuals lumped together in a tradition." Their study of the behaviour of British civil servants hinges upon a "decentered analysis; that is ... unpacking the actual and contingent beliefs and actions of its individual adherents ... [to] provide 'thick descriptions' of the world ... by means of an ethnographic form of inquiry ... [that] encourages the researcher to get out there and see what actors are thinking and doing."

There are also important limitations to this method, the primary of which is generalizability. Participant observation sacrifices representativeness for greater analytical depth (Belfry Munroe and Munroe 2018, 140; Sayers 1999, 14). The participating campaigns cannot constitute a representative sample of local campaigns, and those who are willing to host an outside researcher may be systematically different from others. The issue of access to subjects for participant observation research is a common problem and constitutes an important limitation of the study.

Ultimately, only campaigns that accept the presence of a researcher can be observed.

Primary source documents are the third major data source employed in this book. They include public and private materials: internal party guidelines for local campaigns, including campaign talking points, and partisan campaign literature such as candidate pamphlets and other promotional materials. EDA guidelines were also examined, which typically feature a balance of information from party and local sources. In rare cases, confidential emails and memoranda were made available. Such documents proved useful as further evidence of internal party dynamics and the local-national relationship. In some cases, these documents were readily accessible during interviews and participant observation. In others, participants made contact after their interviews to provide electronic or physical copies, and some materials were independently located online through party websites.

Given the potential limitations of each research method described here, the investigation of multiple data sources including interviews, campaign documents, and observational research, permits the triangulation of information to improve its inferential validity (Fielding 2012; Kara 2015). The inclusion of ethnographic methods such as participant observation ensures that social realities are not excluded or abstracted from research. Observation of active campaign dynamics can help to test whether data gleaned elsewhere "falter[s] on the shoals of lived experience" (Yanow and Schwartz-Shea 2012, 28). Conflicting data inspire greater reflection and further investigation to account for discrepancies.

Constituency Campaign Organization: Party Expectation versus Reality

What is the role and purpose of constituency campaigns? How do their main functions and activities shape national-local party relations? Carty's franchise model asserts a division of labour between national and local party strata but does not elaborate on the substantive content of this arrangement. According to Sayers (1999, 68–71), local campaigns feature three levels of essential personnel: an inner circle executes core specialized functions, secondary workers are regularly available to perform labour-intensive tasks, and sympathizers perform volunteer work on an ad hoc basis. Despite their diversity, constituency campaigns share common activities and objectives, which are derived from central party guidelines. For the three major parties, these training guides set the general expectations for local campaigns. These confidential documents are created by party headquarters and are therefore not available for external study or reproduction. Nonetheless, party strategists allude to their underlying logic and the general expectations for local campaigns.

Strategists generally suggest that the efforts of local campaigns should be oriented towards canvassing and building an effective get-out-the-vote (GOTV) operation. This approach translates to a tight focus on identifying and mobilizing supporters. According to a Liberal strategist, local campaigns must:

> start with their existing list of voters in the riding. They'll start by contacting the friendly people to make sure they're still Liberals. If you can identify a certain number that we've determined you need to win the riding, you can do it without contacting people who might not support us. In other ridings, you need to go beyond [voters listed as most likely supporters] and try to get the number up. All the canvassing is to find these voters and put them into the system, so we can do calls, doorknocking, mail ... and once you have all your people identified, you need to remind them to vote, ideally a lot, and especially on election day make sure they actually vote. It all leads to the GOTV operation.

As of 2015, the Liberal Party's digital campaign platform included a "campaign dashboard" that breaks down these responsibilities in a formulaic manner for each local campaign (Bennett 2019). In 2019, some local campaigns routinely accessed an online dashboard with a spreadsheet-like functionality that indicated the number of votes the party projected would be needed to win the constituency, the number of voter IDs required to win,[12] and the current number completed.

These targets are drawn from the "back end" of the central party dataverse, which relies on data obtained by the party, as well as commercially purchased bulk data. These data feed into an algorithm that produces constituency vote targets and projections. According to a Liberal strategist, these projections were proven accurate in 2015 and would be again in 2019.

The Conservative Party benefited from similar technologies and was first to develop a modern digital voter database, in 2004 (Patten 2017, 53). According to a Conservative strategist, the party today demonstrates slightly less enthusiasm for the reliability of big data: "the Liberals since 2015 adopted data as religion ...[W]e see it as a piece, a very important piece, but it can lead you astray if you don't make careful big-picture decisions."

From the local perspective, the Liberal campaign dashboard is generally described as logical and user-friendly. As a 2019 Liberal candidate in Ontario suggests, "this is basically how to build a hamburger, if you follow it." In this particular case, the ingredients included four door-knocks per household, two direct mail drops, and two phone calls. At the same time, another 2019 Liberal candidate stresses that they "barely looked at [the party database]." This observation underlines a crucial point in local-national party relations. The central party can develop the most sophisticated, precise, and intuitive technologies available, but they ultimately require local faith, acceptance, and cooperation, to ensure their proper implementation (Patten 2017, 54).

Overall, Conservative and Liberal strategists expressed scepticism towards constituency campaign activities that might disturb central party strategies. Conversely, NDP strategists appeared more permissive, as an NDP strategist explains:

> [in most ridings] the national narrative isn't going to be enough for us to win. The only frontrunner campaign we've run was in 2015 … that means instead we rely on pockets of strength … including some very strong, effective local candidates … in the past we've had some problems with rogue candidates … if our polling shows what it did in 2019, I would be less concerned … let's say if you're already down by four goals, you're in a different spot than if the game is on your stick and as the coach … you know what has to be done to win.

NDP candidates who have run in multiple elections echo this interpretation, stating that party strategy and directives appeared to be more cautious and controlling in 2015, suggesting less risk tolerance for local activities. These views raise the question of how local actors view their own roles and responsibilities. In other words, how do central party expectations for local campaign behaviour translate to the realities of the campaign trail?

Some local campaigns undoubtedly share central party priorities. As a 2019 Conservative campaign manager explains, "I totally agree that running the ground game means knocking on doors, making phone calls, contact[ing] people again and again wherever we can, getting volunteers in here, and getting out the vote, not wasting time on other [stuff]." Similarly, a 2019 Ontario Liberal candidate agrees with the need to stay focused on canvassing, noting that "there's so much you can waste time on, you can get into a social media war, you can get into a sign war,[13] none of that is a good idea." However, many other local campaign actors disagreed with party interpretations of their roles. For example, a 2019 Conservative candidate suggests that party directives to focus on voter IDs and GOTV are overly simplistic and narrow:

[i]f you have a certain local profile, it's not just a mechanistic science of hitting a certain number of IDs ... because you can try to keep this positive reputation that will spread in other ways like word of mouth and earned media ... And that can be an efficient way to build support ... [that means] showing up at lots of community events ... supporting local [causes], being involved [in the riding] way before the campaign started actually, whether you're the incumbent or not.

Indeed, a more complex picture of local campaign ambitions can be observed in their daily operations. In addition to a campaign manager and an official agent,[14] campaigns typically feature executives in charge of canvassing operations, finance, election day coordination, multimedia communications, and volunteer coordination (Richler 2016, 111). In some cases, these core roles may also exercise secondary functions such as office management, graphics and design for promotional materials, outreach for specific socio-demographic groups, election sign coordination, and managing the candidate's itinerary. Some local campaigns also feature precise positions such as a "sign captain" and other well-resourced campaigns conduct oppo research to investigate opposing campaigns' strategies and weaknesses.[15] Each campaign observed in September and October 2019 more or less adhered to this structure, with exceptions for some with very few resources, where a small number of people must fill key roles (Koop 2011, 117).

Noah Richler's 2015 NDP campaign team in the Liberal stronghold constituency of Toronto–St. Paul's featured three co-campaign managers, an official agent, candidate handler, and people in six additional organizational pillars: election planning, volunteer coordination, office management, campaign strategy, social media, and finance (Richler 2016, 86–7). Further, each of the six pillars was comprised of multiple subcommittees. For example, social media included web administration, audiovisual managers, and a video team. Richler's campaign structure illustrates the potential complexity of constituency campaign organization, even for his long-shot candidacy. All of this suggests that Sayers's (1999) three-tiered conception of constituency campaign organization has grown increasingly complex as specialized talent is called upon for tasks such as social media management and graphic design. Similarly, NDP candidate Marlene Rivier (Ottawa West–Nepean) has employed a consensus-style campaign organization during each of her five federal campaigns from 2004 to 2015. Rivier explains: "when I had my first training to be a candidate ... the trainer said, very jocularly, 'candidates, you're a piece of meat. We send you out in the morning and we bring you back in at night' ... But of course, we never worked that way." Instead, Rivier's local campaign teams have prioritized deliberation and compromise: "we always worked by consensus ... we have to still like each other when the campaign is over, because there will always be another one ... and we need to continue to work cohesively in the meantime." Such thinking transcends the single-minded focus on canvassing that parties often seek to engender.

Richler (2016) states that most of his campaign team was recruited due to their personal connections with him, the candidate. Indeed, many local staff or volunteers are relatively uninterested in the party relative to the candidate (Carty and Eagles 2005, 76; Koop 2011, 116).[16] As 2015 NDP candidate Daniel Beals (Kingston and the Islands) recounts, "I chose the campaign manager I wanted ... instead of a party person ... I gave myself more freedom just by choosing someone who wasn't beholden to the party for their future." This may help to explain constituency campaign decision-making, since a local campaign's perceived purpose and obligations are driven by its senior staff (Sayers 1999). As explained below, constituency campaigns do not reliably view their interests as aligned with those of the central party.

Perceptions of Constituency Campaign Interests versus
Central Party Interests

In executing the functions discussed above, do constituency campaigns largely view themselves as emissaries of the central party or as distinct entities? Table 3.1 sheds light on this question by addressing constituency campaigns' perceived alignment of their interests with central party interests. According to these findings, only 28 per cent of constituency campaigns feel that their interests are always aligned with their party's interests. Nearly 40 per cent of constituency campaigns in this sample identify potential conflict in their interests and the central party's interests. A 2015 NDP candidate in Quebec mentions why they struggle to perceive an alignment of interests: "I think we look after ourselves ... That's what the party is doing [for themselves] ... and [they] would probably throw us under the bus if it got [the leader] a two-point bump [in the polls]." In this view, the consequentialist logic of the national campaign may lead them to sacrifice certain constituencies for the overall good of the party. In a more extreme illustration, a 2019 local campaign manager expressed a desire for their own party to lose the 2019 election and for this to result in their leader's resignation

Table 3.1 Perceived Alignment of Local and National Campaign Interests

Our local interests are the same as the central party's interests ...	Percentage*
All of the time	28
Most of the time	35
Some of the time	33
None of the time	5

*May not add to 100 due to rounding; n=87

or replacement. With a long view towards more durable victory for their party, they anticipated that the winning party in 2019 would lead a short-lived minority government, setting up a newly installed opposition leader for a major victory by 2021.[17]

Others argue that the central party's focus on the median constituency clashes with their distinct needs. As 2015 NDP candidate Daniel Beals (Kingston and the Islands) declares, "my belief is Kingston's a different kind of riding than anywhere else in the country. So why not do what we think will work best in Kingston?" A 2019 Liberal campaign manager argues similarly that "we are not the median riding ... These [generic instructions] aren't going to help ... We need to do some critical thinking about ... which instructions actually make sense." Similarly, national campaign messaging intended to generate broad generic appeal can be ill-suited to particular constituencies. As Liberal MP Rob Oliphant (Don Valley West) explains, the Liberal Party's 2015 messages appealing to "the middle class and those working hard to join it" were inappropriate for his riding, because "I just didn't have enough middle class. I had wealthy and I had poor."

In fairness to the central office, they face the formidable task of managing all local campaigns alongside a national campaign, media strategy, and endless logistics. An NDP strategist describes this as "juggling flaming swords on a tightrope." These challenges are not always respected by local campaigns who, according to Conservative strategist Hamish Marshall, often possess an exaggerated view of their own uniqueness. NDP strategist Karl Bélanger agrees with this viewpoint: "[local campaigns] all say their riding is unique and they're all wrong." Therefore, it is important to consider these honestly held competing views, adhered to by local campaigns and the central campaign. Party headquarters pursues its core campaign goals, while local campaigns realize that their fortunes are intertwined, but not interchangeable.

The perceived misalignment of national and local interests is an important finding in anticipating the importance of undisciplined campaign behaviour. If most local campaigns felt their interests were interchangeable with their parties' interests, it may not even occur to them to disturb party cohesion or act in defiance of the central party. Since this is not the case, these results anticipate the existence of undisciplined behaviour.

Identifying Undisciplined Behaviour

Given that the major roles and responsibilities for constituency campaigns are determined by the central party, how closely do these campaigns adhere to them? Federal parties maintain guidelines and expectations for the practice of local campaigns. This chapter contends that when constituency campaigns depart from these guidelines, they engage in undisciplined behaviour.

There are four definitional parameters for undisciplined behaviour, which broadly refers to actions or practices that contravene party directives.

First, undisciplined behaviour must entail *campaign* behaviour. In other words, it does not encompass the private lives of candidates or campaign staff. It does not include non-campaign practices that nonetheless occur during a campaign such as, for example, a candidate's use of illegal drugs. While this example would undoubtedly frustrate the central party, it does not constitute a campaign practice. Second, undisciplined behaviour must originate from core campaign staff and candidates themselves, rather than from volunteers, most of whom cannot be said to represent the campaign. In observing undisciplined behaviour, only the actions of seniormost campaign team members are considered.[18] Third, undisciplined behaviour can result from either action, such as releasing unsanctioned campaign materials, or inaction, such as failure to complete paperwork. Fourth, undisciplined behaviour can be either intentional or unintentional. This semantic precision indicates that intent is less important than outcome. In other words, local campaigns may defy party procedures unintentionally, but the result for the party in failing to maintain discipline is the same as if they had done this intentionally. Given these parameters, I seek to develop indicators through which to identify undisciplined behaviour. I introduce six key indicators, based primarily on party documents and information obtained from party strategists.

As discussed in Chapter 2, the central party requires local campaigns to identify and mobilize their supporters, amplify party messages, and communicate regularly with the party. But parties are also preoccupied

Table 3.2 Undisciplined Behaviour Indicators

Indicator	Percentage yes
1. Ignore party instructions	42
2. Distribute unvetted material	37
3. Critique party leadership (privately)	30
4. Contradict party's position	19
5. Cooperate with opposing party	8
6. Critique party leadership (publicly)	5

n=87

with expectations for what behaviours or activities local campaigns must avoid. These expectations are all relevant in understanding the parameters of undisciplined behaviour. To help identify significant prohibited campaign activities, I examined the three major parties' constituency campaign guidelines from the 2015 federal election. Confidentiality prohibits sharing direct quotations from these materials, however, guidelines for all three parties feature common directives for acceptable and unacceptable[19] constituency campaign activities and behaviours. This chapter focuses on items that were significant enough to be mentioned for all three parties. Information was supplemented with secondary accounts from the literature (Belfry Munroe and Munroe 2018; Cross 2004; Eagles and Hagley 2010; Flanagan 2014; Thompson 2016) and from strategist interviews, which help to represent the party's general views on undisciplined behaviour.

Party strategists were asked the following open-ended questions: "Is there anything that local campaigns can do that would cause concern for the central party? Based on past experience, what activities or behaviour would you want local campaigns to avoid?" Party strategists offered a variety of responses, which validated the initial eight indicators that emerged from party documents and the existing literature. Party strategist responses are amalgamated to create six broad indicators, intended to be general enough to cover a range of constituency campaign behaviours. The six indicators of undisciplined behaviour are not mutually exclusive and are as follows: contradicting the party's position, publicly critiquing the party, privately critiquing the party, ignoring instructions from the party, cooperating with personnel from an opposing party, and distributing unvetted campaign materials.

The finalized indicators of undisciplined behaviour[20] are displayed in Table 3.2, which gives the percentage of local campaigns that identified their participation in each aspect or indicator of undisciplined behaviour.[21] At the lower end, 5 per cent of campaigns publicly criticized their leader or party and 8 per cent cooperated with an opposing campaign. The most frequent form of undisciplined behaviour is the 42 per cent of campaigns that ignored a directive from party headquarters.

Typologizing Campaign Discipline

What conclusions can be drawn from these data? The nature of variation within these indicators suggests there are distinct local campaign types that vary based on the propensity to engage in undisciplined behaviour: some abstain entirely, many indulge intermittently, and other campaigns are persistently undisciplined. Moreover, the indicators of undisciplined behaviour vary in their severity: publicly criticizing a party leader is more severe than privately criticizing the leader.

Based on these findings, local candidates and their campaigns are classified as conscientious, conflicted, or maverick, based on frequency and type of undisciplined behaviour. These labels are preferred to the more straightforward terms disciplined and undisciplined because of the connotation of carelessness or laziness that the latter entails. The term maverick helps to convey a conscious defiance of central party preferences.

As shown in Table 3.3, local campaigns that display zero indicators are classified as conscientious. Campaigns are labelled as conflicted that exhibit one or more of the following four indicators: ignore party instructions, distribute unvetted materials, privately critique party leadership, or contradict a party position. Last, candidates that cooperate with an opposing party and/or publicly criticize party leadership are assigned the maverick campaign label. In this manner, we see that 45 per cent of candidates in this sample can be classified as conflicted, 42 per cent as conscientious and 13 per cent as maverick.

These broad categories mask fundamental differences in local campaign attitudes towards their roles within the party organization and towards the central campaign. Conscientious candidates, and by extension, their constituency campaigns, broadly suggest that undisciplined behaviour is unacceptable and party discipline must always be maintained. These candidates represent 42 per cent of respondents. They broadly feel that local campaigns must always follow the national party line, and in cases of uncertainty, should do what they feel the party would prefer. As a conscientious Conservative candidate (2015, Quebec) explains, "There is no room for conflict with your own party. You sign the candidate agreement ... so you know exactly what you're getting into ... [The party has] enough to worry about." Similarly, when asked if they ever openly disagreed with their party, a Liberal candidate

Table 3.3 Local Campaign Typology by Degree of Discipline

Campaign profile	Undisciplined constituency campaign indicators	Total percentage of respondents*
Conscientious	None	42 (37)
Conflicted	Ignore instructions; distribute unvetted material; privately criticize leadership; contradict party position	45 (39)
Maverick	Cooperate with other party; publicly criticize leadership	13 (11)

*May not add to 100 due to rounding; n=87

(2015, Ontario) adds, "Absolutely not. Never speak up like that during a campaign. What is that accomplishing? If you are a real team player, you can nod and go along until the campaign is over and then you might have some other channel."

In the face of uncertainty, these campaigns feel that the party must be consulted. As a 2015 Liberal candidate in Alberta suggests, "yes, absolutely ask, and make sure. Much better safe than sorry." Conscientious candidates tend to view their campaigns as an extension of the central party, rather than as distinct entities. As an NDP candidate (2019, Quebec) explains, "When you think about it, we're actually one and the same." A Liberal Party campaign manager (2019, Ontario) agrees with this view: "I don't usually think of 'the party' [as separate] ... We're the party as much as they're the party." These candidates are also preoccupied with unintended consequences of their actions and potential repercussions for other candidates. Former NDP MP Matthew Dubé (Beloeil–Chambly) emphasizes that "solidarity is really important. You're part of a team ... You don't want to damage someone else's chances ... particularly in the era of social media where an off-the-cuff comment can easily find its way out." Similarly, 2015 Liberal candidate Karen Leibovici (Edmonton West) suggests that "it's not all about yourself but also ... other candidates that are running. If you become the focal point that makes the difference between someone else winning or losing just so you can win ... that's a selfish attitude."

Conversely, conflicted candidates are prone to certain undisciplined campaign behaviours, as listed in Table 3.2. In other words, they are more tolerant of undisciplined behaviour and exhibit a moderate commitment to party cohesion. These candidates indicate they have ignored party instructions, contradicted a party position, distributed unvetted campaign materials, and/or privately criticized their party leadership.

Conflicted candidates represent 45 per cent of respondents. Despite openness to undisciplined behaviour and questioning the necessity of unwavering discipline, conflicted candidates are reluctant to distract from the national campaign or to face repercussions from central party officials. Therefore, they articulate conflicting sentiments regarding their party obligations. For example, Marlene Rivier, 2015 NDP candidate in Ottawa West–Nepean explains that she generally sought to comply with party instructions despite her own "strong philosophical beliefs." Former Conservative MP Brad Butt (Mississauga–Streetsville) is similarly conflicted on whether candidates should deviate from their parties: "I think it depends what the issue is. There might be a very important issue for a candidate or an MP in a certain part of the country, where they have to say, 'I'm sorry, I cannot support the party's position on this issue … it's up to you to communicate it properly.' If you're a lousy communicator then God help you."

Conflicted candidates do not perceive a strong obligation to seek party guidance in the face of uncertainty. A 2015 Liberal candidate in Quebec explains that they sought to use their "best judgment … [I]f you're a candidate and you've gone through that process, I'd like to think you can make the right decision on your own, at least 99 per cent of the time." Nor do conflicted candidates view their campaigns as extensions of the central party. As a 2015 Alberta Liberal candidate explains, "I sometimes did what I wanted even if it wasn't what the party wanted because I felt like: (A) They didn't know what I was doing and were far away, and; (B) They didn't really care anyways." Meanwhile, a 2015 Conservative candidate in Ontario claims that "you have to be very careful if you're going to say something that goes against the platform or official line … It's been a tension in the past maybe, although if it came up, I would essentially say no comment or avoid it somehow."

Lastly, there are two indicators for maverick candidates: cooperation with an opposing campaign and publicly criticizing party leadership. Either indicator is sufficient to receive this maverick label. Every maverick candidate also indicated that they had engaged in more than one other less severe form of undisciplined behaviour, such as ignoring party instructions. Maverick candidates represent roughly 13 per cent of respondents, or eleven people in a sample of eighty-seven. Maverick candidates speak openly of party discipline as inauthentic and proclaim their devotion to the constituency above partisan loyalties. According to 2015 NDP candidate Ken Kuzminski (Yellowhead), "[voters] can tell if you're just spouting the party line. They see that on TV, on the radio, they see the ads, and they're sick and tired of it."

These candidates offer concrete examples of this approach to local campaigning. NDP candidate Daniel Beals (2015, Kingston and the Islands) explains that his maverick attitude stemmed from an allegiance to local party members: "NDP members in Kingston chose me as the NDP representative. I won a nomination where our members in Kingston were the ones that picked me to be the candidate, both times. They're the ones that I owed my first allegiance to ... And I might not have been elected by the riding, but I was elected by those people to be their voice." Accordingly, when Beals opposed his party's official positions on energy and climate change, he "decided I was going to make it very clear that I believe that the oil sands in Alberta should, in fact, be called the tar sands and we should leave the oil in the ground. That was not a talking point that the party wanted anyone to use ... It wasn't done expecting nothing to happen. I thought that I'd hear about it later ... I did it on purpose." Beals provides further evidence of his efforts to represent and motivate local members by advocating for particular issues.[22] In this case, Beals contends that stepping around party directives allowed him to sustain a satisfied and engaged local activist base.

In another case, a maverick candidate in Ontario recalls critiquing one of their party's policy commitments and related communications. The candidate indicated their refusal to repeat these messages, recounted heated discussions with the central party, and claimed they ultimately faced no discernible party repercussions. These maverick candidates include both long-serving incumbents with ample campaign resources and less experienced politicians running in uncompetitive constituencies. For example, after seven federal campaigns, Liberal MP John McKay (Scarborough–Guildwood) is confident in his ability to discern when party messaging is misguided for his community. When provided with such messaging, McKay is comfortable responding: "[a]re you kidding, I'm not saying that, I'm going to throw it in the garbage." Conversely, a first-time Conservative candidate (2015, Quebec) explains that when openly disagreeing with their party, "I speak in the 'I' when I say this [issue position], I don't claim it's the party position. I speak for myself and justify the issue."

Variations in Campaign Discipline: Riding and Candidate Attributes

Which types of candidates and campaigns are more likely to display undisciplined behaviour? In seeking to explain the propensity for undisciplined behaviour, it is worth returning to figures 3.1 and 3.2 on sample characteristics and considering variables such as party affiliation and riding density. These data serve an illustrative purpose more so than an analytical one. Caution and nuance are required in drawing conclusions due to small sample sizes, for example, of rural candidates.[23] Nor were these eighty-seven candidates and local campaigns identified through randomized probability sampling.

Previous studies of personalized campaigning (for example, Pruysers and Cross, 2018) have benefited from several hundred survey responses in determining which factors are associated with personalized campaigns. Conversely, this research aims to maximize internal validity while obtaining sensitive political information (e.g., Sayers 1999; Koop 2011). Despite limited breadth, the findings outlined below help to reveal how local campaign behaviour may differ based on key candidate and riding characteristics. Interestingly, there is minimal variation in disciplinary tendencies across the variables. Sample characteristics for the eighty-seven interview subjects are displayed on page 49 in Figure 3.1 and Figure 3.2, which feature breakdowns by candidate and riding attributes relevant to the propensity for undisciplined behaviour. Political parties may have different disciplinary norms, and the NDP historically has fewer resources that can be dedicated to campaign cohesion (McGrane 2019). Moreover, existing research shows us that women candidates are treated differently than men by parties and the media (e.g., Goodyear-Grant 2013), and this may be reflected in candidates' behaviours. Figure 3.1 also illustrates how many candidates in the sample were successful in their elections. Elected candidates may be more prone to undisciplined behaviour due to their campaign viability and likelihood of possessing substantial campaign resources.

Figure 3.2 displays riding-level characteristics relevant to the analysis. Candidates are differentiated by province, as regional differences may generate different attitudes towards campaign discipline and party cohesion. Riding density and riding competitiveness are also considered. For the former, rural candidates are more prone to running personalized campaigns (Cross and Young 2015) and may also be prone to undisciplined behaviour. In terms of competitiveness, parties may be more tolerant of undisciplined behaviour in constituencies where they are unlikely to win. Parties also pay greater attention to seats where the outcome is uncertain. Competitiveness is measured here with a simple distinction between battleground and stronghold ridings (Bodet 2013) based on margin of victory, as per Blais and Lago (2009, 95). In battleground ridings, the candidate of interest won or lost their race by 10 percentage points or less. In strongholds, the candidate of interest won or lost by over 10 points. Rural, urban, and suburban distinctions are based on population density, as per Sayers (1999, 111–18).

Table 3.4 Constituency Campaign Discipline by Candidate and Riding Characteristics: Proportions (raw counts)

	Conscientious (37)	Conflicted (39)	Maverick (11)	Totals (87)
Conservative	.39 (11)	.46 (13)	.14 (4)	1 (28)
Liberal	.41 (11)	.52 (14)	.07 (2)	1 (27)
NDP	.47 (15)	.38 (12)	.16 (5)	1 (32)
Men	.38 (25)	.48 (31)	.14 (9)	1 (65)
Women	.55 (12)	.36 (8)	.09 (2)	1 (22)
Elected	.38 (10)	.54 (14)	.08 (2)	1 (26)
Not elected	.44 (27)	.41 (25)	.15 (9)	1 (61)
Alberta	.54 (15)	.32 (9)	.14 (4)	1 (28)
Ontario	.26 (6)	.61 (14)	.13 (3)	1 (23)
Quebec	.44 (16)	.44 (16)	.11 (4)	1 (36)
Rural	.50 (8)	.31 (5)	.19 (3)	1 (16)
Suburban	.40 (16)	.45 (18)	.10 (4)	1 (40)
Urban	.42 (13)	.52 (16)	.13 (4)	1 (31)
Battleground	.41 (11)	.56 (15)	.04 (1)	1 (27)
Stronghold	.43 (26)	.40 (24)	.17 (10)	1 (60)

n=87

Table 3.4 displays results for undisciplined behaviour based on candidate and riding-level attributes. For greater readability, findings are reported as proportions that total to 1, as seen in the far right-hand column. Contrary to expectations, there is limited variation in undisciplined behaviour by candidate and riding attributes. As shown in Table 3.3, 13 per cent of candidates in the sample are mavericks, who display the most strident undisciplined behaviour. Table 3.4 shows only 7 per cent of Liberals in the sample are maverick candidates, versus 16 per cent of NDP candidates. However, the small sample size is such that if just one additional Liberal candidate qualified as maverick, the figure would increase to 11 per cent. Apparent variation in proportion or percentage terms must be viewed alongside the modest variation in raw counts.

Women candidates are the most disproportionately conscientious in this sample, with 55 per cent, compared to a sample average of 42 per cent. Women candidates are also slightly less likely than men to display maverick behaviour (9 per cent versus 14 per cent). There is no apparent difference in discipline based on whether candidates were successfully elected. Aside from a disproportionate concentration of conflicted candidates in Ontario, there is minimal variation by province. Somewhat surprisingly, Ontario candidates did not express a more harmonious relationship with the central party than those in Quebec or Alberta.[24]

The clearest disproportionate concentration of maverick candidates is found among rural candidates and those in stronghold ridings, with proportions of 0.19 and 0.17, respectively, compared to the all-candidate average of 0.13. This is consistent with findings that rural candidates are better known in their ridings than non-rural candidates (Carty and Eagles 2005) and are more likely to personalize their campaigns (Cross and Young 2015). It also suggests that central party attention, which is focused on battleground ridings (Flanagan 2014), may serve as a check on undisciplined behaviour. But these differences are fairly modest when considering the overall number of rural and battleground candidates.

Insubordination, Innovation, and Incompetence

At least in this sample, there is limited variation in undisciplined behaviour based on candidate and riding attributes. But are there other explanations or common features of undisciplined behaviour? In fact, interview and observational data reveal three broad features of undisciplined behaviour that shed light on why candidates sometimes refuse or fail to follow party directives. In reviewing these data, individual instances of undisciplined behaviour appear to be driven by insubordination, innovation, and incompetence within local campaigns. These concepts are not mutually exclusive, as certain instances of innovation also constitute insubordination.

Insubordination

Insubordinate campaign behaviour is defiant towards the central party. This entails knowledge of central party expectations and a decision to discount them. There are abundant examples of such behaviour among local campaigns in 2015 and 2019. The central party is often unaware of insubordinate behaviour. For example, a 2019 candidate in Ontario recounts how their campaign was instructed not to accept volunteers affiliated with a particular advocacy organization. However, they proceeded to accept several volunteers without the party's knowledge. In other cases, the party communicates directly with an insubordinate campaign. For example, in 2015, party headquarters asked a candidate to drive two hours to stand behind the party leader as a media backdrop during a speech. Despite the party "pulling all the strings," including by suggesting that the leader "would really appreciate it," the local candidate refused to attend, relying on a creative excuse.

Interestingly, party strategists do not generally anticipate significant insubordination from constituency campaigns. A Liberal strategist contends that "if there's a respect and buy-in to the purpose of the campaign, I think [there is] excellent compliance from the local level ... [What you] may call discipline or uniformity is the result of hard work that brings everyone on the same page and that's why it seems heavily scripted." Similarly, a Conservative strategist suggests that "by the time the campaign starts, and the local campaigns have been through the vetting and the training, we're pulling together, which of course actually means we're on the phones making sure no one is screwing up ... and [local campaigns are] doing their best to follow the instructions and stretch their resources and generally be an asset for [the central party]." However, in several key domains of local campaign activity, evidence reflects insubordinate behaviour, including through obstinate and disjointed local execution of party preferences, as well as fractious relations between local, regional, and national party offices.

Insubordination often results from a sense of local alienation or frustration with supposedly out-of-touch directions imposed by the party. In such cases, constituency actors claim to contravene party directives in favour of local or regional representation or simply to accommodate local preferences. Andy Brooke, 2015 Conservative candidate (Kingston and the Islands) recalls, "I was told early in the [2015] campaign to not even address or speak on local issues." In the end, Brooke "only tried it for about a week," after perceiving this to be an ineffective approach for the riding. In Brooke's view, a national focus would generate poor voter engagement and negative local media coverage. Conservative MP John Barlow (Foothills) recalls trying to remain "as hyper-local as possible" in 2015, despite party requests to amplify national talking points. And longtime Liberal MP John McKay (Scarborough–Guildwood) contends that candidates require much greater leeway to address local issues, although he personally feels free to do so. In terms of contradicting central party messages, McKay suggests "[y]ou do try to minimize your inconsistencies, but the Lord himself was not entirely consistent on all matters ... We're all inconsistent. Parties, frankly, more so."

A 2015 NDP candidate in Alberta illustrates party concerns with local message tailoring, noting that "some of the statements by the Ontario and Quebec candidates [on oil sands production] were killing us." Likewise, a Conservative strategist suggests that "in 2015, almost every Liberal and NDP candidate [in Quebec], outside of Montreal, and even some within Montreal, was contradicting their parties' stance on [the right to wear face coverings at citizenship ceremonies] ... On pipelines, [candidates] in Quebec and other provinces were also clearly taking opposing positions." This is consistent with controversies where candidates have distanced themselves from their parties' locally unpopular stances (e.g., Laschinger 2016, 209).

Some of these episodes are also linked to local reactions to key campaign events. For example, during Justin Trudeau's infamous blackface makeup scandal (Noël and Blouin 2019), local Liberal campaigns were initially asked to downplay the issue, preferably by avoiding it and directing electors to national talking points. However, one campaign noticed an immediate uptick in volunteers, donations, and political interest in the days after the scandal, and chose to go out of their way to discuss it at public events.

Why would the party bother to discourage a localized campaign focus? A Conservative strategist suggests that "once you're deep into [local issues] there's a heightened risk of making a mistake ... something with an implication you haven't considered." Similarly, NDP strategist Karl Bélanger notes that "the messages chosen by the party were tested and selected in order to maximize the ability to gain votes ... once you depart from them, you're in uncharted territory and you're going on local instinct. Some have strong instincts and others have less strong instincts, it's the latter I'm concerned about if we were to loosen this." Bélanger perceives minimal need to address local issues, since "it's a federal election, not a local referendum." Nonetheless, these contentions sit poorly with some local campaigns.[25]

Innovation

In other cases, candidates and campaign managers contravene party directives through their innovative campaign practices. Innovative constituency campaigns do not confine themselves to the typical activities anticipated by the central party, and some adopt novel ways of completing routine campaign tasks. Their atypical tactics and behaviours can result in the contravention of party directives. As a 2019 NDP campaign manager suggests, "Some of [our activity] ... is more creative [and] falls outside the bounds of what's typically expected." As an example, they mentioned certain volunteer appreciation events they had organized in the past.

Constituency campaign resources are a strong predictor of innovation. In other words, high-resource campaigns are prone to experiment with atypically sophisticated, bold, or novel campaign tactics. Such campaigns also typically have more autonomy from the central party (Sayers 1999). Other local campaigns with substantial resources are uninterested in innovative behaviour and use their resources to focus exclusively on core campaign activities, for example, by meeting or exceeding their parties' canvassing targets and fundraising goals.

Innovation can also occur among resource-poor constituency campaigns, when scarcity promotes improvisation that results in deviation from party rules. For example, in one area of Quebec, local campaigns from two opposing parties shared some campaign resources including certain voter information, volunteers, and storage space. Although his campaign enjoyed considerable resources, Liberal MP Adam Vaughan sought to achieve efficiencies through innovative canvassing techniques: "If you went knocking on doors, you wouldn't find anybody home, if you went to the park, you'd find two thousand voters there … [and] everyone drinks illegally in the park … [so] we took small brown paper bags, we got a small rubber stamp that said "hide your beer, don't hide your vote," and gave them [information] for where the advance polls were." While their campaign was told by the central party not to attempt this tactic, they decided to ignore the directive. Vaughan recalls, "when we first proposed to do this, the party went nuts … this looked like we were encouraging lawbreaking and public disorderly conduct … if this gets back to the churches in the suburbs that we're doing this and we'll be just as lax with illegal drugs … but we did it anyways because we knew it was going to stay in the park … and it was very successful, and it didn't blow up beyond the park." In Vaughan's view, this experience reinforced the idea that the central party is not always in touch with local realities. He explains that "the central party if you ask them they'll shut it down because they want a regimented military message-of-the-day campaign but locally that's not breaking through, and you've got to find a way to communicate to people where they live and how they live."

As this example illustrates, innovative behaviour may or may not overlap with insubordinate behaviour, as an instance of insubordinate innovation. For Vaughan's campaign, diverging from typical party practices was necessary in order to implement a novel canvassing tactic. Conversely, constituency campaign innovation may unintentionally disregard party procedures. For example, a local candidate in 2015 recounts hiring a group of musicians to accompany them around major streets in the constituency while playing music and waving campaign signs, but later discovered this affiliation was a conflict of interest for the musical group. As we have seen, not all campaign scenarios are accounted for by candidate training and party handbooks. Accordingly, when experimenting with innovative campaign techniques, an NDP strategist recounts that the guiding principle from the central party's viewpoint is "to be smart and follow the spirit of the rules."[26]

While local actors are hardly forbidden from pursuing innovative campaign practices, these must be cleared with field organizers and other party officials. When pressed for why they did not seek official party approval, local campaigns typically pointed to impracticality, delays, and the possibility of having the request refused. As a 2019 Conservative campaign manager explains, "I'm moving ahead [with this] because I'm very confident that what they don't know won't hurt them." They added a familiar idea heard from several local campaign actors: "beg for forgiveness, not permission." An NDP candidate in Ontario echoes this view: "I think there's a randomness to getting the green light [for this campaign practice] ... if I show it to [a certain person], they'll be fine with it, someone else might be quite sceptical ... I'm not in a place to navigate that right now so better to just go ahead and tinker later if [someone objects]."

By far, the most common manifestation of constituency campaign innovation in 2015 and 2019 surrounded the creation of digital advertisements and online promotional videos. An example of the latter is recounted by Richler (2016, 237–44), who stood for election as a long-shot NDP candidate in the constituency of Toronto–St. Paul's. Richler employed a digital animation team to create viral parody videos where he inserted animated versions of himself into scenes where he could disrupt and correct other major parties' leaders. The central party eventually forced Richler to take down these videos, but Richler's team purposefully lagged in following this instruction long enough for the videos to achieve their desired effect of attracting viral attention. The video also triggered the central party's fears of angering the CBC, due to the depiction of former anchor Peter Mansbridge.

Digital advertisements allow micro-targeting of electors based on postal code, cultural-linguistic group, or other categories (Bennett 2019). Campaign observation revealed that the Liberals and Conservatives provided centrally regulated digital advertising packages, through party-aligned suppliers, which local campaigns could opt in to and purchase. However, certain local campaigns declined this service in order to exercise greater creative control. Campaign observation also revealed how digital advertisements have become highly effective in micro-targeting. Some advertisements consist of video clips, typically lasting ten to thirty seconds, while others are simply images with moving text. Their approach demonstrates local creativity, in terms of using humour, parody, and music. In contrast to the party's digital ads, they may speak to local or niche political issues. Other advertisements include non-official language messaging. Local teams were asked whether the central party would view these advertisements before their appearance on platforms such as Facebook. A 2019 Liberal campaign manager stated, "I don't think so. If they ask then we will [show them] … they're there if they want to see. We're not hiding anything." Other campaigns expressed similar sentiments, explaining that the central party was not part of this process and they would not seek party approval for digital advertisements. In their view, the party could verify content once it is posted online.

In some cases, digital advertisements reinforced the central party's core messages. However, others evinced tensions, if not outright contradictions, for different candidates of the same party. Although the content of these ads cannot be identified for confidentiality purposes, in certain cases, they varied significantly, to the point of tension, with national party messages. For example, some Conservative candidates in Quebec announced support for the 2019 Quebec secularism law that their leader took pains to avoid discussing (Vastel 2019). In all, digital advertising may facilitate regionally and locally dissonant campaign messaging, on a variety of contentious issues.[27]

Incompetence

A final source of undisciplined behaviour stems from the incompetence or incapacity of local campaigns. This classification does not necessarily signify poor judgment, but rather an inability to follow party directives due to insufficient resources, training, or other restrictions. Unlike insubordination and innovation, which entail more purposive departures from party directives, incompetence is always non-instrumental. Nonetheless, the result is the same: central party preferences are obstructed or distorted in their adoption by constituency campaigns.

A 2015 candidate explains that as national campaign momentum shifted against their party, and volunteers and resources trickled away, they could no longer meet party expectations to do "anything other than don't say something stupid … and even that's not a given." Other campaigns echoed the sentiment of being ill-equipped to handle the demands imposed by their parties. A 2015 NDP candidate in Alberta explains their gradual exhaustion, since "at the start [a volunteer] and I were driving three hundred kilometres plus a day to keep up … [but] we've pretty much stopped now." In the case of another 2015 candidate in Alberta, the accumulation of unmet campaign obligations was a highly stressful experience. The candidate explains that "I knew what they wanted and why we couldn't [achieve this] … I didn't like the constant reminders. I felt that I'd tried … [A]t one point … I just hung up [the phone] on them and stopped returning calls."

Accordingly, incompetence frequently stemmed from local campaigns being unable to act in accordance with party preferences due to a lack of resources. In other words, a lack of local capacity can result in undisciplined behaviour through error or omission. As explained by a 2015 Liberal candidate in Ontario,

> There were problems left and right ... we didn't commit our data, we sent the wrong data, we had one person who had done [party training] but he wasn't available and there were all sorts of mistakes ... our volunteers did a whole canvass entering the information backwards and it's already submitted [on the canvassing app] ... [T]hat happened more than once. You can fix it afterwards but in some cases I don't think we had time.

Similarly, in the middle of the 2019 campaign, one candidate realized they had not technically been nominated when Elections Canada uncovered dozens of signatures from people outside the constituency on their nomination form. This problem resulted from a miscommunication between volunteer members of the local constituency association. Such cases illustrate the difficulty of running a textbook campaign, given significant inequalities in campaign competencies and resources. This is especially notable as volunteers tend to be overworked during the campaign period and they are typically younger or much older than the average citizen. Given substantial inequalities in local financial capacity, vertical or horizontal transfers to under-resourced constituencies (Currie-Wood 2020; Westlake 2022) could help to mitigate this type of undisciplined behaviour and its attendant challenges.

In other cases, undisciplined behaviour through incompetence occurred when local candidates or campaign managers simply made a mistake that contradicted party preferences. Along these lines, insufficient training can also help to explain incompetence. After experiencing a challenging all-candidates meeting, a 2015 Liberal candidate in Alberta explained, "that debate was a total disaster. I just didn't know what I was doing, I didn't know what to say and ... said [things] I shouldn't have said ... [it was] a learning experience."

Local actors offered a variety of explanations when asked to justify their undisciplined behaviour. When asked to explain why they chose not to follow party instructions, their rationales included to reflect the wishes of their constituents, for political advantage in their election race, to advance the career or reputation of the candidate or campaign staff member, because the party's advice was ineffective, and to follow personal convictions. In other constituencies, careerism may underpin undisciplined behaviour. As a 2019 Liberal campaign manager suggests, "don't underestimate how many campaign decisions are made in the narrow ... career interest of the campaign manager."

As such, how close a local race is does not clearly relate to the likelihood of engaging in undisciplined behaviour. Local campaigns in tightly contested elections may be more risk tolerant in seeking to gain electoral advantage and adapting to local preferences. But they are also more closely monitored by the centre. In safe seats, candidates are more likely to be established incumbents with confidence to act independently from their party. At the same time, their winning trajectory carries low motivation to adopt undisciplined or atypical campaign tactics and to risk upsetting the central party. Finally, for those in unwinnable districts, there is little electoral payoff from undisciplined behaviour. But there is typically greater indifference towards the central party and the campaign itself, which may lead to deviation from party instructions. Indeed, some candidates in these ridings accepted to run as a favour to their parties and may have a lower threshold for additional sacrifices in time, effort, or compromise to their preferences.

Implications of Undisciplined Campaign Behaviour

During a period of campaign observation, a Liberal campaign manager quipped, "if a local campaign ignores the [party], but they don't find out, did it even happen?" This question highlights the importance of the tangible implications that arise from undisciplined behaviour. First, the frequent expressions of undisciplined behaviour identified in this chapter call into question perceptions of domineering party headquarters or subservient constituency campaigns. In his 2014 book *Winning Power: Canadian Campaigning in the Twenty-First Century*, Tom Flanagan contends that "Local candidates mostly repeat talking points furnished by the national campaign. They are urged to spend their time doorknocking and meeting voters in person, not generating new policy positions. They are, for all practical purposes, a regionalized sales force for a national firm" (31). While this language evokes Carty's franchise model, it does not align with the reality of local autonomy to run the ground campaign, as identified by the work of Carty and Cross[28] and reaffirmed here. Some campaigns do largely repeat national talking points but most are preoccupied with tailoring messages to their communities and specific audiences within them. Based on perceptions of diverging interests and the nature of undisciplined campaign behaviour (see Tables 3.1 and 3.3), it appears that many constituency actors neither perceive themselves nor behave as local sales agents for the central party. Each major party encompasses considerable regional, ideological, and socio-demographic diversity. This undoubtedly leads to varied local perceptions of, and potential tensions with, the centre.

In this respect, undisciplined behaviour highlights the importance of individual personalities and idiosyncratic local forces in the campaign ecosystem. Party cohesion depends upon local decision-making and compliance. And there are diverse local responses to party influence. Some local actors are profoundly shaped by party influences, as stated by one such candidate: "I'm a party hack, guilty as charged ... I can't help it." Others are relatively unfazed by party norms, resistant to disciplinary expectations, or sceptical towards their own parties. One such candidate suggests that "I generally believe in the party but not over [my community], or my instincts and boundaries."

A second implication concerns campaign operations. Undisciplined behaviour may cause disruptions or inconveniences to the central campaign, even if party officials are unaware of their source. This is especially clear when campaign planning requires local participation or collaboration. Indeed, through the course of the campaign, the central party deploys the leader, campaign surrogates, and other resources to target regions and ridings. Yet several constituency campaigns viewed these exercises as poorly executed or unwelcome burdens. As a result, they effectively resisted or even undermined central party efforts. In one case, the central party had planned an announcement targeting members of a particular ethnocultural community. The party requested that a constituency campaign send members of this community to attend the announcement event. However, members of the local campaign declined this request by exaggerating the hardship they would endure and misrepresenting their ability to meet it. In another case, a 2019 campaign manager who was asked to provide advance team services for a leaders' visit recounts that "they asked me to drive the route that the [leaders' entourage] was going to take ... except I couldn't [do this] and they wouldn't listen. I didn't do it and they never knew." Luckily the leaders' tour passed through smoothly, even without verification of the route.

Visits by party leaders are perceived to be desirable to local campaigns (Carty and Eagles 2005, 112). Yet some candidates contend that these visits command an extraordinary amount of their resources and distract them from local objectives, with minimal political benefit. When it came time to coordinate with the leaders' tour, some campaigns aimed to release a minimal number of volunteers, even when parties persistently sought out crowds of supporters to surround the leader. As Liberal MP John McKay explains, "if the Prime Minister or party leader is coming, basically you have to take your team off the campaign for two days, organize the event, make sure you've got enough bodies there to make it a crowd, and then do the cleanup afterwards … " Some local actors go further, suggesting to the party that the leaders' presence would be unhelpful, and they should not bother visiting their riding. Others hesitate to pitch in with party requests for leaders' visits. A 2019 local campaign manager recalled telling the party that "we have a volunteer shortage" and releasing the "the minimum volunteers possible." While seemingly minor disruptions, these examples illustrate potential risks for the party when local campaign support is needed to benefit from earned media and build a sense of campaign momentum.

A third implication is the potential electoral consequences of undisciplined behaviour. A Liberal strategist describes their worries about such behaviour, suggesting that "in a high-stakes election, which is [every election], that's enough for me to say absolutely not please." A lack of campaign discipline may even have contributed to recent election defeats at the provincial level. Alluding to recent examples at the time of their interview, an NDP strategist suggests that candidate blunders cost the Ontario NDP dearly in the 2018 provincial election: "it fed into a narrative that the party was not serious and not prepared and the media was very happy to run with that … amateur hour narrative … [building] momentum of [the NDP] as not fit to govern." Likewise, in Alberta, Flanagan (2014, 184) identifies factors that led to the surprise late-campaign decline of the Wildrose Party in 2012: "inadequate opposition research on our own candidates, candidates not consulting the war room before talking to the media, leader and candidates being overeager to answer questions that should have been deflected." And strategist John Laschinger (2016, 208) contends that insufficient discipline among Progressive Conservative candidates effectively cost the party the 2007 Ontario provincial election.[29] As the campaign progressed, Bill Murdoch and Garfield Dunlop, two PC MPPs, contradicted party policy on extending public funding for religious schools. Laschinger writes (209) that "The Murdoch/Dunlop disease was threatening to extend to other candidates," which forced the party to make politically dubious modifications to its previous policy. Ultimately, "Dalton McGuinty was returned to Queen's Park with a majority government thanks mainly to two MPPs … " (209).

NDP strategist Brad Lavigne emphasizes that different forms of undisciplined behaviour are not equally consequential. But even benign actions may be enough to worry campaign strategists. Regardless of electoral impact, undisciplined behaviour sheds light on the scope and magnitude of central party authority. It bears emphasizing that parties are frequently unequipped to prevent this behaviour, despite what we may expect in terms of their organizational abilities.

A fourth implication of these findings concerns organizational cohesion. The prevalence and nature of undisciplined behaviour indicates tensions in the relationship between the central party and local actors. During initial discussions held with national and local campaign actors, most claimed they were appreciative of their counterparts. However, these sentiments changed as details emerged, whether during interviews or campaign observation, with many highlighting frustrations and disappointments. Broadly speaking, the central party may feel that constituency campaigns have an unwarranted sense of their uniqueness. While parties designate officials to support local campaigns, their senior strategists who deal with large-scale trends and vast amounts of precise data may not appreciate local demands. Conversely, local campaigns often feel that the party is unavailable when needed, distant and detached from ground-level realities, and guided by optics and efficiency, with little regard for local actors or their well-being.

In sum, many constituency campaigns have the motivation and audacity to contravene party preferences. They do not reliably view their interests as aligned with those of their parties. In addition to self-interested motivations, constituency campaigns also act to maintain local independence and diversity. In a campaign context, centrifugal forces, including significant sociocultural and regional diversity, are powerful enough to withstand party machinations intended to suppress them through candidate vetting, training, socialization, and monitoring of constituency campaigns.

Regarding the question of how closely constituency campaigns adhere to central party norms and expectations, this chapter shows that constituency campaigns regularly act in defiance of such preferences and do so in varied ways. In establishing definitional parameters for undisciplined behaviour, it is possible to separate constituency campaigns into three categories – conscientious, conflicted, and maverick – when it comes to their adherence to party norms and procedures. By identifying patterns of undisciplined behaviour by local campaigns, it is possible to categorize such undisciplined behaviour according to their primary causes: innovation, insubordination, and incompetence. Altogether, the level of undisciplined behaviour is higher than anticipated in existing research, and this points to the limitations of central party authority during a campaign period. The next chapter expands the study of undisciplined behaviour by asking how party directives interact with local realities during the practice of voter canvassing and the development of partisan campaign literature.

Chapter 4

Voter Canvassing and Campaign Literature

Voter canvassing and campaign literature are among the most essential elements of a local campaign. Even long-shot candidates typically take on these responsibilities, while credible campaigns dedicate extensive time and resources. Canvassing and campaign literature also notably require local campaign messaging, as local actors may decide how to transmit party messages appropriately in their communities. It bears examining what disciplined and undisciplined local campaign behaviour look like in practice through these specific case studies. The first case study of public-facing communications explored in this chapter asks to what extent local campaigns follow central party directives and procedures in voter canvassing practices. The second considers the development and distribution of partisan campaign literature.

Parties rely on the voter data and other benefits garnered by canvassers, but local campaigns do not necessarily follow canvassing protocols and procedures. This chapter identifies extensive variation in voter canvassing practices. Some campaigns are highly enthusiastic and diligent about their canvassing duties, while others are ambivalent or even hostile to them. Moreover, the six indicators of undisciplined campaign behaviour, as explained in Chapter 3, can all be observed during canvassing.[1] The chapter also considers the consequences of undisciplined local canvassing, some of which result in improved voter engagement as local campaigns that ignore party directives facilitate more substantive canvassing interactions.

Turning to the creation and distribution of partisan campaign literature, the chapter draws from a sample of ninety-six campaign leaflets from the three largest federal parties in order to determine the extent to which they deviate from central party templates. Working with this sample, it is clear that local campaigns are consistent in the aesthetic presentation of their campaign materials but are more likely to deviate from the party's national campaign brand and themes in their substantive content. There is minor variation in locally distinct branding based on political party, region, and riding population density, but less undisciplined behaviour overall in the development of constituency campaign literature relative to voter canvassing. With constituency campaign literature, undisciplined behaviour manifests in more subtle ways, particularly involving the distribution of unvetted materials and the creation of literature in non-official languages. The case studies together show that public-facing campaign communications provide venues for the negotiation of local autonomy and the reassertion of local campaign preferences. In this respect, the prevalence of undisciplined behaviour indicates that local campaigns are not strictly confined to party rules and scripts.

Voter Canvassing: Purpose and Process[2]

During their interviews, eight party strategists were asked, "during a federal election, what would you say are the most important things that local campaigns must do?" Respondents were permitted to list as many activities as they desired. As Table 4.1 illustrates below, canvassing and distributing campaign literature were the two most popular responses.

Voter canvassing is mentioned by all eight of the strategists interviewed, while campaign literature is mentioned by six. Get-out-the-vote (GOTV) is one aspect of canvassing, which occurs only on election day and is intended to ensure that previously identified supporters have actually voted (Thompson 2016). For its part, canvassing refers to direct unmediated contact with voters, either by phone or in person.[3] To canvass by phone, volunteers and campaign staff rely on voter lists, typically aided by automated dialing software, and read scripted campaign messages during live phone interactions or less frequently by voicemail. Party strategists underlined the importance of phone canvassing in ridings with a small volunteer base or a large geographic area, both of which pose challenges for door-to-door canvassing. Volunteers with mobility challenges may also prefer to canvass by phone. Candidates may also conduct follow-up phone calls with voters who expressed a desire to speak to them directly. That said, door canvassing is generally perceived to be more effective than phone canvassing. A shrinking number of households have landlines and cell phone numbers can be difficult to obtain. Compared with door canvassing, the mobilizing effect of a phone canvass is generally weaker, refusal rates are higher, and communication barriers are more pronounced (Gerber and Green 2000; Green and Gerber 2001, 2019).[4]

Table 4.1 Local Campaign Activities' Perceived Importance by Party Strategists*

Activity	Number of Strategists Mentioning
Canvassing	8
Get-out-the-vote	7
Distributing campaign literature	6
Fundraising	5
Recruiting volunteers	5
Attracting positive media coverage/credibility	3
Attending local events	3
Erecting lawn/public signs	3
Other	2

n=8
*See Appendix C

Scholars and party strategists agree that face-to-face contact is essential for mobilizing and persuading potential voters, as well as building and updating lists with voter information (Black 1984; Gerber, Green, and Green 2003; Green, Gerber, and Nickerson 2003). A Liberal strategist explains that "seeing an actual human is extremely effective." Other strategists emphasize the valuable data on voter preferences and demographics provided by canvassers. They also note that door canvassers typically obtain more data and more reliable data. Moreover, people are generally reluctant to answer phone calls from unknown numbers due to telemarketers and scam artists.

For these reasons, door canvassing is seen as the "centrepiece of any strong constituency campaign ... [and] the most important activity carried out by these campaigns" (Koop 2015, 42). Local campaigns with a strong partisan base have the luxury of interacting mostly with supportive voters, whom they seek to identify, ask for a financial contribution or volunteer commitment, and eventually get to the polls. Identifying supporters is the central goal, whereas other campaigns must frequently interact with hostile or indifferent citizens. Due to the significance of canvassing for local campaigns, this is a critical area in which to examine whether party instructions are followed or whether and why undisciplined behaviour occurs.

Party Expectations for Canvassing

Parties typically ask local campaigns to meet daily or weekly canvassing targets that vary based on constituency competitiveness and local resources (Richler 2016; Thompson 2016).[5] Candidates and campaign managers are repeatedly made aware of the canvassing demands imposed on them. As explained by a 2015 Conservative candidate in Ontario, "if there's one thing that was drilled in [during campaign training], it was to canvass all the time, go knock doors, make contact as much as possible. Try not to get distracted. Follow the canvassing procedures and whatnot. Sometimes I would ask an unrelated question and the answer from the party would be 'go knock doors.'"

Aside from helping the party to prevail in close local races, there are further reasons why parties require diligent canvassing. NDP strategist Brad Lavigne contends that the central party is at a significant disadvantage without substantial accurate data collected by local campaigns. Lavigne lists several benefits of these data, which include understanding the changing demographic and partisan composition of the electorate, providing valuable information for micro-targeting electors, staying in long-term contact with supporters, and keeping up with the tactics and practices of rival parties.

Party databases, with their extensive information on individual electors, have become crucial for voter outreach (Patten 2017, 47). The data that feeds these databases are continuously changing, and canvassing provides fresh information on voter locations, political leanings, and demographic information, to continuously feed these databases (56). This view is shared by a Liberal Party strategist who suggests that "we do depend on that data to update [our systems] about where our voters are, who's moved, who's a Conservative now, and who's dead … [canvassing is] probably most of what [local campaigns] do all day." Another Liberal strategist suggests that although there are other ways to obtain voter data, the campaign setting and the organizational structure of local campaigns create a rare opportunity: "this is our chance … we have volunteers activated and interested in door knocking and giving us a sense of the [electorate] … it's not unusual for each campaign to hit thousands of doors and it's some of the best information money can buy, except it's free … that's why we need [local campaigns] to optimize their canvassing game." The Liberals and Conservatives have special uses for these data, as they have begun to employ predictive algorithms to determine vote choice based on information in their database (Bennett 2019; Patten 2017, 57). The algorithms' predictive power improves as they gain information on past political leanings, principal political concerns, and demographic attributes. The Liberals and Conservatives also draw from "commercially purchased bulk data" (Belfry Munroe and Munroe 2018, 146; see also Marland 2020, 151), which are lists of voter contact information and sometimes more personal information such as languages spoken or consumer habits.

Party strategists are unanimous on the importance of following canvassing protocols. Since local canvassing abilities vary based on available resources (Robbins-Kanter 2022b), parties maintain clear but variable expectations for their local campaigns. As a Liberal strategist suggests, "my expectations for door-to-door would obviously be different based on the riding ... the targets vary based on what's appropriate ... and if you can't meet them, get in touch so we can hopefully fix the problem." A Conservative strategist adds that their canvassing instructions are always the same and "it doesn't matter if you have two volunteers or ... two hundred volunteers." Similarly, a Liberal strategist recounts, "You have to be good at getting to [the doors] and if you're not keeping up, you shouldn't be running." In addition, party strategists agree on their preferred nature and duration of voter interactions during door canvassing. When asked what canvassers should be doing and saying at the door, an NDP strategist suggests, "introduce yourself and ask if they can count on your support, note the information [they provide] and move on. It's quick and it shouldn't be a policy discussion because there are many, many doors to [visit]." A Conservative strategist agrees that candidates should spend "thirty seconds or less at the door ... it's not door-to-door debating. It's rare to persuade someone to change their mind ... that would be very infrequent." And a Liberal Party strategist notes that some candidates "might have a tendency to get into a long discussion or argument even ... that is not a good use of time and resources and will be reflected in the number of doors you can visit." These expectations are understood by local candidates, as a 2015 Liberal candidate in Ontario explains: "they want to know who lives [where], how many [party supporters], what language they speak ... and to keep this data as up to date as possible. Getting good data is the key. It's how we win and keep [winning] long term." It is thus far unknown whether local actors respect these party guidelines for canvassing interactions.

How are party preferences for canvassing established and enforced? The three major parties rely on field organizers or regional desk officers to monitor canvassing progress, and to follow up with campaigns that lag behind on assigned targets. As Koop (2015, 43) explains, the central party is committed to ensuring that local campaigns follow their canvassing guidelines:

> the canvass provides an example of how central party campaigns attempt to direct local operations. For instance, in 2015 the central Conservative campaign mandated the number of supporters local organizations would be required to identify each day of the campaign. Those that fell short

of their targets could expect to receive a disapproving phone call from "national"… [P]arties appreciate the role of constituency campaigns in identifying supporters and subsequently getting them to the polls.

Similarly, Marland (2020, 152) notes that parties routinely admonish MPs who lag behind their peers in canvassing and data entry duties. And Belfry Munroe and Munroe (2018, 139) explain how canvassing activity can be tracked through party software. This is consistent with the experience of 2015 Conservative candidate Andy Brooke (Kingston and the Islands), who recounts, "they can actually look at me live as I move on the map." Parties have begun to develop standardized practices for database-based canvassing, which they intend to mandate for all local campaigns (Belfry Munroe and Munroe 2018). The authors anticipate this has produced further campaign centralization. While adherence to standardized procedures would suggest minimal undisciplined behaviour in voter canvassing, there is no guarantee that party directives are willingly and competently followed by those who receive them.

National Directives, Local Realities

When asked to elaborate on their canvassing practices, local candidates expressed a variety of conflicting views on their voter contact obligations.[6] Candidates were asked to describe how often they reached their door canvassing targets on a five-point scale, ranging from "none of the time" to "all of the time" (see Table 4.2). They were also asked, "did the campaign use any original or creative canvassing techniques?"

Interview and observational data reveal substantial variation in door-to-door canvassing attitudes and activities. Some candidates delighted in reporting the tens of thousands of doors they had personally visited. For example, a 2015 Conservative candidate in Alberta explains, "I hustled every single day to get these numbers, since … eight months before the campaign started." As Table 4.2 indicates, 48 per cent of cases claimed to regularly meet their door knocking targets, with 28 per cent meeting all and 20 per cent meeting most of them.

Others, labelled neutral in Table 4.2, accounting for 22 per cent of campaigns, made some effort to meet targets, and expressed regret at failing to do so. These candidates tended to recall difficulties in meeting canvassing targets with limited resources. A 2015 NDP candidate in Quebec suggests, "I understand where the party is coming from with their canvassing [targets], but that's not going to happen here." Conservative candidate Yves Labecge (2015, Bécancour–Nicolet–Saurel) experienced similar troubles, with a modest volunteer base and uninterested

Table 4.2   Attempts to Meet Canvassing Targets*

Canvasser type	Meets canvassing targets	Percentage of cases (n)
Enthusiastic	All of the time	28
Diligent	Most	20
Neutral	Some	22
Ambivalent	Rarely	24
Hostile	None	7

*Question: Would you say that your campaign attempted to meet the party's canvassing targets all of the time, most of the time, some of the time, rarely, or none of the time?

n=87

central campaign. Laberge explains, "the terrain is difficult for the Conservative Party ... I was not a target riding and they didn't have the resources or ability to keep track of what I was doing."

Others, accounting for 31 per cent of cases, labelled as ambivalent or hostile, rejected the canvassing objectives mandated by their parties and de-prioritized door canvassing as an element of the campaign. While also often mentioning insufficient resources or futile terrain, they expressed less interest in the process itself and sometimes even admonished their parties for forcing the issue. Many felt their parties were either unduly concerned with data collection or viewed the constant instruction to canvass as a misguided effort to redirect their energies from more diverse and fulfilling uses of their time. For example, a Conservative candidate (2015, Ontario) explained that they felt pressure to increase their canvassing numbers but felt this was unfair to their small team of volunteers. Sensing volunteers were overworked, they pushed back against the party and ultimately stopped following canvassing instructions. Similarly, an NDP candidate (2015, Quebec) contends that "my job isn't to enable a data harvesting fetish." A like-minded Liberal candidate explains they prefer not to provide the party with their electors' contact information because the party will "spam [electors] with messages," usually leading them to disengage and ignore future appeals. In a concrete sense, these attitudes and behaviours can result in missing or ignoring canvassing targets, as well as misrepresenting canvassing data. For example, on one local campaign, a volunteer was told to mark swaths of electors who were never actually canvassed as "not home" in order for the numbers to register in the party system. In this respect, minor acts of rebellion denote difficulties in imposing party procedure.

The 31 per cent of cases classified as ambivalent and hostile (see Table 4.2) exemplify undisciplined behaviour, given their failure to meet canvassing targets and stated rejection of party objectives. For the reasons stated above, largely low motivation resulting from a lack of resources, most had little patience or interest in pursuing them. That said, undisciplined behaviour can also originate from a place of strength for local campaigns with ample resources which do regularly meet canvassing targets. For example, some local campaigns directed their canvassers not to use the party's centrally mandated smartphone canvassing app and instead managed and kept their own voter data.

At times, concerns with the central parties' canvassing mandates arose from a perceived disconnect between party instructions and local realities. A 2015 NDP candidate in Quebec suggests that "if I followed [the party procedures] it would take me much longer." They note that canvassing apartment buildings and gated communities can pose particular challenges that the central party does not account for. This sentiment is consistent with Belfry Munroe and Munroe's (2018, 151–2) research, which describes how parties' overly generic protocols led Liberal canvassers in British Columbia astray:

> the highest density polling division, composed of townhouses and apartments inhabited by middle income Canadians to whom the party's messaging was chiefly directed, was not extensively canvassed. Less dense polling divisions consisting of single-family homes, which would have been middle class in Ontario but which are more likely to house Conservative supporters in the high-priced Vancouver area, were canvassed extensively. In Whistler, meanwhile, volunteers were at times sent to polling divisions with significant numbers of vacation homes inhabited only for a few weeks every year and not to the neighbourhoods where residents actually lived.

As this experience suggests, party procedures can sometimes benefit from greater local discretion. Similarly, several local campaigns expressed a desire to develop relationships with various socio-demographic groups in their constituencies. This may entail a particular canvassing strategy that they preferred not to justify to the party, and some rejected their party procedure as overly generic, impractical, or even culturally insensitive. Altogether, local canvassing practices do not reflect a consistent adherence to party procedures. A substantial portion of local campaigns in this sample are hostile or otherwise resistant towards their canvassing obligations.

Some constituency campaign actors share the central party's dedication to door canvassing but disagree with designated canvassing procedures. An example of this is found in the previous chapter where a Toronto-area campaign manager defied the central party by canvassing a wider selection of voter tiers than requested by the party. Here, the party asks local canvassers to only visit the topmost promising tiers (of confirmed party supporters), but the campaign manager prefers to canvass nearly all tiers. In following up with the campaign manager two weeks after this interaction with the party official, they mention benefits of their decision to ignore the party directive: "It was good for everyone ... it was good for [the candidate] to speak with people who weren't just [confirmed supporters], it was good for more [electors] to see [the candidate] ... we reached more people and it wasn't just an echo chamber ... You get much more substantive interactions than a five-second 'remember to vote for me' drop by. And most of those [in the top supporter tier] are going to [vote] ... no matter what."

Along these lines, while the central party calls for brief interactions that glean morsels of demographic and political information from citizens, local actors do not necessarily share these priorities. Instead, as a 2015 Liberal candidate explains,

> the party demands a very frenzied pace ... [that is] very much quantity instead of quality in terms of your interactions with people ... what they want is more to confirm that what's in [the party database] is correct and to update if it's not ... I do think [the party approach] works some of the time, but you have to feel people out and that's not something the party can teach. So they have this one-size-fits-all instruction that I think typifies why local campaigns should use more of their own discretion.

Another Liberal candidate (2015, Quebec) agrees with this sentiment, explaining that from their viewpoint, "in [this constituency] that can be rude to just pop in and out ... some of my most enlightening, most affirming experiences in politics have been when you hear personal stories at the door or even get invited into someone's home. I wouldn't deprive myself or our volunteers of that." This is consistent with Richler (2016) and Thompson (2016) who cite canvassing as among the most rewarding and productive elements of their constituency campaigns. A 2015 Conservative candidate in Alberta adds that they minimally rely on party directions for door canvassing with "no script, no rules for that. If I'm going to knock on that many doors, I'll do it my own way. I tell all the volunteers the same thing, I'm grateful for their time." Similarly, Conservative candidate Yves Laberge (2015, Bécancour–Nicolet–Saurel) recalls that "we didn't have a user guide for door-to-door canvassing ... my approach was always to listen first. To ask [citizens] how they are doing. This was a very interesting approach from a purely human point of view." Laberge views the benefits of this approach as extending to his party and constituents: "essentially there's a need to show that the party is actually listening to voters ... [and] to show voters that they can have a proximity to their elected officials." NDP candidate Ken Kuzminski (2015, Yellowhead) similarly suggests that "at the door it's 100 per cent me and not what the party is saying. I listen to what their issues are. I tell them what I believe." In terms of meeting party expectations, an NDP candidate (2015, Ontario) suggests that they "can't stomach the scripted mechanized way they want you to canvass ... there's no way I'll win or lose ... based on whether I do 50 or 250 doors per day."

This lack of adherence to parties' canvassing procedures arguably produces benefits for voter engagement and representation. A higher number of citizens may encounter politicians and campaign volunteers than the party would otherwise allow, for example, when parties' digital algorithms direct canvassers to ignore unlikely voters. Moreover, those who are visited by canvassers may experience more substantive interactions than party canvassing practices typically facilitate. Along these lines, Morden (2020, 50–1) contends that it is vital for representatives "to get democratic engagement right. Citizens feel out of touch with their political institutions, despite MPs spending more time and resources in the riding." This view is shared by a Liberal candidate (2019, Ontario) who suggests that their party is "chipping away at some of the unscripted ... things we used to do because they're not useful or there's a risk ... " In terms of canvassing, they contend that "most people rarely see a politician in person, and they can tell the difference between 'am I just being counted' or [approached] cynically, or 'am I being heard.'" In their view, while "the party discourages it ... it's not at cross purposes to win an election and actually listen to people." This manifestation of undisciplined behaviour demonstrates local impulses to meaningfully engage citizens that can withstand party objectives and constraints. Furthermore, many local actors remain sceptical of the party's efficiency-based objectives.

Canvassing and Message Dissonance

Stephenson et al. (2019, 75) suggest that local campaigns typically emphasize different issues in different regions. But canvassing behaviour shows they may also seek to distance themselves from party positions on key issues. In some cases, candidates are upfront with electors if and when they hold a personal difference of opinion with their parties. Liberal MP Randy Boissonnault (Edmonton Centre) suggests that candidates can break with their parties if they do so in a constructive way that clarifies to electors why they would have done something differently. Similarly, NDP candidate Marlene Rivier (Ottawa West–Nepean) notes that "if it was something that I felt strongly about, then I would not have a problem saying, 'it's not quite the way I see things, and I anticipate, being active within the party, to shift that position.'" And a 2015 Conservative candidate in Quebec recounts that they often identified points of disagreement with their party while canvassing, and promised citizens they would work to change those positions from within the party.

In other cases, candidates and canvassers appeared to strategically obscure or even misrepresent their parties' positions. As a Liberal candidate (2015, Quebec) explains, "[my opponent] had confused the debate so much … [at the door] I heard again and again [voters] thought we were in favour of [a project] … and they mixed up the positions." These message ambiguities or dissonance may pose an accountability problem, as electors are not necessarily attentive to party platforms, political news, and campaign events. Most canvassing interactions are not subject to public scrutiny, and canvassers who stray from party positions may confuse electors and even hinder their ability to make the "correct choice," defined by Gidengil et al. (2004) as voting consistently with their stated preferences.

When asked whether message dissonance was a common occurrence, most candidates and campaign managers denied personally contradicting their parties. A small number admitted to this, and others suggested that their opponents employed this tactic, but they did not. This trend was observed consistently for each major party, and with varying degrees of severity that did not predictably follow party lines.[7] As previously noted, a Conservative strategist pointed to Liberal and NDP candidates as contradicting their parties in 2015 on pipeline construction and the so-called niqab controversy. However, a Liberal strategist also emphatically suggested their party is least likely to have contradictory messaging among candidates, as the more ideological nature of Conservative and NDP activists makes these parties more susceptible to message dissonance.[8] Given the widespread recognition of this phenomenon, and uneven levels of campaign training and resources, it may be anticipated that each of the three major parties feature some intended or unintended local campaign message dissonance.[9]

Irrespective of positive or negative implications, the extent of local input in canvassing remains notable, given the extent of party investment in this activity and its perceived tactical importance. Local campaigns that display undisciplined behaviour and disregard party procedures do so in the context of their most essential political activity (Koop 2015, 42). Although parties have begun to develop standardized practices for data-based canvassing (Belfry Munroe and Munroe 2018), these efforts have not yet produced uniform or predictable canvassing logics. These findings suggest there is greater local discretion and more difficulty imposing parties' canvassing preferences than anticipated by existing research. At the same time, it is unsurprising that the central office experiences challenges in overseeing the activities of hundreds of organizational units during a campaign. Since many local campaigns have a relatively large and diverse roster of volunteer canvassers, the activity is susceptible to local whims. Other tasks, such as the creation of partisan campaign literature, are restricted to a smaller core of local actors, such as a graphic designer, candidate, and campaign manager. How are message consistency and local autonomy reflected there?

Campaign Literature: Purpose and Process

Along with voter canvassing, the creation and distribution of campaign literature is a core function of local campaigns, as noted by strategists who view it as an essential activity. These materials offer insight into the curation of a local face for national party brands. The present analysis consists of three questions related to campaign literature. First, what are the general rules and principles that inform the creation of campaign literature? Second, how distinct are local campaign materials from national party brands, and which factors affect the degree of variation from party templates? Third, to what extent is undisciplined behaviour detectable in the production and distribution of campaign literature? These elements reveal how local campaigns interpret party directives, the extent of local decision-making authority, and the degree of localized branding that exists under a centralized and nationalized party framework.

Campaign literature refers to print materials such as flyers and pamphlets that are distributed by local campaigns to promote their candidate and political message (King 2002). There are three distinct stages involved in the development of partisan campaign literature within local campaigns: creation, authorization, and distribution. At the first stage, local campaigns and the party collaborate, to varying degrees, to determine the desired content and design for campaign materials. At the second, the candidate's official agent and a party official grant a formal approval before literature is printed. In some cases, the product is sent electronically to the central party, and a regional organizer may grant approval, but other local campaigns view this as a mere formality and may even ignore this step. Third, the materials must be distributed within the riding and circulated to wherever they will be encountered by electors: usually to their homes, but also to local businesses or public events where they can be handed out by volunteers. In most cases, the materials are hand delivered by door canvassers or sent as direct mail.

According to local and national party officials, campaign literature is rarely intended to persuade, but it can ideally leave a brief favourable impression on the recipient and may exert cumulative effects. This is consistent with scholarly researching showing only modest effects in terms of voter mobilization or persuasion (e.g., Brown, Perrella, and Kay 2010; Gerber and Green 2000; Miller and Richey 1980). Citizens rarely read campaign literature with care or in detail. In discussing literature, campaign strategists mentioned a "seven second rule," whereby a campaign leaflet has up to seven seconds of a voter's attention, the rule being named for the amount of time it often takes to carry a flyer from the front door to the recycling bin. As a Liberal strategist explains, "some voters will barely glance at the flyer. For others they'll be reminded that there is an election. But for the average person there's the walk from the door to the bin and that's what I have in most cases if I want to them to process what's on a flyer ... seven seconds can actually be longer than it seems, even if they just remember smiling face and party, it's something." Liberal MP John McKay (Scarborough–Guildwood) agrees, suggesting that "if you can get their attention for fifteen seconds, I consider that a win."[10]

Because campaign leaflets are designed to be quickly thrown away, they often feature little substantive content. Their text typically includes key messages in large lettering that encapsulate keywords and priorities for the minimally attentive. In addition, these materials frequently include biographical details, and thus represent one of the few opportunities for candidates to present their curated political portrait to citizens. An NDP strategist describes other components that have the possibility to register in a voter's mind during their brief encounter: "does it look professional? Do they have an appealing image? Maybe they'll remember the person and party and maybe if we're lucky one issue. The brain processes quickly, but then it goes onto processing other things in life and [people] forget. That's why you need other interactions."

In terms of initial composition or creation, parties typically offer templates to local campaigns that feature minor variations in aesthetic and messaging. Local campaigns can then choose their preferred content from this predetermined menu. This was the case for most Conservative candidates in 2015. For example, as a Quebec Conservative explains, "we were given a catalogue of [around] forty different prepared messages to choose from and within those, there was the option [to] make your own, but it has to be approved. Or take one of these templates, we'll put your [information] on it, and send it to your campaign office."

Constituency campaigns often appreciate this assistance, as the central party facilitates and simplifies the process, in exchange for providing some basic information and a portion of their campaign budget. As a Liberal candidate (2015, Quebec) explains, "I wanted to originally [create my own] but didn't have time so I just said show me the most popular ones and I'll take those." Other campaigns with sufficient resources may prefer to create their own campaign literature, tailored according to both local conditions and party requirements, and must have them receive party approval for their final product.

To facilitate centrally produced campaign literature, the central party typically asks campaigns to submit biographical details and a professional headshot that can be used to create pamphlets that are sent back to the campaign. This is seen with the NDP's 2015 campaign guidelines displayed in Figure 4.1.

To be sure, this does not signify that all NDP local campaigns in 2015 followed this procedure. Many chose to create their own campaign literature and others used a mix of nationally and locally produced campaign materials. In another case, NDP candidate Marlene Rivier (2015, Ottawa West–Nepean) received permission from a neighbouring NDP candidate to use their regionally specialized flyer template and substituted her own name and photo.

While some candidates care deeply about their literature, others barely give a second thought to its creation. A Conservative candidate (2015, Ontario) typifies this nonchalant attitude: "I barely looked at it and didn't really care, it's standard pamphlets." Conversely, a 2015 Liberal candidate recounts grappling with the personal implications of their campaign pamphlets:

> Having your great big face on thousands of [pamphlets] is a curious thing … [because] you're like an actual product that's presented. I was thinking, who will see this? My family, friends, acquaintances, people I went to high school with? I think that's why some people running can be a little touchy about [campaign pamphlets] … It's naive to think it doesn't touch your ego.

These concerns are partially shared by a Conservative candidate (2015, Ontario) who suggests that "in this riding, local candidates are definitely not invisible. I was recognized constantly, that's what happens when your face is all over the place. Because of the pamphlets and signs." Despite the fleeting and limited visibility of most campaign

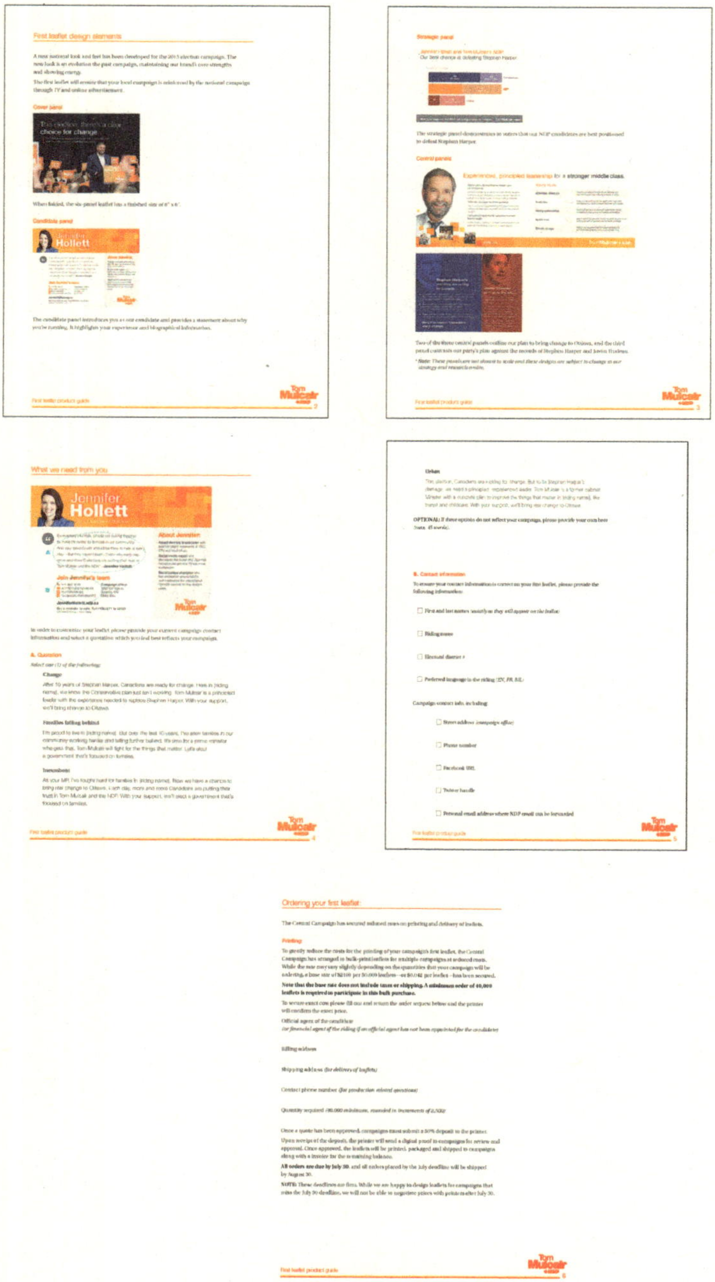

Figure 4.1 NDP Leaflet Guidelines

literature, this candidate was led to reflect on the social and professional implications of their candidacies: "I had no chance of winning, but I still thought about the [campaign literature] and like everything else in the future, how it might affect [Google] searches of my name. You're tied to the party in many ways and you have to think about how that can affect you [and] your business ... "

In such a situation, local party officials can seize opportunities to shape their campaigns' public-facing communications. Liberal MP John McKay (Scarborough–Guildwood) indicates the limitations of party authority with respect to campaign literature: "[t]hey would send [campaign literature] out to you, with a high expectation that you would use it ... I don't think we ever used that stuff ... we would generally take out the [points] that we thought [were] useful, and plug ... my own stuff in." Along these lines, candidates reported various reasons for choosing to deviate from party templates for campaign literature. Most offered one of three closely related reasons: party templates were too generic, messaging options were unsuitable for the riding, and they wanted to distance themselves from the party. To an extent, efforts to tailor campaign literature to local concerns and sensibilities are encouraged by the central party. As a Liberal strategist recounts, "I suggest [local campaigns] throw in some eye-catching local content that can be recognizable to people: a high school name, charity work with a local club, an infrastructure project we got done." According to a Conservative strategist, "if they aren't satisfied with templates, we are fine with [local campaigns creating materials] from scratch if it gets approved." Thus, localized branding does not necessarily represent undisciplined behaviour or entail deviation from the party if it has been approved. Local campaigns that produce their own materials are obligated to seek party authorization before it is distributed.

Party Branding, Localized Branding, and Campaign Literature

According to political marketing scholarship, political leaders and parties can be conceptualized as brands (Cormack 2012; Cosgrove 2012; Esselment 2012; Scammell 2015; Wesley and Moyes 2014). Like all brands, a political brand is comprised of symbols or images that identify the product and differentiate it from its competitors. Cosgrove (2007) describes political brands as summaries for consumers about parties, policies, or candidates. Similarly, Marland (2016, 36) explains that "[a] brand evokes emotional connections to specific images and stimulates loyalty among target audiences. Brands are complex concepts comprised of a multifaceted combination of tangibles, such as a logo, and intangibles, such as emotional attachments ... "

(see also pp. 39–40). Political branding allows citizens to readily identify political figures or messages and categorize them within the larger
brand universe. This task is made more difficult by the dynamic nature of
political brands: parties or leaders often engage in rebranding in order to
react to events or their changing political strengths and weaknesses (e.g.,
Gillies and Wisniewski 2023; Lees-Marshment 2019). Indeed, brands are
subject to continuous revisions based on performance or track record of
the brand in question, along with evolving media and public perceptions.

Marland (2016) differentiates between a party's master brand, which
aligns with "a core philosophical stance," but is also complemented by
"specialized and changing sub-brands." For example, the Conservative
master brand under Prime Minister Stephen Harper was "comprised of
strong economic stewardship and tough-on-crime measures" (21). For
their part, sub-brands may be used to ensure brand relevance across
diverse geographic areas.

Existing research mostly implies that branding is practised at the
political centre by a core group of party strategists. Savoie (2019, 167)
declares that "local party candidates are there to defend their party
leader's brand, not to create a separate one." And as Marland and
Wagner (2020) argue, election candidates for Canada's major parties
are required to serve as "brand ambassadors," meaning they relinquish
individual expression and amplify the centre's brand priorities. Implicitly, there is little to no space for local management of party messaging.

Nonetheless, the existence of sub-brands and prior research on decentralized campaign personalization (e.g., Balmas et al. 2012) suggest the
potential for local campaigns to influence local party branding. This may
even be welcomed by the central party if it does not interfere with or contradict their national branding and allows the party to benefit from a locally
popular candidate. As a Liberal strategist states, "we typically suggest that
the leader is front and centre but of course there are exceptions to this …
there's nothing wrong with playing up local strengths of a well-known
candidate … and what they're bringing to the party." Cross and Young
(2015) explain that campaign personalization occurs when individual candidates and their personal characteristics are emphasized over parties or
policy questions. Localized branding is related to campaign personalization, as both indicate local initiative or assertiveness. But candidates may
pursue distinctive branding or messaging without necessarily personaliz-
ing their campaigns. Therefore, localized branding can be understood as a
distinct concept from decentralized campaign personalization.

In sum, we lack firsthand data on whether or how brands are potentially adapted by local actors. Understanding the practice and prevalence
of localized branding could in turn help reveal the predominance of the

centre and its branding choices. And campaign literature is a key venue to assess these possibilities. Accordingly, the present analysis investigates the extent to which Canadian campaign literature employs localized branding. It starts from the premise, outlined by King (2002), that "candidates make decisions about what goes into their campaign literature and how it is presented based on their perceptions of the voting public […] [T]hese perceptions can be identified through examination of their outputs, i.e., written campaign literature … "

Aside from party influences, there are few mediating forces between the campaigns' desired message and the promotional material that is produced. Indeed, campaign literature embodies candidates' self-images, through their curated issue selections, biographical information, and design choices (Cwalina, Falkowski, and Newman 2011, 203). Materials can help reveal how candidates perceive their communities, as well as their own strategic impulses. As King (2002, 32) argues: "[a]nalyzing campaign literature from local elections is an especially productive way to examine the relationship between candidates and their perceptions of potential voters." In Canada, candidates and their volunteers rank partisan literature as an important component of the campaign effort and dedicate a substantial portion of their budget to its production (Brown, Perrella, and Kay 2010; Carty 1991). Similarly, partisan campaign literature can reveal changing trends in political communications and electoral politics, for example, as some versions begin to migrate online (Kaid 2012). Despite this, the study of Canadian campaign literature is extremely rare, with scholarly attention focusing instead on national-scale advertising (Brown, Perrella, and Kay 2010).

The persuasion effects of campaign literature are ambiguous and difficult to measure. Lilleker (2005) notes that leaflets can reinforce citizens' awareness of specific candidates and potentially increase voter turnout. Reeves (2013) adds that, in conjunction with other modes of communication such as print advertising and canvassing, campaign literature can have a compounding and non-trivial effect on vote choice. Regardless of impact on vote choice, the medium of print literature remains ubiquitous during campaigns and is viewed by parties and candidates as a worthwhile investment, even as digital forms of advertising gain in appeal (Brown, Perrella, and Kay 2010; Pimlott 2011; Basen 2009).

The Localized Branding Index

This chapter focuses on elements of localized branding that are recognizable in partisan campaign literature. To assess local campaign development and presentation of literature, it draws from a sample of ninety-six

Sample Characteristics

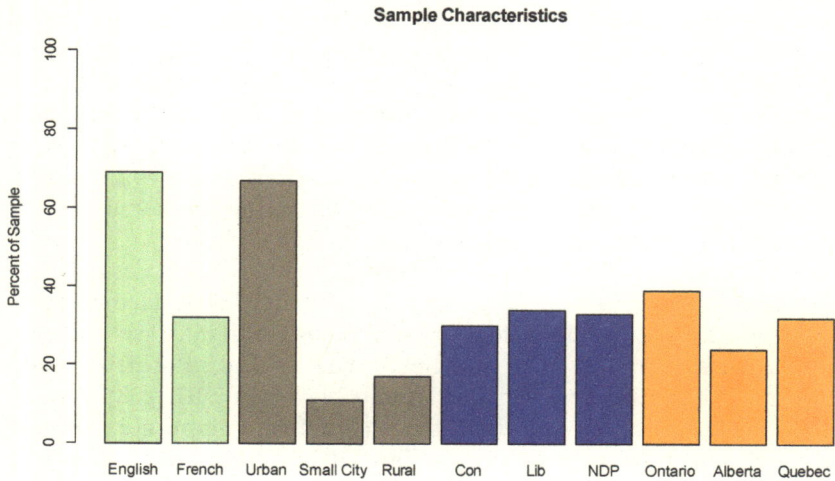

Figure 4.2 Campaign Literature Sample (n=96)

pieces of campaign literature from thirty-two different constituencies in Ontario, Quebec, and Alberta (see Figure 4.2). Of these items, thirty-one come from the Conservative Party, thirty-four are from the Liberal Party, and thirty-one from the NDP. The provincial breakdown is as follows: thirty-nine from Ontario, twenty-four from Alberta, and thirty-three from Quebec. Urban constituencies account for sixty-seven items, small city ridings for twelve, and rural constituencies for the remaining seventeen.

Thompson (2016, 213) mentions three different forms campaign literature can take: promotional flyers often printed as two-sided "door-knockers," smaller candidate cards with brief messages and campaign contact information, and brochure-style tri-fold flyers with more elaborate information and policy details. In order to analyse reasonably comparable materials, this excludes candidate cards and includes only materials that are between 4½ and 8½ inches in width and 5½ to 11 inches in height.[11]

Campaign literature from 2015 was obtained by: 1) personally collecting electronic and print materials during the 2015 campaign period; 2) contacting EDAs during the summer of 2018 and asking for copies of campaign literature; or 3) conducting an internet search focused on candidates' Twitter and Facebook pages to locate additional literature. The writs of election for this campaign were issued on 4 August 2015 and the election was held on 19 October 2015. This sample contains literature from both the pre-writ period and formal election period.

Branding research emphasizes design features and substantive meanings as complementary aspects of a brand (e.g., Guzmán and Sierra

Table 4.3 Substantive Code Options

Substantive	Issue focus	Party slogan	Leader presence
0	National	National slogan	Name and photo appear
1	National and regional/local	No slogan	Name or photo appears
2	Regional/local only	Local slogan	Neither name nor photo appear

Table 4.4 Aesthetic Code Options

Design Code	Colour	Font	Logo	Backdrop
0	Party colours only	Official party font	Generic party logo	National/party/neutral backdrop
1	Features colours other than party colours	Features font other than party font	Amended logo/no logo (incl. colour change)	Depicts local or regional imagery

2009, 210; Smith and French 2009). In this case, a localized branding index is derived from substantive (text) and aesthetic (design) elements of campaign literature, which together account for key local branding decisions.[12] The purpose is to compare localized branding between local campaigns and candidates, by using this ten-point scale. The substantive portion of the scale consists of three dimensions: issue focus, party slogan, and leader presence (see Table 4.3). Each of these dimensions is coded on a zero to two scale, with six as the highest possible total score. The aesthetic component features separate measures of design consistency: colour, font, logo, and backdrop (see Table 4.4). These four measures are coded either as a zero or a one, with a four as the highest possible total score. Together, substantive and aesthetic components constitute a ten-point scale, with zero representing the greatest possible congruence with the national campaign and ten indicating the greatest localized branding. The scale is skewed towards greater importance for substantive elements, although each can also be separately examined.

Substantive criteria: Political branding entails choosing key terms and phrases to convey substantive priorities and build affinity with a target audience (Lees-Marshment 2021; Lees-Marshment and Malik 2023). Three substantive elements are scrutinized for localized branding of campaign literature. First, issue focus ascertains whether the campaign material concentrates on national, regional, or local issues. This item is coded as a zero if it focuses exclusively on national issues, one for a mix of local and national issues, and two for regional or local only. National issues are pan-Canadian in scope, while content without pan-Canadian implications is

Table 4.5 Major Federal Party Slogans, 2015

Party	English Slogan	French Slogan
Liberal	Real Change	Changer ensemble
Conservative	Proven Leadership for a Stronger Canada[13]	Un leadership qui a fait ses preuves (pour une économie plus forte)
NDP	Ready for Change	Ensemble pour le changement

coded as a local or regional issue focus. The latter includes tailored appeals based on electors' place of residence, as well as localized appeals based on the disproportionate concentration of certain groups in the constituency, for example, farmers or military families. Second, the presence or absence of the party's national slogan is also recorded. A zero signifies that the national slogan appears, a one signifies that neither a national nor local slogan appears, and a two signifies that a local or regional slogan is used in place of a national slogan. The parties' official English and French slogans are displayed in Table 4.5.[14] Third, leader presence assesses whether the material mentions or depicts the party's leader. A zero signifies that the leader's name and image appear, a one signifies that only the leader's name appears, and a two that neither their name nor their image appear.[15]

Aesthetic criteria: Aesthetic design features such as symbols and colours identify the brand, attract consumer interest, and evoke wider and deeper substantive meanings (Cormack 2012, 209; Lilleker 2006; Liu et al. 2017, 83; Plummer 1984–5). In this case, aesthetic elements consider whether the design of the promotional material is consistent with the national campaign's aesthetic. Parties typically provide aesthetic guidelines for the creation of campaign literature. The development of the aesthetic criteria was guided by the Liberal and NDP 2015 campaign literature production guides (see Figure 4.1).

In terms of colour, a leaflet is coded as zero if only official party colours are depicted and one if it uses colours other than official party colours. Font choice is coded as zero for the use of the party's centrally chosen fonts and one if a locally distinct font appears. For party logos, a one signifies that the standard national logo appears. A zero indicates that a modified version of the national logo appears or that the national logo does not appear. Lastly, background choice is coded as zero if there is neutral or national imagery depicted in the backdrop, rather than local or regional imagery, which receives a score of one.

Shown below are examples of campaign literature with varying levels of aesthetic consistency. Major parties create a generic literature template for local candidates. Design consistency is assessed with reference to the default party template. Figure 4.3 shows examples of

Figure 4.3 Conservative Leaflets with Consistent National Brand Aesthetic

Figure 4.4 NDP Leaflets with Consistent National Brand Aesthetic

Conservative candidates employing their party's standard baseline for the 2015 campaign. The Conservative baseline aesthetic features dark blue and white colours, with a standardized party font, logo, and layout. The examples found below in Figure 4.3 receive a localized branding score of zero on their aesthetic components, meaning they do not deviate from the party template.

Likewise, the examples in Figure 4.4 represent the generic orange and white NDP aesthetic from 2015 and would receive the same coding score of zero.

Figures 4.5a and 4.5b provide examples of candidates employing the Liberal Party's standard baseline for the 2015 campaign. Unlike the Conservatives and NDP, they mandate a separate template for Quebec.[16] To speculate, this is likely because the Liberals may wish to evoke Canada's flag and unofficial national colours, which are also their party colours, in English Canada, but not in Quebec.[17] For example, in 2015, the party's distinct Quebec template was darker in appearance than for English Canadian literature. As seen below, some Quebec candidates also used the English Canada template. In each case, the materials below receive a localized branding score of zero on aesthetic elements.

Conversely, some materials clearly deviate from party templates. Documents in Figure 4.6 feature moderate cohesion with the templates and would receive coding scores of one or two.

The Rayes example features a distinct background and colours but consistent party logo and font. Interestingly, the backdrop depicts the

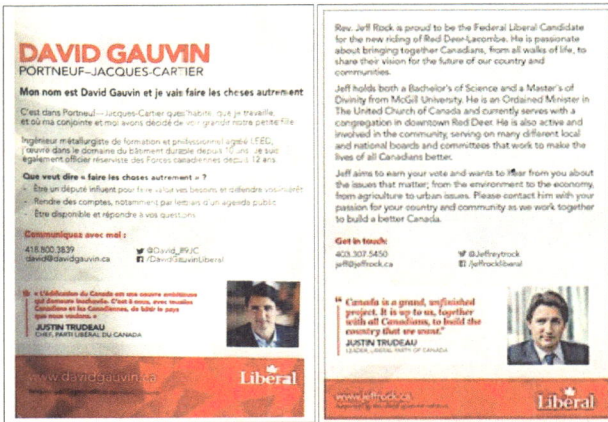

Figure 4.5a Liberal Leaflets with Consistent National Brand Aesthetic

Figure 4.5b Liberal Leaflets with Consistent National Brand Aesthetic (Quebec)

Figure 4.6 Assorted Leaflets with Mixed National/Local Aesthetic

candidate with a regional party figure, Denis Lebel, rather than the Conservative prime minister. The Grant leaflet features consistent font, logo, and colouring, but with a local backdrop. For its part, the Souraya example uses a familiar NDP backdrop with faded light orange squares, but with a map of the constituency and does not display the official NDP logo or font.

Lastly, the examples in Figure 4.7 are noteworthy for the use of localized branding. They would receive an aesthetic coding score of four out of four, signifying their differences in terms of font, colouring, logos, and backdrop. Liberal candidate Nirmala Naidoo's literature employs red, purple, and white colouring and the party leader does not appear. Conservative candidate Andy Brooke's literature shows images of law enforcement and the Canadian military and a fully distinct aesthetic. And NDP candidate Craig Scott's sample material prominently uses green along with orange, without the party font or logo.

The examples in Figures 4.3 to 4.7 also feature differences in their substantive content. With the clearest illustrations of localized branding, Figure 4.7 shows how regional or local issues can overshadow parties' national messages. Naidoo's messaging prioritizes pipeline construction and local roots, Brooke does not mention policy issues, and Scott's leaflet highlights proposed investments in Toronto infrastructure.[18]

Findings

Despite the motivations and abilities to create tailored messages that deviate from the central party, there is limited variation in the design elements of campaign literature and moderate variation in its content. Many local campaigns begin with a party template and make constituency-level adjustments. Others may use an unmodified party template. Still others create their own materials from scratch.[19]

The overall picture suggests that candidates generally rely on their central party aesthetic for campaign literature. As outlined in Table 4.4, this component was measured on a zero to four scale, with a zero signifying perfect congruence and a four signifying a unique aesthetic. To score 100 per cent on this scale, or four out of four (perfect aesthetic dissonance), a leaflet must contain distinct font, backdrop, logo, and colours. Table 4.6 displays the average score on the zero to four scale of 0.8 out of four. It also indicates the average brand consistency for both aesthetic and substantive elements in percentage terms.

There is considerable variation in the substantive content of campaign literature. A leaflet scores six out of six (or 100 per cent) in substantive dissonance if it features only local political issues, a local slogan, and

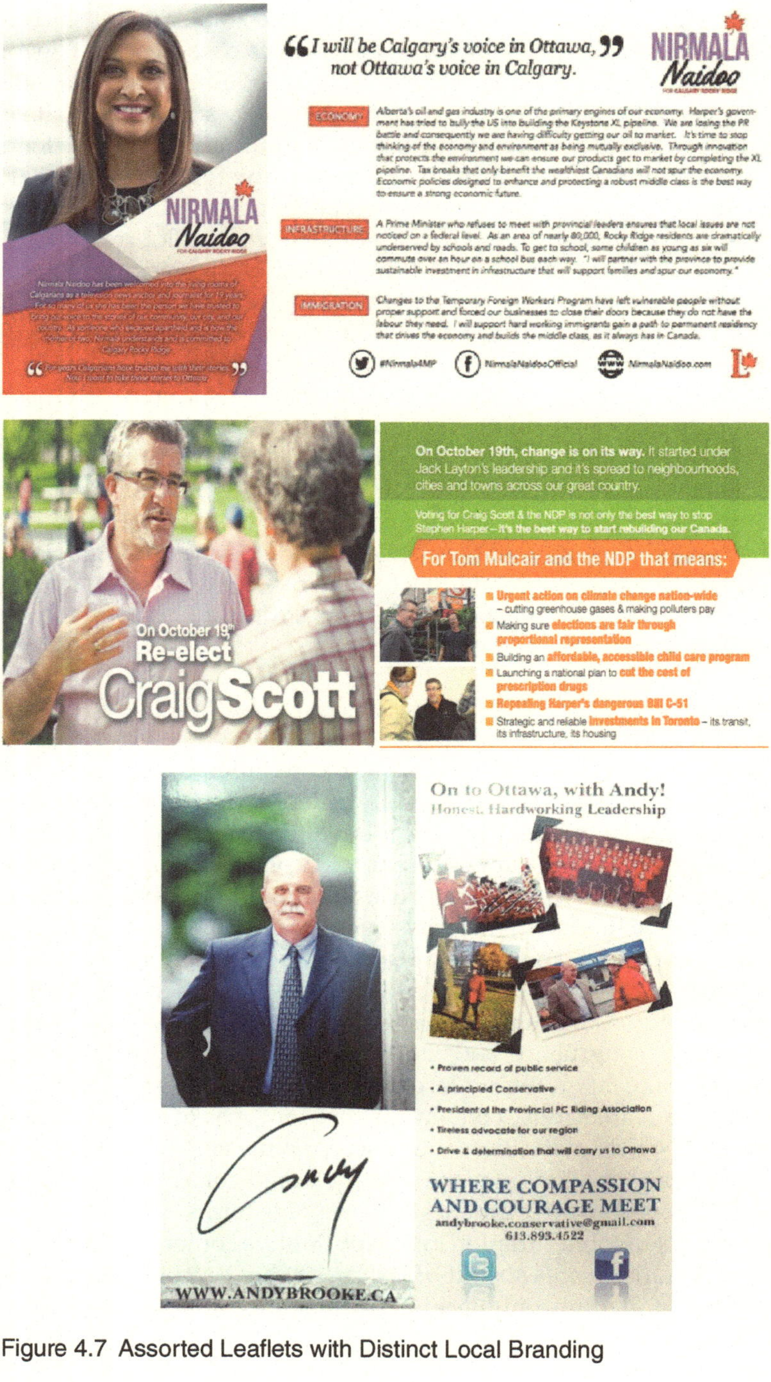

Figure 4.7 Assorted Leaflets with Distinct Local Branding

Table 4.6 Average Scores on Aesthetic and Substantive Localized Branding Scale

Criteria	Constituency material dissonance score	Score as percentage on dissonance scale*
Average aesthetic	0.8/4	19.7 per cent
Average substantive	2.9/6	48.2 per cent
Composite average	3.7/10	36.8 per cent

*This figure converts the local distinctiveness score on aesthetic and substantive scales to a percentage of that scale

the party leader does not appear. According to this sample, many leaflets emphasize a regional or local message over the leader and national campaign. They also vary in their depiction of party leaders and slogans. The average score on substantive content was 2.9 out of six, which roughly equates to 48 per cent dissonance from the central party.

Four factors may influence the content and presentation of campaign literature. First, brand consistency may differ by political party. In 2015, the Conservative Party featured a relatively unpopular leader in Stephen Harper, who had served as prime minister since 2006. Although the Harper government was known to exercise strong message discipline (cf. Flanagan 2014), the party is also known to feature a relatively decentralized organization which affords greater freedom than other parties to its regional components (Pruysers 2014b). Therefore, the Conservatives may demonstrate less brand consistency than the other major parties. For their part, the Liberal Party campaigned with a relatively popular leader and the party typically employs a more centralized party organization. The Liberals are anticipated to feature the greatest brand consistency. Lastly, the New Democratic Party (NDP), with its relatively popular leader and centralized party organization, may fall in between the Conservatives and Liberals in terms of brand consistency.[20]

Second, brand consistency may differ by constituency type. Rural electors are more likely to vote based on their local candidate (Roy and Alcantara 2015). As Cross and Young (2015) explain, rural candidates are also more prone to personalize their candidacies. Accordingly, rural constituencies may feature less brand consistency. Conversely, the residents of urban ridings tend to view elections in more national and party-oriented terms, while candidates in these areas are typically less well known relative to their parties (Carty and Eagles 2005).

Third, regional differences may affect localized branding decisions. Here, region is inferred along provincial lines and materials from Ontario, Alberta, and Quebec are examined. Ontario's lack of regional distinctiveness and congruence with the national political agenda (Cross

Table 4.7 Summary of Brand Dissonance Scores by Party, Region, and Riding Type

Party	Riding Type	Region
CPC 3.8	Urban 4.0	ON 4.0
LPC 3.6	Small city 4.0	AB 4.7
NDP 3.6	Rural 2.0*	QC 2.6
Avg. 3.7	Avg. 3.7	Avg. 3.7

*Sample size of <10

et al. 2015) should entail that its constituencies feature the greatest brand consistency. Meanwhile, Quebec's sociopolitical distinctiveness may result in the least brand consistency and Alberta constituencies are anticipated to fall somewhere between the other two provinces.

With this in mind, what major differences are apparent? Table 4.7 summarizes these findings, which are then displayed in figures 4.8, 4.9, and 4.10. The highest possible brand dissonance, with no similar elements to party templates, would be a score of ten. Interestingly, there is essentially no difference in brand consistency among political parties. The composite scores on brand distinctiveness fall just under four out of ten for each major party, with 3.8 for the Conservatives, 3.6 for the Liberals, and 3.6 for the NDP. The Liberal and NDP leaders are frequently depicted in party literature, while the Conservative leader, Stephen Harper, is slightly less likely to appear. In some cases, a regionally significant Conservative figure such as Jason Kenney or Denis Lebel is present. Additionally, Conservative literature is most consistent in displaying the party's campaign slogan, emphasizing a message of economic stability. Meanwhile, the change-oriented slogans of the other two parties appear relatively rarely on candidates' campaign materials.

Contrary to expectations, urban constituencies feature greater brand inconsistency than rural constituencies. The urban constituency score on distinctive leaflet branding is roughly four out of ten versus two out of ten for rural constituencies. Materials from ridings in small cities are roughly equivalent to urban materials, with an average score of four. These findings are attributable to two main factors. First, urban literature displayed a marked focus on local issues, especially regarding infrastructure and transit projects. Second, this finding is inhibited by the relatively small selection of rural and small city campaign literature included in the sample.

In terms of provincial differences, brand consistency is strongest in Quebec, with an average score of 2.6 out of ten. This likely stems from the Liberal and NDP campaigns' focus on leadership and their national brand within Quebec. Both parties were led by Quebecers and their personal brand appears to have been leveraged to a greater extent in

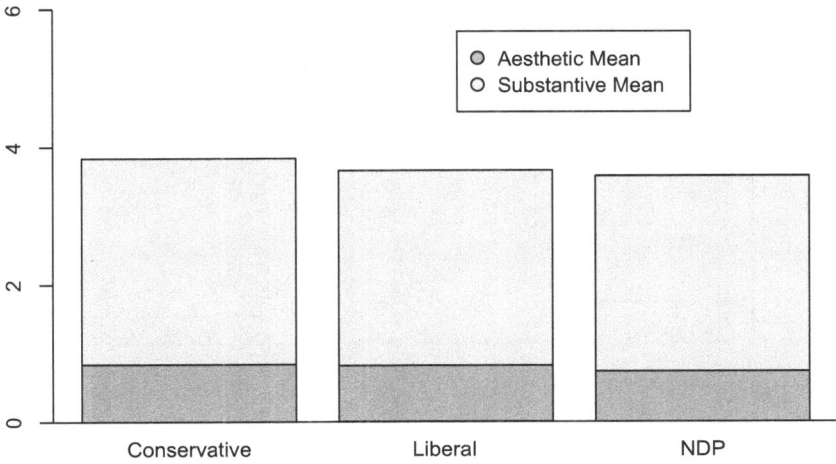

Note: 0 signifies consistency with central party, 10 signifies inconsistency

Figure 4.8 Localized Branding by Political Party

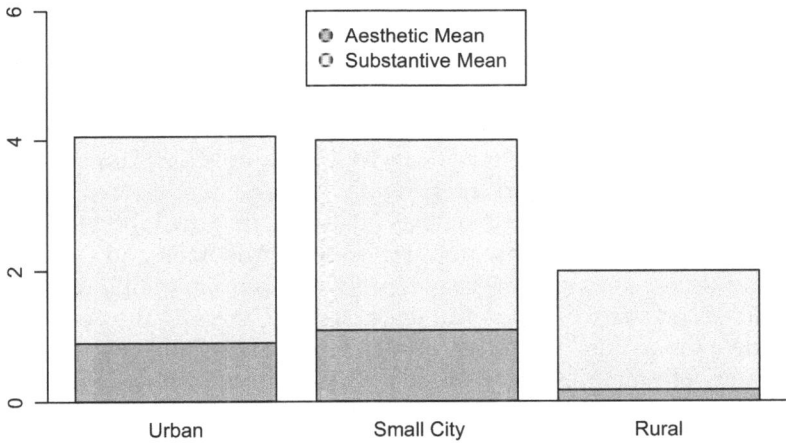

Note: 0 signifies consistency with central party, 10 signifies inconsistency

Figure 4.9 Localized Branding by Riding Type

local Quebec campaigns than those in other provinces. Conservative leaflets in Quebec did not feature this extent of national brand consistency. Ontario constituencies have an average score of four out of ten and Alberta campaign materials demonstrate the greatest propensity for localized branding, with a score of 4.7 out of ten. Alberta campaign

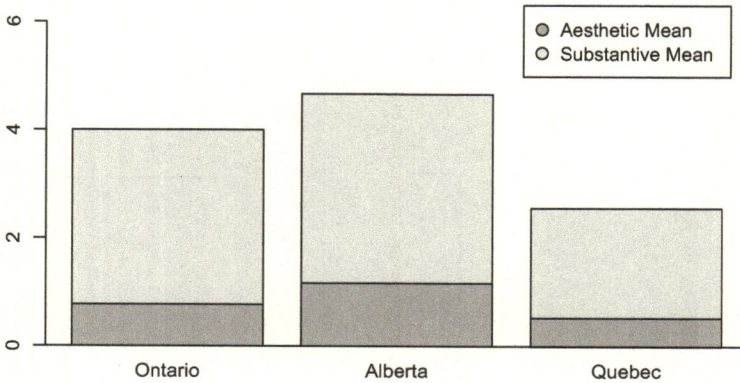

Note: 0 signifies consistency with central party, 10 signifies inconsistency

Figure 4.10 Localized Branding by Region

literature often discussed pipeline construction and energy issues. Liberal and NDP candidates in Alberta appear to have sought out greater distance from national party brands. Ontario leaflets fall in between Alberta and Quebec in terms of brand consistency.

What might account for greater-than-anticipated brand consistency? This finding is surprising, given the capacities of local campaigns to produce and distribute their own literature, but it may be derived from particularities of the 2015 election, as well as sample size limitations which necessitate caution in interpreting these results. According to party strategists, the 2015 election was notable in that the Liberal Party and NDP were led by broadly popular leaders (Anderson and Coletto 2015) and local campaigns may have preferred to prominently feature their leader and party brand. As a Liberal strategist recalls, the decision to mandate the words "Team/Équipe Trudeau" on candidate signs and other campaign materials was based on "research that showed [Justin Trudeau] was almost certain to have a coattail effect for local campaigns ... and somewhat surprisingly [based on the mixed legacy of Pierre Trudeau in Quebec] it was particularly true in Quebec." An NDP strategist reports similar tendencies: "[Mulcair] had strong numbers and quite evenly across the country ... for all our eventual struggles it wasn't because the leader was unpopular." An NDP candidate (2015, Ontario) illustrates both the perceived popularity of the leader and their desire to engage in localized branding: "I didn't use the party materials. I did all of my own ... [but] I put [the leader] on almost everything because I knew he played well."

The Conservative leader, Stephen Harper, had relatively low personal popularity in 2015. But Conservative candidates are only marginally more likely to employ localized branding. According to one Conservative candidate, the party was known to prefer that the leader appear on campaign materials: "they thought that if [Harper] was on there along with some positive accomplishments it was part of a certain strategy." This view is consistent with the former prime minister's reported preference for personalized branding, for example, in preferring the label of Harper Government to the Government of Canada (Marland 2016).

Public-Facing Campaign Communications

Alongside the final product of completed campaign literature, the processes surrounding the design and circulation of campaign literature are also revealing of how national directives interact with local realities. Local autonomy and undisciplined behaviour are apparent at three stages in the production of campaign literature: composition, authorization, and distribution.

At the creation or composition stage, undisciplined behaviour entails the production of literature that does not adhere to party guideline for campaign literature. The major parties detail the distinctive aesthetic and substantive elements for campaign materials, such as the Liberal Party's logo guidelines seen below in Figure 4.11.

When campaign literature is produced independently by local campaigns, they may hire a graphic designer or rely on expertise from their team of employees and volunteers. In so doing, they are expected to follow party guidelines. These guidelines can sometimes be overruled with party knowledge and approval, so the use of localized branding does not necessarily indicate the presence of undisciplined behaviour or local autonomy. Indeed, the central party may endorse localized branding as politically advisable in some constituencies. The specific nature of party involvement and local-national party interactions are important to consider in assessing undisciplined behaviour.

At the next stage, undisciplined behaviour consists of distribution of unvetted campaign materials. Some local campaigns neglected to ask for party approval for their final products, despite this party requirement. NDP strategist Karl Bélanger contends that this is a significant problem, as the party seeks to ensure that leaflet guidelines have been followed. Bélanger states that all party literature should echo the baseline national format since "brand penetration is really hard to achieve. If your brand is confusing, then people aren't paying attention to you." Bélanger further suggests that unique leaflets can attract negative media

Figure 4.11 Liberal Party Guidelines for Logo Display

attention and undermine the party, if they are viewed as unprofessional or as an indication of disassociation from the national campaign.

Most local campaign actors who did not ask permission reported they neglected to do so because they felt it was an unnecessary step that would slow down the process. NDP candidate Ken Kuzminski (2015, Yellowhead) recounts, "They like to review stuff but ... To hold your breath and wait for the campaign to get you literature [or an answer], you wouldn't be doing anything."[21] Others contend that they knew the party would not approve their campaign materials and avoided the authorization process in order to circumvent this verification. As a 2019 Conservative candidate in Quebec explains, "there was one [campaign leaflet] that I knew they wouldn't like, and we thought it over and felt it was important, so it went out." From the central party perspective, a Liberal strategist claims that the lack of party scrutiny and approval for campaign materials, "can be more serious than [local campaigns] realize, first in undermining the purpose of solidarity and open communications, but also because every once in a while there's a problem that we would have brought up and it ends up meaning they reprint everything." By far, lack of party authorization was the most common form of undisciplined behaviour with respect to campaign literature.[22] In fairness to local actors, errors with campaign literature also occur

Mulcair's PLAN

Better transit

Together we'll change Ottawa.

Tom **Mulcair** ✦ **NDP**

We face it every day.

If you live in Toronto Centre and use the TTC, you know. Packed buses, delayed subway trains and frustrated riders. Toronto's transit system can't keep up with growth. But the Conservative transit plan doesn't include a single new dollar until 2018. And Justin Trudeau would force Toronto to compete with other cities for private pension investment. That's not along-term plan.

Andrew and Tom Mulcair's NDP will:

✓ Invest $1.3 billion a year for 20 years to fix the transit backlog.

✓ Transfer funds straight to Toronto and other cities so projects get off the ground sooner.

✓ Provide long-term investment for roads, bridges and vital infrastructure.

Andrew **Thomson**

📞 647-286-9098
AndrewThomson.ca

Figure 4.12 Misprint in NDP Campaign Literature

at the central party. For example, the leaflet in Figure 4.12 identifies candidate Andrew Thomson's riding as Toronto Centre, rather than the candidate's actual riding, Eglinton–Lawrence.

Lastly, undisciplined behaviour can occur at the distribution stage if materials are not circulated in the constituency according to party wishes. During interviews and campaign observation, multiple candidates and local party officials reported being asked to distribute literature viewed as ill-conceived and seen to reflect poorly on their candidacies. While many chose to follow the instruction from their parties, others did so partially and half-heartedly, while a select few ignored the instruction altogether. For example, one 2019 Liberal campaign simply left their party flyers in a storage room in their campaign office, refusing to hand them out. In a case of tepid acquiescence, another Liberal candidate (2015, Alberta) states that, "I wasn't going to go out of my way to distribute these ... flyers. If we had a surplus of volunteers with nothing to do ... then yes, I did part of that ... "

Similarly, several NDP constituency campaigns noted that the party asked them to distribute leaflets that framed their party as a strategic vote to defeat the Conservatives. Local actors viewed this message as out of step with polling realities, which placed the Liberals well ahead of the NDP. Former MP Matthew Dubé (Beloeil–Chambly) recalls "that message was resonating but not giving us the expected ... result, in other words ... [it was] pointing people towards the Liberals." An NDP candidate in Ontario contends that this message "was going to kill us and we didn't even put it out. We just left the boxes in the corner because we thought that doesn't make any sense." Accordingly, most of these local campaigns neglected to distribute these leaflets, out of fear of undermining their own electoral prospects. In another case, an NDP candidate (2015, Alberta) recalls, "there was this terrible pamphlet I didn't want and didn't ask for ... it was my face but it was pointless for the riding ... The pamphlets came and my campaign manager and I looked at each other and said, well it's not going out."

Other constituency campaigns created literature distribution plans that conflicted with party procedure. For example, rather than canvassing strategic party targets, they simply distributed pamphlets to every single home in an area of the constituency with a high concentration of supporters. In another case, volunteers chose where and when to distribute materials, rather than following party priorities. In this respect, what constituency campaigns choose not to do with their campaign materials is also relevant in assessing campaign discipline, as evidenced in the occasions where materials do not reach their intended audience.

Returning to Carty's model, voter canvassing and the production of campaign literature exemplify local variations on a franchise. These campaign activities enable us to observe the contours of centralization and varying effects of central party influence. Canvassing procedures and campaign literature are in many ways centrally controlled. Nonetheless, constituency campaigns pursue an array of canvassing practices and literature outputs in order to assert their particular ambitions and autonomy to operate the ground campaign. These diverse responses to the confines of party expectations underscore the relevance of local decision-making under a political franchise model.[23] In addition, this chapter emphasizes asymmetries between local franchises, as constituency campaigns view their roles and responsibilities in distinct ways and behave accordingly.

To conclude, this chapter expands upon the examination of undisciplined behaviour identified in Chapter 3 by reviewing patterns of discipline and autonomy in local campaigns' most important public-facing activities. While parties are highly preoccupied with canvassing, many local campaigns do not attempt to follow their directives and procedures. Furthermore, the production of campaign literature sheds light on the constraints of their party brand and directives as well as local campaigns' adaptations. The creation, authorization, and distribution of campaign literature comprises an important locus of activity where candidates confront potential tensions between national and local political imperatives, as well as strategic and practical concerns for how to operate an effective local campaign. With varying levels of central party involvement, local campaigns seek to produce campaign literature that allows them to benefit from their parties' locally perceived strengths and minimize vulnerabilities, while employing these materials as part of an overall strategy to make brief, repeated, and positive impressions on electors. In examining brand consistency in campaign literature, I find moderate variation in the substantive presentation of these materials, along with minimal variation in its aesthetic features. The results indicate relatively modest differences based on party, with Alberta materials being less consistent with central party branding than those in Ontario and Quebec. These findings are limited by potential idiosyncrasies of the 2015 campaign and by the relatively small sample size.

The use of localized branding in campaign literature does not necessarily stem from federal parties granting candidates meaningful autonomy in their print communications. Indeed, parties may allow or even encourage these practices if local campaigns can effectively distance themselves from the trappings of the leader and party brand, without damaging or distracting from the overall campaign (Stephenson et al. 2019, 78–9). Moreover, localized branding does not necessarily constitute undisciplined behaviour when this is a party-approved tactic. A process-oriented approach that includes the composition, authorization, and distribution of campaign literature facilitates greater understanding of the balance between central party authority and local decision-making.

This chapter further reveals key cases where local campaigns disregard party guidelines and where the central party does not endorse or discover such tactics. In this respect, campaign centralization has not yet eliminated key elements of individuality and creativity among local actors. To better understand the contours and limitations of central party authority, the next chapter examines on-the-ground realities of intra-party communications and party capacities to monitor local campaigns.

Chapter 5

Internal Party Communications

There is a popular cliché that successful relationships are built on effective communication. This sentiment arguably applies not only to interpersonal relations but also to large organizations such as political parties. Indeed, internal communications channels are a vital part of parties' smooth operations. This chapter examines how internal communications channels shape party authority, campaign discipline, and local-national party relations more broadly.

Communication processes between national and local components of political parties remain understudied (e.g., Datts and Gerl 2023). Generally speaking, during an election, the centre communicates party preferences and helps local actors to meet them. Local actors are also expected to communicate information to the centre regarding local conditions and provide data to facilitate party objectives. In essence, central party authority depends upon the party's communications channels. But in recent Canadian elections, parties' internal communications channels have reliably failed to maintain central authority, despite being constructed for this purpose. Indeed, on-the-ground realities of intra-party communications help to reveal why parties fail to prevent undisciplined behaviour.

This chapter begins by assessing existing research that implies that parties can maintain discipline by monitoring and regulating local campaign behaviour. This requires effective intra-party communications channels. The chapter focuses on the three largest parties' internal communications practices during the 2015 and 2019 elections. Since they cannot be physically present in most constituencies, parties rely on continuous communications through national and regional offices in order to react to campaign developments. Yet local campaigns vary considerably in their integration and engagement with communications channels. This undermines the transmission of timely and accurate information. Some local campaigns communicate primarily through formal party networks while others prefer irregular channels that bypass the centre. And the central party cannot reliably communicate with insular local campaigns who intentionally or unintentionally ignore them. These communications processes illustrate the limitations of central authority under a decentralized franchise system and in a vast country. Despite this, it bears repeating that most local campaigns in this study tend to behave in a disciplined manner, in accordance with central party preferences. A more suitable explanation for campaign cohesion is therefore warranted.

Can Internal Communications Prevent Undisciplined Behaviour?

How effective is the central party in controlling or influencing local actors? The stratarchical bargain between national and local party organizations has always been tilted in the central party's favour (Cross, Pruysers, and Currie-Wood 2022). In recent elections, organizational and technological changes have fed notions of a hegemonic central party with minimal local autonomy. Scholars highlight an atmosphere of permanent campaigning characterized by hyper message discipline, instantaneous digital communications, and monitoring of candidate activities (e.g., Marland, Esselment, and Giasson 2017, 17). Some question whether centralized party control is such that local campaigns are reduced to party mouthpieces (Flanagan 2014).

The present chapter contends that the central office's ability to regulate local actors depends on intra-party communications. They must know what local actors are doing and saying, correct missteps, and sanction rule-breakers, preferably all in a timely manner. This requires a continuous flow of information to the central office regarding constituency activities (Belfry Munroe and Munroe 2018; Patten 2017, 56). Some scholars have noted parties' apparent abilities to monitor candidate behaviour. As Savoie explains (2019, 174), in a lament of campaign centralization, federal candidates are "always under the watchful eye of party leaders and their courtiers." Similarly, Marland (2020, 44) recounts that federal "candidates are told that someone somewhere is observing everything that they say or do." Yates echoes this sentiment (2022, 287–8):

> Unsurprisingly, political parties usually keep tight control of local campaigns' messages and promises ... curbing candidates' inclinations to craft their own messages; centralized decision making and control over messaging remain very strong. A political party will call to order a candidate who veers from core messages. The correction can go as far as revoking the endorsement and appointing a new candidate.

Marland and Wagner (2020, 63) identify how this surveillance occurs, as well as potential consequences for rule-breakers: "public remarks are monitored by party staff who practice rapid response ... a brand ambassador who freelances is required to apologize and is ostracized by the leadership. Those whose public behavior seriously threatens the brand are dropped as candidates or evicted from the party caucus." There are other ways for party headquarters to track local activities: by monitoring local media, social media, and party databases (Laschinger 2016, 160–1; McLean 2012, 57–8). The latter has become increasingly important, as the central office can rely on real-time data to view and analyse local movements (Belfry Munroe and Munroe 2018, 139). McLean (2012, 59) reminds us that parties monitor public statements from other parties and their candidates, in addition to their own. The ability to enforce discipline is common to all three major parties, as the NDP has recently reached a level of campaign professionalization that approaches its more established opponents (McGrane 2019, 121). For these reasons, candidates are said to be constrained in their behaviour and made to do the central party's bidding (Flanagan 2014, 31; Marland 2016, 10; Marland, Giasson, and Esselment 2017).

In assessing long-term changes, some local candidates agree that the central party has gradually increased its abilities to influence their activities. Liberal MP Rob Oliphant (Don Valley West) has been involved in political campaigns for over fifty years, since his childhood. Oliphant recalls, "[t]hrough the '70s and '80s the central campaign wanted to have influence, but things were delayed ... There wasn't an ability for the central party to observe and find out what you're doing and what they needed to tell you to be doing. I think the party's capacity to [influence] local campaigns has grown immensely, given the changes in communications."

But local campaign behaviour in 2015 and 2019 once again shows a more varied and disordered picture. Parties possess finite resources during a campaign, including demands on workers' time and attention. Cross (2004, 139) suggests this results in substantial party attention directed towards competitive constituencies, while non-competitive districts are left to local actors (see also Cross 2006, 171). Local campaign behaviour in 2015 and 2019 confirms uneven levels of party involvement in local activities. Andy Brooke, 2015 Conservative candidate (Kingston and the Islands), states that "they weren't over our shoulders because they couldn't be ... but [they would] like to be." Fellow 2015 Conservative candidate Yves Laberge (Bécancour–Nicolet–Saurel) also feels that the party did not have the resources to keep track of his activities and was generally unaware of them. Parties sometimes possess imperfect information on local activities. This is particularly true for the NDP, which has traditionally had fewer resources at their disposal than the other major parties. As strategist Brad Lavigne explains, "we rely on goodwill of [local campaigns]." Further, NDP strategist Karl Bélanger suggests that party surveillance of local campaigns is unfeasible, for logistical and financial reasons.

Yet, given unlimited resources, parties indicate that they would seek to scrutinize all constituency campaigns, including those in non-competitive districts. A Conservative strategist highlights this reasoning, explaining that campaign mistakes can come from anywhere, even from experienced candidates, and they are often "costly and usually unnecessary." Savoie (2019, 162) shares this view, reminding that "one misstep by a candidate in one region can have a highly negative impact in another region that dominates the news cycle for several days." This reality often worried Karl Bélanger: "The party is fixated on avoiding blunders, which are often caused by actors within the party who stray from the game plan. When you're off track defending yourself against something, instead of what was planned to talk about, you're wasting tens of thousands of dollars a day or more." These concerns are under-scored by recent election controversies stemming from candidates in uncompetitive constituencies who nonetheless attracted negative media attention and distracted from national or provincial campaigns.[1]

Moreover, evidence presented in this book suggests that parties are often unaware of undisciplined behaviour, and when they are, it may be difficult to address effectively. NDP candidate Daniel Beals (Kingston and the Islands) recalls after speaking against the party's position on pipelines and energy projects, "They did [ask me to retract] ... I said no, whether you want to take it any further is up to you ... I'm not tak-ing it back and if they want to remove me, they can try." During a fast-moving election period the options for addressing a recalcitrant local campaign largely consist of removing a candidate and offering explicit or implicit punishments.[2] These are not always effective options during a dynamic campaign period where fractious relations can also harm the central party. Conservative strategist Hamish Marshall suggests that "screaming at people" is an ineffective way to instil local discipline and onerous long-term trust and relationship building are instead required.

Indeed, party strategists from all three parties suggest that inter-nal communications are intended to relay campaign expectations and hold local actors accountable. Unfortunately, intra-party communica-tions are minimally studied and poorly understood (Strömbäck 2007). Communications intrinsically involves the transmission of a desired message (e.g., Hallahan et al. 2007) and political party communications typically evokes public-facing activities aimed to shape public opinion (Esser and Strömbäck 2012, 239).[3] Internal communications involves sharing information up and down communications channels within an organization (Robson and Tourish 2005). These activities are not public-facing and are thus more difficult to study. Scholarly accounts of internal party communications are generally based on firsthand campaign experiences (e.g., Kinsella 2007; Laschinger 2016; Lavigne 2013) and almost exclusively undertaken from the perspective of the central party rather than local campaigns.[4] Moreover, they tend to focus on particular incidents rather than general communications activities.

Carty (2004, 10) explains the importance of a shared understanding of organizational roles for national and local actors:

> To structure the relationship, and institutionalize the rules ordering the system, franchise contracts spelling out the rights, responsibilities and obligations of each guarantee their autonomy and mutual interdependence. This design allows each element to perform its functions relatively unhindered by the others. It ensures that the central office can penalize a local affiliate if it fails to meet the organization's standards and provides mechanisms for local units to hold the central organization to its policies and responsibilities.

Findings from this chapter suggest that within a campaign environment, neither the central office nor local units fully respect their portion of the franchise bargain, and neither is able to reliably hold the other accountable. While different organizational rules and roles exist for local and national actors, communications barriers can prevent them from being reliably followed. Carty and Cross's reminder that parties can penalize local branches merits further examination. Given the importance of message discipline and party cohesion in contemporary campaigns, what concrete tools are actually used to enforce party standards and demands?

The central party cannot be present in all places at all times and its authority depends upon internal communications networks that monitor and manage local activity. As March and Simon ([1958] 1993) contend, the authority of any organization depends upon planned and spontaneous communications channels. Strategists from the three major parties emphasize this reality.

According to 2019 Conservative campaign manager Hamish Marshall, in terms of party awareness of local activity, "the primary method we have is we're talking to them every single day ... if we're talking to them every day and knowing what they're doing and we're seeing the data come in ... and are collecting it, we know what's going on." In addition to information in party databases, Marshall highlights how regional organizers monitor local campaigns through regularized phone and online check-ins, following up areas of concern. The Liberals have been notably data-driven, as a Liberal strategist explains that

> there are check-ins through data all the time with [constituency campaigns] and they have to commit their data to the [party software system] ... [we will] bug you if something isn't right. We have a good sense of what is and isn't possible in different ridings but the challenge is how that changes during the campaign ... [So] we keep in touch, and I'd say we mostly keep in touch through calls, check-ins, and minding the data.

And NDP strategist Brad Lavigne suggests there are three major sources of information on local activity for the head office: the local campaign team, the riding association, and members of the central campaign in "field operations" who reach local campaigns by phone, text, and email.

While Lavigne is confident that the party almost always receives accurate information from these sources, spending time with local actors quickly reveals that party strategists do not always enjoy a complete picture of their activities. To illustrate, in 2019, a major party's campaign headquarters sent occasional messages to local campaigns that began by stating "We'd like to remind everyone that ... " At least one local campaign found these reminders to be instructive and helpful. Another local campaign found them to be passive-aggressive and unnecessary, suggesting the party was actually saying "if you're going to do something, fucking do this." And a third campaign did not even receive them. This situation demonstrates the top-down nature of intraparty communications and challenges faced by parties in seeking to reach local actors while appearing to respect local agency.

The present chapter considers three major aspects of internal communications that affect parties' abilities to supervise and regulate local campaign behaviour: the frequency and closeness of interactions between constituency campaigns and their parties, whether these interactions take place through formal or informal channels, and the role and authority of regional party offices. During interviews and campaign observation, research subjects were asked, "what communications channels exist between local campaigns and the central party or its regional offices?" While this question elicited a variety of responses, participants generally identified six principal communications channels: phone calls, text messages, emails, in-person meetings, campaign software, and party websites and online discussion boards. These six outlets are denoted as communications channels, meaning the technical mode of communication or the medium through which messages are diffused. Moreover, political communications are imbued with meanings and intentions not directly captured by message content or their technical means of transmission. Research participants were asked two additional questions on this topic: "to what extent is intra-party communications important to [your (local) campaign or to the central party]? What do you hope to accomplish from these interactions?"[5]

Based on these data, a communications profile can be ascertained for each constituency campaign by examining the nature of their interactions with the broader party. Two major dimensions help to reveal local campaigns' communications tendencies. First, integration or insularity is determined by the closeness and frequency of interactions with the central party. Second, formality indicates whether constituency campaigns tended towards official or informal channels in their communications. In terms of the former, campaigns in competitive ridings and those in Ontario tend to be more integrated with the national campaign, while others are more insular. And campaigns with professional and personal networks throughout the party tend to exploit these informal network opportunities.

Communications Integration and Insularity

Some constituency campaigns experience close daily contact with the party and others claim they experienced virtually no interactions. Highly insular campaigns may be compared with those closely integrated into the broader party and even to other local campaigns. Table 5.1 reports local candidates' responses to questions on this topic, with columns displaying percentages rather than raw counts. Constituency campaigns that tend to strongly agree or agree with the statements in the left-hand column are more integrated, while those who tend to disagree are more insular.

This variation in closeness and frequency of communications is summarized in Table 5.2. The scale runs in ascending order of integration from zero to ten, categorizing subjects based on responses to the questions in Table 5.1. Local campaigns are highly dispersed across the spectrum, rather than clustered around the mean of five. Highly integrated campaigns regularly engage in communications with the centre, seek out party interactions, and perceive strong party interest in their affairs. They also indicate that intra-party communications are an important aspect of their campaigns. Twenty-seven per cent of campaigns in the

Table 5.1 Local-National Integration in Constituency Campaign Communications

Statement	Strongly agree (percentage)*	Agree	Disagree	Strongly disagree
1. Our campaign was regularly in touch with the party by email, phone, or other forms of communication.	33	28	20	18
2. Our campaign stayed informed of changing party expectations through their emails, conference calls, and other forms of communication.	46	21	20	13
3. Our campaign usually sought party input when making major decisions.	19	20	43	18
4. When our campaign encountered a problem, someone from the party helped to resolve it.	24	28	31	17
5. The central party had a good sense of what was happening on the ground for our campaign.	39	18	23	20
6. The central party sent staff to personally support or monitor our campaign.	9	10	29	53
7. Party communications were collaborative: the party spoke and also listened to our local campaign.	20	24	18	38
8. Our campaign regularly communicated with other local campaigns (horizontal integration).	26	29	26	19

*May not add to 100 due to rounding; n=87

sample can be classified as fully integrated. Those constituency campaigns score between eight and ten on the scale displayed in Table 5.2. A further 35 per cent are neither integrated nor insular. These campaigns score between four and six on the scale in Table 5.2.

Insular campaigns passively receive party communications, are less likely to make requests of or coordinate with their parties, and perceive minimal oversight. Fifteen per cent of campaigns in this sample as seen in Table 5.2 (scores between zero and two) are fully insular, with rare interactions with the party. This insularity conflicts with preferred campaign management styles. As a Liberal strategist explains, "they [must] take the [messages] to heart, follow what's going on in the national campaign, what the leader is saying. There's no point in shouting into

Table 5.2 Integration Scale for Constituency Campaign Communications[6]

Integration scale:	0 (most insular)	1	2	3	4	5	6	7	8	9	10 (most integrated
Frequency: (percentage)	3%	7%	5%	12%	9%	11%	15%	10%	12%	10%	5%

n=87

the dark. And once campaigns aren't responsive ... if we aren't on the same page, that's when the problems can start." Another Liberal strategist contends that "there's some contact and some follow-through that we expect, especially if it involves the media. Even candidates [in unwinnable ridings] have to be careful and we can help most of the time." A Conservative strategist shares this viewpoint, noting that "if [a local campaign is] not aware and up to date on our messaging, strategy, expectations, for your riding, then that's a problem."

Yet some local actors claimed to ignore the bulk of party communications or to do the bare minimum to placate the party. Insularity persists because the central party cannot effectively micromanage local operations across the country. As a Conservative candidate (2015, Alberta) suggests, "There were a few tough phone calls with the party, but the moment I get off the phone, they don't know what I'm doing ... Maybe they have some doubts or frustration, [but] they know I want what's best ... and not just for me personally ... I don't mind being a red-headed stepchild in [the party's] mind as long as they tolerate [us]." And some insular campaigns highlighted resource constraints. As one such candidate (2019, Quebec) explains, "It's possible they phone and get mad, why haven't you done this [but] I don't have much patience for that. If you want it done, send me ten volunteers."

Another dimension of communications integration involves horizontal linkages between local campaigns. In 2015 and 2019, some local campaigns were relatively disconnected from the central party but maintained strong ties with other local campaigns, while others kept ties with both the centre and other local campaigns. Horizontal linkages were more common in dense urban areas where neighbouring ridings could easily share resources and conduct coordinated activities such as canvassing and fundraising. Exceptionally, seven local campaigns in 2015 and one campaign in 2019 disclosed that their horizontal communications included cooperation with opposing campaigns, albeit in other ridings. One campaign manager claimed that they regularly shared information and advice with campaign managers from other parties. This was intended to give their candidates a competitive

Table 5.3 Campaign Communications Integration by Constituency Competitiveness

District competitiveness[8]	Mean integration score
30%+ margin	4.2
25%–29% margin	4.8
20%–24% margin	6.0
15%–19% margin	7.4
10%–14% margin	7.0
5%–9% margin	7.0
1%–4% margin	8.1

n=87

advantage and help each other prevail in their respective races, even at the price of harming their own parties' candidates in other ridings. The campaign manager explained that the benefit of gaining other points of view was that it "get[s] us out of the bubble of [our party]."

These arrangements were made possible by pre-existing personal or professional relationships between members of different campaign teams. Evidently, the central party would not appreciate or permit this type of activity. Whether between local campaigns of the same party or opposing parties, these horizontal linkages demonstrate and perpetuate local independence from the centre.

Why are some local campaigns more integrated with the central party? Unsurprisingly, as depicted in Table 5.3, riding competitiveness is an important factor. The table classifies local campaigns by race competitiveness and provides a mean insularity-integration score for campaigns in that category.[7] As in Table 5.2, zero signifies most insular and ten signifies most integrated. The data show a greater tendency towards communications integration in more competitive races. Constituency races with a margin between 1 and 4 per cent have a communications integration score of 8.1. This score drops to 7 for races with a 5 to 9 per cent margin of victory and 4.2 for those with a margin greater than 30 percentage points.

It is unsurprising that marginal seats are targeted by the central party, receiving special attention (Flanagan 2014), and are thus more integrated in their communications. A Liberal strategist explains that this is "the same for all parties ... For [those ridings] we're calling and checking up multiple times a day, and closer to e-day, even multiple times an hour. Ideally there's also someone to drop by in person and help out." NDP strategist Karl Bélanger agrees that "headquarters reacts according to public demand." He suggests that the party invests its attention where there are prospects for success.

Table 5.4 Local Campa gn Communication Integration by Province

Province	Mean integration score
Alberta	5.2
Quebec	5
Ontario	7.3
All provinces	6.1

n=87

But strategists also prefer that less competitive campaigns remain connected with the centre. As a Liberal strategist states, "sometimes the weaker ridings actually need a lot of help ... they're less experienced, have fewer volunteers and so forth." Non-target constituencies can also elicit substantial party attention and communications resources; Noah Richler's 2015 NDP candidacy demonstrates this dynamic. Despite running in an unwinnable district, Richler's campaign occupied disproportionate party attention. Richler (2016) reproduces extensive phone and email conversations of his negotiations with the central party, for example, in crafting satirical viral campaign videos (178–9, 211–14). Similarly, a Liberal candidate (2015, Quebec) reports, "we weren't a target [constituency] but we had extensive contact with the party ... we were in close collusion and that wasn't always a good thing."

Regional differences also matter. As displayed in Table 5.4, Ontario constituencies featured relatively integrated communications, while Quebec and Alberta constituencies are more insular. The density of campaign communications in Ontario ridings may be attributed to physical and even the cultural distance from the central office outside of this province.

Candidates in other provinces express less interest in asking for advice or assistance from the party. Forty per cent of Ontario candidates said they would frequently ask for party assistance, versus 20 per cent in Alberta and 18 per cent in Quebec.[9] In NDP candidate Ken Kuzminski's (2015, Yellowhead) case, his rural Alberta constituency was both uncompetitive and geographically distant from party headquarters. Kuzminksi notes that he correctly predicted minimal central party involvement, due to his geographic location. Similarly, Ontario candidates were more likely to find party directions to be helpful and to feel that the party knew what was happening in their constituency.

Finally, variation in communications practices also stems from idiosyncratic local personalities. As 2019 Conservative national campaign manager Hamish Marshall explains, certain campaigns were flagged as problem areas with potential for distraction. Marshall notes:

when you're managing people, it doesn't matter if you work in politics or in a bank, people are people. I'm sure RBC has got some bank managers that they have to keep an eye on ... that's just management ... some people are team players, some people are not, some people always [think they] know better, even when they don't. Some people do [know better]. There are some smart individual riding campaign mangers out there.

Similarly, an NDP strategist contends, "some [local actors] have a reputation. And you know they'll need a bit of extra guidance." These constituencies elicited intensified central party supervision, and thus, additional resources. Although parties attempt to screen for potentially rebellious personalities during candidate search processes, the rigour of vetting can be inconsistent. A 2015 Liberal candidate explains the nature of their vetting process: "when I had my green-lighting committee, there were supposed to be three people interviewing me that had booked an hour. Only one of them showed up ... and said 'you're not going to do anything to embarrass us are you?' I said 'No.' ... it was a one-question green-light committee." Although the candidate was subjected to an online background check and offered campaign training (they declined the latter), this was insufficient to prevent the stoking of a past controversy by an opposing party during the campaign period.[10]

Formal and Informal Communications

The central party faces further challenges in communicating with local actors. While parties establish procedures for internal communications, these are not necessarily known or followed by local actors. Local campaign behaviour in 2015 and 2019 demonstrates that a substantial amount of internal communications takes place outside of official party channels. Official channels are party-sanctioned outlets or procedures such as regular campaign check-ins via party software. Some local actors prefer to communicate informally, with the party or other relevant political actors, through unsanctioned channels such as group chats on instant messaging platforms.

Effective internal communications inevitably requires "balanced management of both formal and informal communications" (Pich, Dean, and Punjaisri 2016, 103). These venues are intended to be complementary, but some local actors disregard conventional party channels. Roughly 56 per cent of 2015 candidates claimed they primarily relied on formal channels, versus 44 per cent who used mostly informal channels. In explaining their reliance on these channels,

Table 5.5 Constituency Campaigns' Use of Personal Networks for Intra-party Communication

	Yes (percentage)*	No (percentage)
Did you have a pre-existing professional or personal relationship with someone at party headquarters?	37	62
If so, were you in regular contact with this person or these persons during the campaign? (exclude no respondents from Q1)	72	28
If so, do you think this relationship helped your campaign gain special privileges? (exclude no respondents from Q1)	44	56

*May not add to 100 due to rounding; n=87

some local actors felt that official party venues were not an effective use of their time or that they could better achieve their objectives elsewhere. As shown in Table 5.5, this relates to the importance of personal networks. Many local actors enjoyed pre-existing relationships with central party staff and sometimes used these contacts to gain privileges, such as quick responses to questions or insights on central campaign strategy. A Liberal strategist suggests that such channels are fairly common "in the insular and incestuous world of Canadian politics." Indeed, many party officials have previously worked on local campaigns, and some local actors have previously worked for the central office.

As such, local campaign officials can mobilize informal networks and enjoy privileged access to the centre. For example, Richler (2016, 169) recounts that his personal networks allowed him to transmit requests directly to the central party's seniormost advisors. Another 2015 candidate explained that their campaign manager once worked in an important party position, which signified that they "had the ear of [the party] ... including to make things happen for us [at the local level] ... it was a huge help and just [required] ... sending a text." Similarly, one local campaign manager explains that they texted the national campaign manager every day, admitting that "I don't think they like it but it's much, much faster to get answers that are final, that are ... the right answer." And despite requests not to overburden communications channels, another campaign manager sent frequent emails that "blind copied" up to six senior party officials, hoping to receive the desired response from at least one.

Local campaigns which do not enjoy such access may resent informal channels. For example, in 2019, an Ontario campaign manager explained that the party's candidate in a neighbouring riding enjoyed favoured access to the leader's office because their campaign manager knew members of their core team. Their perceived special treatment, such as collaborations with popular party surrogates, was "disappointing and demoralizing." To the extent that they foster resentments, consume disproportionate resources, or disturb party strategy, these practices may be detrimental to other campaigns or the national campaign. Meanwhile, local campaigns that enjoy these benefits feel they have saved time and resources, engaged in problem solving, and demonstrated their resourcefulness in gaining advantages for their campaign. In their own estimation, as a 2015 Liberal candidate in Ontario states, they "violate the letter of the law, but not the spirit of the law." Importantly, rather than deterring this type of informal communication, some central party actors continue to allow it, perhaps because the alternative would place strain on their friendships.

Communications Hierarchies and Their Effects

Prior expectations suggest that intra-party communications are hierarchical, with virtually no ability for local campaigns to influence the central campaign. Indeed, interview and observational data indicate that most intra-party communications is unidirectional and initiated from the central party. A Liberal strategist summarizes these issues in hierarchical terms: "[o]f course, we are not coequals. No one locally really has a direct line to the centre because that would be chaos. As much as I don't want to say our communications are just [party HQ] telling [local campaigns] what to do, that's pretty much what's happening." Similarly, a Conservative strategist explains that "internal party communications means that we stress what the campaigns need to be doing more and less of … areas for improvement … and keeping morale up. There's not really room or time to have two-way conversations for the most part."

Others echoed the notion of regular demands based on implicit obligations to more carefully listen and comply with particular party instructions ("we'd like to remind everyone that … "). A 2019 Conservative campaign manager stresses that "the messages don't overtly say, do this and do that, or else dot dot dot … [but] the threat of some sort of sanction is always there. Hopefully it never comes to that, at least for us … I don't know about other campaigns. I hear things all the time, but this is a stressful period."

NDP campaigns in 2019 were less likely to identify hierarchical campaign logic. As an NDP campaign manager claimed, "I don't think we're necessarily being told what to do, I think the information from the party is there when you need it, I actually wish there was more coming from [the party]." This marked an apparent change from 2015, where most credible candidates felt that the party generally behaved in a hierarchical manner, for example in their unilateral action and micromanagement of select campaigns. This change might be attributed to the party's stronger electoral prospects in 2015, since greater resources and expectations may foster a more rigid central office (McGrane 2019). An NDP candidate who ran in both elections suggests that "one of the reasons I enjoyed [2019] more was not just that expectations were lower but also there was more humility and less hierarchy coming from the party." Similarly, former NDP MP Matthew Dubé (Beloiel–Chambly) suggests that party demands increase as their resource capacities and investment increase: "certainly there's a bargain that's made in so far as if the party is providing a lot of support, paying for things . . it's kind of like when your parents are paying for your wedding. They're going to have a bigger say."

Some evidence suggests that parties are unwise to enforce strictly one-way communications and neglect local viewpoints. In recalling the 2015 election, Dubé regrets the central party's unapproachability. In Dubé's view, the central party's inability to listen to constituency campaigns may have cost several popular NDP incumbents their seats, as the central campaign erroneously focused on a message of strategic voting to replace Prime Minister Stephen Harper:

> At the end it sounded like [we] were saying vote Liberal. We should have instead turned to, well who do you want to replace him with? ... We were clearly getting a sense on the ground that what we were communicating wasn't benefiting us ... it was very distinct ... we tried to communicate this to the party, and we didn't really feel we were getting responsiveness on that ... I look at it as when it's a big apparatus ... like a big ship, trying to get it to turn around [is] more difficult than getting a little speed boat to turn around.

Numerous other candidates and party strategists agree that local campaigns can serve as early warning systems based on their experiences on the ground. While they are no substitute for polling data, improved two-way communications and local inputs may benefit parties. This is particularly important for the NDP, which generally has lower quality data.

The hierarchical nature of intra-party communications was generally confirmed through observational research that featured a continuous flow of instructions and guidance from the centre. Interviewees frequently described the communications aspect of national-local party relations using language of hierarchy in identifying "top-down," "centralized," or "one-way" communications.

The most forceful way to advance party preferences is to send central party staff to visit a local campaign in person. However, an NDP strategist conveys why they prefer not to do this: "we already have people for that, regional [organizers] ... to send people from [the central party] is expensive and you lose that person helping out at [party headquarters] ... it's also not a guarantee you'll fix any problems, unless you're sticking around for a long time." An NDP candidate (2015, Quebec) feels that there would "be a revolt if [the party] tried to take over from the local [campaign]." Similarly, a Conservative candidate (2015, Ontario) in a highly competitive riding declares that "unless [the party] wants to literally send a squad of people here ... [like a] hostile takeover, they have limited say in the day-to-day decisions." Conservative candidate Andy Brooke (2015, Kingston and the Islands) recalls determining that, in an attempt to influence his campaign's behaviour, the party recruited a volunteer to join the campaign and report back to them. Brooke did not appreciate this, and reports that "we sensed something was wrong and we had to release [this] person from the campaign."[11] For their part, a 2019 Liberal campaign manager suggests that it is rare for central party employees to be physically present within local campaigns: "the party isn't actually here though, they're not telling me what to do with my time, we check in [with the party] and chat, and go back to the [campaign]." Nonetheless, in 2015, the Liberal Party decided to send a large number of central party interns to constituencies across Canada, asking them to report back to the party on local activities. This practice was not repeated in 2019.

In terms of email communications and conference calls, some campaigns viewed messages regularly transmitted by the party to be helpful, while others found them to be unnecessary or distracting. A 2019 Liberal campaign manager explains: "every day we have some points on the messaging and strategy, and I think we need to know these things, it's useful information for the most part ... [I] actively use something from it every other day." Conversely, when addressing the party's daily email messages, a 2019 candidate states that "we have a place for that, it's called the trash." When their campaign manager laughed at this remark, the candidate retorted, "[they] think I'm kidding." Similarly, a Liberal candidate (2015, Quebec) recalls that "they sent me talking points every morning, but I never read them." Along these lines, a Conservative campaign manager explains that "at a certain point it's mostly just noise, and we honestly ignore a lot of what the party's saying because we're not the typical riding." Ultimately, if top-down communications evoke images of a one-way street, this road is a metaphorical dead end if messages are sent but not meaningfully received.[12] Influence on local attitudes and behaviour is contingent on their campaigns' willingness to engage with an internal communications network.

Regional Party Offices

Do regional offices serve to secure and advance central party authority? Party strategists frequently mentioned these campaign staff as constituting crucial communications linkages with constituency campaigns. As a Liberal Party strategist explains, "our real eyes and ears are the [regional organizers]." Regional offices constitute an ambiguous aspect of the party hierarchy. These offices are an important component of federal party organization that is relatively absent from Carty's (2002) franchise analysis. Fourteen local and national party officials with previous experience at a regional party office were interviewed for this project. Regional offices serve as an intermediary between the central party and local campaigns. Typically, one party organizer is assigned to support a particular group of ridings in a defined geographic area. For example, the Toronto area featured multiple Liberal Party field organizers during the 2019 campaign, who reported to the regional director for the twenty-five Toronto ridings, Ian Perkins. At the time, the Liberals tended to refer to people staffing these posts as field organizers, while the Conservatives used the term desk officers.[13] Party organizers are also assigned to aid with target seats and fill support roles such as data software assistance.

Their intermediate position in a campaign hierarchy is such that some local campaigns claimed to view a regional organizer as their boss, while others resisted this idea. A 2019 Liberal campaign manager states: "I report to [this field organizer] and he reports to [a regional director], so there is a chain of command I would say. If I'm in trouble with [a regional director], that's not something I want to have happen." A 2019 NDP candidate agrees that, "yes, ultimately, if I don't do something that's a problem for [the regional office], it will get run up the command chain and I can have some sort of consequences." However, a 2019 Conservative campaign manager suggests that "they are not my boss and if they tried to act that way they wouldn't get very far."

The position of regional offices is difficult to classify in organizational management terms. As a former regional organizer recalls, "there [are] limits to how much you can order around a local campaign as a field organizer. I'm not really sure how [regional offices] fit in that scheme … You're not the big bad wolf and you're not technically there to discipline ... but you are supposed to sort of guide things along, like a guard rail ... I always thought I was more of a resource than supervisor." Similarly, another former regional organizer explains that "part of that job is to make sure the campaigns are doing what they're supposed to be ... but [also to] just give them what they need." Nonetheless, regional offices clearly receive their instructions from party headquarters and remain subject to their authority. Conservative strategist Hamish Marshall recalls that local actors sometimes defied or ignored instructions from party desk officers. He describes a dynamic where "[constituency campaigns] push back on the younger people that work for me and if it's really bad I get on the phone with them and they would do what I told them, especially if they had any chance of winning."

While regional party offices are intended to support local campaign needs and provide more tailored guidance, they are often understaffed. National and local party officials for all parties stressed the fact that constituency campaigns should not overburden their parties' communications channels. This expectation is made explicit in candidate training. Interview subjects also suggested this expectation is reinforced during the active campaign period through conference calls and emails. A Conservative strategist explains that "the party doesn't necessarily have the staff to answer questions all day, we have [field] organizers who do lots of that but we try to encourage problem-solving at the local level. [We're] not happy if phones are ringing with questions all day." An NDP strategist agrees with this sentiment: "we don't have resources to answer every question and so we want to minimize that tendency." This is not to say that parties discourage contacting field organizers, but rather, as a Liberal strategist contends,

> the field organizers have to deal with a lot, multiple campaigns ... each of them, overseeing the day-to-day and a lot of unexpected things that can and will come up. Our local campaigns are generally quite ... street-smart and wise to what they need to be doing, I don't think anyone is so inexperienced that they can't work independently ... If they were, someone would notice and [we would] deal with that by getting someone in there who can ... set things straight.

A former NDP regional organizer explains this challenging position: "I was given twelve campaigns to be in charge of and I never had time to keep up, sometimes it was like pulling teeth, I felt the slow responses from [party headquarters] and a lack of response or cooperation from the local." Altogether, ambiguous roles and responsibilities as well as logistical challenges appear to limit regional party offices' ability to maintain party authority.

Message Not Delivered: Communications Barriers

Given local autonomy to make significant campaign decisions, parties depend on internal communications to exert their influence throughout the campaign. Yet internal communications networks fail to ensure or facilitate party authority despite being constructed for this purpose. They do not necessarily provide a continuous accurate flow of information on constituency activities. As evidenced in this chapter, central authority is challenged by the persistence of insular constituency campaigns, the nature of horizontal campaign communications and cooperation, and the logistical limitations of vertical communications channels.

In any relationship, parties may have inaccurate perceptions of one another when communication does not function as intended. As Pich, Dean, and Punjaisri (2016, 103) surmise, "an open environment ... [and] a two-way communications process is pivotal when building mutual understanding and trust ... within and across departments." Given current internal communications practices on federal campaigns, the central party risks misunderstanding constituency campaigns, just as constituency campaigns sometimes fail to view broader aspects of the national campaign. Potential improvements to facilitate more accurate and reliable intra-party communications might stem from central party efforts to reduce reliance on informal communications networks, codify and abide by clearly established communications practices, reduce unnecessary communications by targeting and simplifying concise messages to local campaigns, and provide increased resources for regional communications liaison desks, including for uncompetitive constituencies. For their part, constituency campaigns might be asked to sign additional communications accountability documents along with candidate contracts. Clearly detailing the proper communications channels and expectations would prevent unsustainable and unfair communications practices, for example, in the case of Conservative National Campaign Director Hamish Marshall, who recounts receiving multiple text messages every day of the election period from a local campaign manager.

Finally, the communications-related practices in this chapter may be examined in relation to other aspects of local campaign behaviour highlighted in previous chapters. Figure 5.1 provides a summary of the major typologies used in this book and how they relate to each other. For purposes of space, the original typologies are not reproduced. The

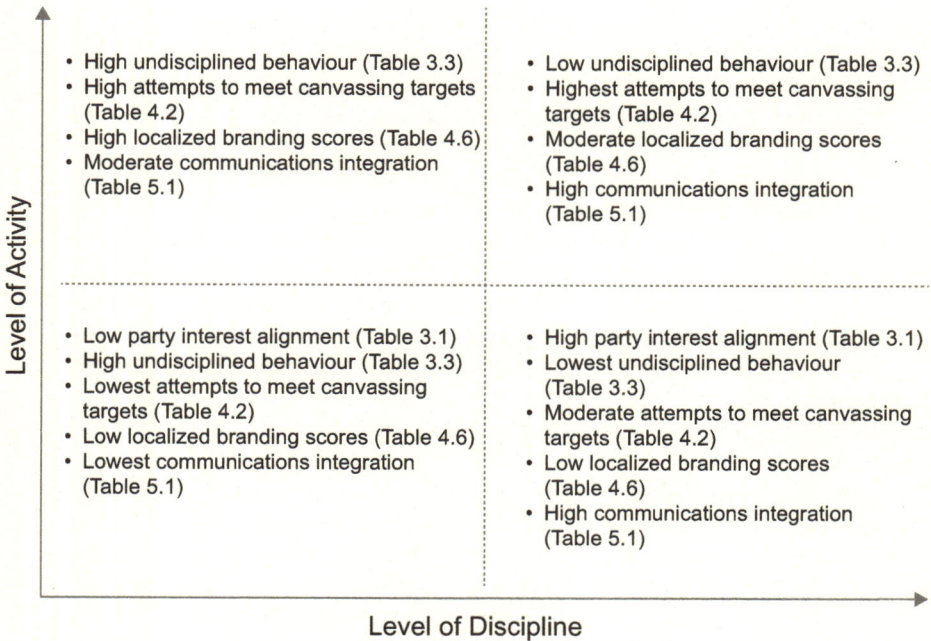

Figure 5.1 Summary of Local Campaign Typologies

figure is composed of four quadrants. The x-axis displays the level of local discipline and the y-axis shows the level of campaign activity. Therefore, local campaigns can be more or less disciplined and separately have more or less initiative to engage in a variety of campaign activities. The bottom left quadrant represents local campaigns that are minimally active and uncooperative. These campaigns are minimally invested in their local race and typically have few resources. As a reminder, undisciplined behaviour can also result from failures to act, which these campaigns are prone to. The top left represents relatively active or industrious campaigns that tend to be undisciplined. These campaigns have ample resources that can be used for entrepreneurial projects such as collecting and storing data independently of the party. The top right shows campaigns that are highly disciplined and highly active. This is the ideal quadrant, from the central party's perspective. The bottom right shows campaigns that are highly disciplined and relatively inactive. They also tend not to engage in undisciplined behaviour since they prioritize teamwork but are relatively quiet on the campaign trail.

To conclude, if local campaigns are told they are always being observed, this is not exactly the case. Despite apparent limitations on the central party's abilities to monitor local activities during a campaign period, federal campaign organizations generally appear to be solidly cohesive and disciplined throughout all levels of their operations.

In examining the capacity of party headquarters to generate campaign discipline, this next chapter highlights limitations in central party authority and gaps in our understanding of how party cohesion is maintained. If, as this chapter has argued, party authority is limited, variable, and contingent, what other mechanisms produce campaign discipline and party cohesion?

Chapter 6

Constituency Campaign Self-Discipline

The Conservative Party ran a relatively successful campaign in 2019, finishing ahead of the victorious Liberals in the national popular vote total and reducing them to a minority government.[1] The party's national campaign manager Hamish Marshall believes that local campaign teams were a major source of strength for the party. Marshall notes that, in many cases, local actors excelled with minimal supervision from the central campaign. Highlighting the limitations of central party authority, he reminds us that ultimately, "[y]ou've got 338 franchises who are staffed by volunteers effectively, and the amount of candidate control that is possible … is minimal." Marshall illustrates an important point about local campaign behaviour. Despite limited central party oversight, campaign discipline and cohesion remain the norm.

While previous chapters in this book focused on the presence and nature of undisciplined behaviour, at the end of the day, most local actors do behave in a disciplined manner. The present chapter seeks to better understand the sources of local campaign discipline, as evidence shows that central party authority does not reliably maintain it. The chapter has two main objectives. First, it offers local campaign self-discipline as a more compelling explanation than party authority for compliance with party preferences. Second, it explains why local campaigns exercise self-discipline, by applying theories of organizational behaviour to an election context.

The chapter contends that self-discipline is encompassed by four distinct logical pathways, or behavioural logics of action for decision-making: the logic of consequences, the logic of appropriateness, the logic of habit, and Kantian optimization. These pathways stem from existing research on organizational behaviour and decision-making within large institutions. The first three logics are derived from organizational theory, made prominent by the work of March and Olsen

(1989) and March and Simon ([1958] 1993). The fourth, Kantian optimization, is a rationalist theory developed by political scientist John Roemer to explain non-altruistic cooperative behaviour. The applicability of these behavioural logics within political parties is imperfect. However, in conjunction with interview and observational data, these frameworks provide cogent and analytically compelling explanations for local campaign self-discipline.

Despite the clear influence of party structures, individual agency remains an important element of local decision-making and campaign discipline. In some cases, constituency campaign behaviour can only be explained in terms of the contingent choices of local actors.

The chapter begins by addressing differences in the attitudes versus behaviours of constituency campaigns. Local candidates are more likely to approve of undisciplined behaviour, and believe in their ability to carry it out, than to actually engage in it. Those who endorse but avoid undisciplined behaviour comprise a substantial proportion of this project's candidate sample. This points to the importance of self-discipline, rather than central party authority, as the most compelling explanation for campaign discipline during federal elections. The chapter further specifies the ways in which self-discipline leads to party cohesion and how it structures key aspects of local campaign behaviour.

Comparing Local Campaign Abilities, Attitudes, and Behaviours

In addition to identifying whether they had engaged in different types of undisciplined behaviour, interview subjects were also asked whether they endorsed these behaviours and whether it was even possible to engage in them. Responses are displayed in Table 6.1, which compares three dimensions of undisciplined behaviour: perceived ability to engage in the behaviour, attitudinal openness or approval, and actual participation in the behaviour. The ability or competence dimension indicates whether respondents believe, given the constraints of party discipline, that local campaigns are actually able to engage in this behaviour. The attitudinal approval dimension refers to whether respondents believe that local campaigns should be allowed to engage in various types of undisciplined behaviour. Lastly, the actualized behaviour dimension asks whether the constituency campaign associated with the candidate has itself engaged in the various indicators of undisciplined behaviour. There are higher scores across ability and attitude dimensions of undisciplined behaviour, when compared to actualized behaviour. These discrepancies anticipate the importance of local campaign self-discipline.[2] For example, 48 per cent believe that local campaigns should be able

Table 6.1 Comparison of Three Dimensions of Undisciplined Behaviour

Indicator of Undisciplined Behaviour	Is it possible for local campaigns to ... (ability/ competence)	Should local campaigns be allowed to ... (attitude/ approval)	Did your campaign ever ... (behaviour)
Ignore party instructions?	61	52	42
Distribute unvetted campaign materials?	77	70	37
Critique (privately) party leadership?	64	55	30
Contradict the party's position?	42	48	19
Cooperate with a local campaign from an opposing party?	16	11	8
Critique (publicly) party leadership?	23	21	5

n=87

to contradict their parties, 42 per cent believe they have the ability to contradict their parties, but only 19 per cent claim to have done so. The average across all indicators underscores this trend, with an average score of 47.2 per cent for ability, 42.8 per cent for attitudes, and 23.5 per cent for behaviour.

Scores on ability/competence indicators in Table 6.1 suggest that local campaigns have relative confidence in their autonomy. For example, 77 per cent believe they have the ability to distribute official campaign materials without party permission and 61 per cent believe they are able to ignore instructions from their parties. Local actors appear unconvinced that the party effectively controls these aspects of their decision-making. Interview data support the view that local campaigns are more autonomous and industrious than anticipated. A 2019 Liberal campaign manager explains, "contrary to what some may think, we're not a glorified door-to-door machine ... We have a lot of projects and so forth that the centre doesn't know about or care to know about." Similarly, a 2019 NDP campaign manager who formerly worked at party headquarters suggests that "there is much more creativity and independence going on [at the local level] than [party headquarters] sometimes realize. If you have an effective person at [the local level] who can work ... in the system there's actually a lot you can do."

A related aspect of these data, which further underscores constituency campaigns' autonomous capacity, is the frequency of their undisciplined behaviour. As seen in Chapters 3 and 4, undisciplined behaviour is higher than anticipated by existing research. For example, 19 per cent of campaigns in this sample have contradicted party policy and 11 per cent think they should be allowed to cooperate with opposing campaigns. Interestingly, notions of a domineering central party were also dismissed by party strategists, who highlight apparent limits of central control and their own desires for conformity. Conservative strategist Hamish Marshall is clear that his party was unable to micromanage local actors in 2019, emphasizing that volunteer workers may not feel beholden to the central campaign. Marshall thus underlines an important difference between campaign and caucus discipline. While elected members face potential career sanctions for undisciplined actions, similar consequences from the central party are not always possible for unpaid local staff or even candidates.[3] Similarly, a Liberal strategist suggests that "some of the ideas of [the central party] mothership are greatly exaggerated ... ultimately, [the party] depend[s] on [local campaigns] to do the right thing." NDP strategist Brad Lavigne offers further reasons why undisciplined behaviour may be more common than some realize: "you've got 338 candidates, 338 campaign managers, you're almost [at] seven hundred people that have varying degrees of experience or time to train on how to run a campaign." These impressions would surely surprise many local campaign officials who do not necessarily believe that the central party is aware of its own limitations.

The fact that many constituency campaigns choose not to exploit their autonomy or behave in an undisciplined manner might be interpreted as evidence of the underlying coercive power of the central party. But this appears not to be true, given the high numbers of constituency campaigns which endorse undisciplined behaviour and declare an ability to engage in it. Substantially lower figures should be anticipated in these dimensions of undisciplined behaviour if party authority could readily prevent and sanction the behaviours.

Based on the available data, three significant explanations for discrepancies in ability, attitude, and behaviour indicators of undisciplined behaviour are apparent. First, the figures for undisciplined behaviour may be under-reported, since local campaigns might be willing to identify the potential for undisciplined behaviour, while remaining hesitant or less than forthcoming in disclosing their own participation. Second, although local campaigns may express openness to undisciplined behaviour, internalized party norms may remain sufficiently powerful, in many instances, to prevent its realization. Third, rather than party structures restricting undisciplined behaviour, the agency and independent decision-making of local campaign actors may explain these results. The first two explanations are indicative of deep-seated central party influence, while the third places greater control in the hands of local actors. This chapter presents evidence of all three options. Ultimately, the extent of independent local decision-making is sufficient to support the claim that constituency actors retain meaningful autonomy over the ground campaign. And local campaign self-discipline is a key factor in explaining lower figures for actualized behaviour indicators in Table 6.1, relative to the ability and attitude indicators. This is consistent with prior chapters' findings on the contingent nature of party authority.

Organizational Theory and Local Campaigns

Our goal is to understand the abilities and behaviours of local actors within party structures and a campaign context. This includes why local candidates act in disciplined and undisciplined ways. For the most part, existing research does not directly address the behaviour of political candidates.[4] However, important insights can be drawn from organizational theory. The most influential work on the behaviour of individuals within complex institutions has been developed by March, Olsen, and Simon. March and Simon ([1958] 1993) employ a novel focus on human behavioural components of organizations. They claim that a solvent or sustainable organization is one that continually produces inducements to recruit and retain members and establishes defined roles for participants (103). Roles for participants are established at a cognitive level, by reliably eliciting certain behaviours. This stems from invoking behavioural responses to stimuli, which are stored in participants' memories and can be later recalled. March and Olsen (1989) elaborate on how organizations establish ordered expectations by creating organizational rules based on anticipated personnel reactions. March, Friedberg, and Arellano (2011, 239) further clarify that there is no sharp distinction between organizations and institutions, as both consist of systems of rules and roles. They summarize that "an institution is a collection of rules and organizations can be thought as instruments for acting within rules."

How do political parties fit within organizational theory? Others have noted that political parties are undoubtedly organizations concerned with rules and roles (e.g., Searing 1994). But the campaign period is a political environment with distinct incentive structures. During elections, candidates are integrated with the party apparatus in various contingent ways. While some candidates experience their parties as an ever-present force, others do so fleetingly and from a great distance. Candidates are unevenly invested in their roles, which are short-term, unstable, and volunteer based. Some candidates and the volunteers around them enjoy the possibility of organizational exit, either due to the temporary nature of a campaign or their options for career and social rewards outside of their parties. The ground-level campaign organization itself that is relevant to candidates is also largely dormant outside of an official campaign period. These realities undermine the entrenchment of organizational roles for election candidates, relative to traditional organizations. However, many candidates are drawn to partisan activism through deeply held values. Social pressures also exist when personal ties fuel party involvement. These realities can bind candidates to their party roles more so than members of other organizations. As such, what behavioural logics might we anticipate for political actors within these institutions?

The Logic of Consequence and Fear of the Central Party

As we have seen in earlier chapters, a significant number of local campaigns behave in a manner that is highly consistent with central party expectations, carefully following party directives and guidelines. As discussed in Chapter 3 (p. 63), 42 per cent of the campaigns in this sample are conscientious because they do not display any indicators of undisciplined behaviour. Many others suggest they are open to undisciplined behaviour but tend not to follow through with it. Local candidates are much more likely to display positive attitudes towards undisciplined behaviour and to believe they are able to engage in undisciplined behaviour than to acknowledge they have engaged in it. Do these campaigns practice restraint and self-discipline because they fear consequences from the central party for deviant behaviour?

Fear of party consequences entails that local actors practice self-discipline because they approximate a "logic of consequences" (March and Olsen 1998). This involves analysis-based behaviour whereby actors weigh the anticipated consequences of their actions, given the structural constraints of their environments. Their decisions are informed by anticipated consequences, and their individual agency is relatively limited (March and Simon 1993, 7). This behavioural logic clearly applies to some local actors. A Conservative candidate (2015, Ontario) explains the essence of fear of consequence-based reasoning: "I wouldn't do anything like that because I could get a phone call from [Conservative national campaign director] Jenni Byrne ... I didn't want to get in trouble." As discussed in Chapter 5, existing research tends to imply that local campaigns uphold party discipline because they fear the repercussions from their parties. Therefore, fear of the central party should constitute a promising explanation for campaign cohesion.[5] However, evidence from 2015 and 2019 campaigns suggests that fear of party consequences is an incomplete explanation for campaign discipline. Most local campaign behaviour is unrelated to this behavioural logic.

Each behavioural logic is inferred here through context-specific judgments, in this case, involving markers of anticipated consequences and fear, based on research participants' responses to questions on undisciplined behaviour, perceptions of the central party, and local campaign decision-making. Reasoning that is rooted in concern for direct and explicit consequences from the party can be understood to represent this type of decision-making. Some local actors clearly believe the party is aware of their everyday activities. They anticipate the party will punish undisciplined behaviour, as well as any behaviours they find objectionable. Table 6.1 helps to identify which campaigns display fear-based motivation. According to these data, a small number of candidates display attitudinal openness to undisciplined behaviour but indicate they do not have the ability to engage in it, nor have they actually engaged in it. For them, fear of party repercussions motivates the exercise of self-discipline. This is because they identify their parties as the reason they do not have the ability to engage in undisciplined behaviour, despite their receptiveness to it. These considerations were occasionally raised during interviews. As an NDP candidate (2015, Alberta) explains, "the problem with [undisciplined behaviour] is quite frankly that you'll get caught. The party will find out and you won't be a candidate much longer, or else there'll be some type of consequence." Similarly, a Conservative candidate (2019, Quebec) states that "you bet I'm worried about what the party can do if you step out of line. There's a reason why we run everything by [party officials] and make sure to go by the book … Things can go south very fast if you get on the wrong side of someone at [party headquarters]." Therefore, some endorse the idea of undisciplined behaviour but anticipate that the party would prevent undisciplined behaviour and enact punishments.

Table 6.1 shows that 48 per cent of candidates feel that local campaigns should be allowed to contradict their parties' political positions, while 42 per cent think they are able to do so. This 6 per cent gap represents candidates who are open to this indicator of undisciplined behaviour, but do not think they are capable of engaging in it.[6] This lack of capacity seems to be attributable to fear of the central party, rather than logistical limitations. As a Liberal candidate (2019, Ontario) explains, "the party definitely holds me back sometimes … from doing certain things. I have a great team, [that] knows what to do … You don't have to have a leash on the local campaigns but unfortunately sometimes it happens …

someone [from the central party] will inevitably find out if you're off the mark and out of bounds from something they wanted." Overall, a relatively small number of local campaigns act in accordance with party expectations because they envision tangible repercussions. Party cohesion is typically maintained through more nuanced processes than sanctions and coercion. As seen below, many more candidates feel they can behave in undisciplined ways but choose not to for other reasons.

The Logic of Appropriateness and the Logic of Habit

The exercise of self-discipline is not sufficiently explained by the logic of consequence or fear of a domineering central party. Evidence from prior chapters suggests that many instances of undisciplined behaviour are neither detected nor punished by the central party. Along these lines, local campaign self-discipline can be attributed to two interrelated factors: the logic of appropriateness and the logic of habit. Local actors are often unaware of their tendencies to comply with party guidelines and execute party preferences. Put differently, local campaigns often behave as if they are being influenced by their parties without actually believing they are being regulated by their parties. Local campaign self-discipline can stem from the logic of appropriateness, according to which social actors make decisions based on ingrained understandings of the rules and norms that exist for their perceived role. As March and Olsen (2011, 478) explain,

> Rules are followed because they are seen as natural, rightful, expected, and legitimate. Actors seek to fulfill the obligations encapsulated in a role, an identity, a membership in a political community or group, and the ethos, practices, and expectations of its institutions. Embedded in a social collectivity, they do what they see as appropriate for themselves in a specific type of situation.

Perceived appropriateness is equally grounded in legitimacy or a belief in the rightness of action, or as Ostrom (1998, 2) contends, "the pursuit of self-interest combined with the capability of acquiring internal norms of behavior and following enforced rules when understood and perceived to be legitimate." The norms that govern behaviour are reinforced through social practices, training, and learning (Weber, Kopelman, and Messick 2004). The totality of these rules governing behaviour represent the desired candidate role, which is initially ingrained through socialization at the stages of candidate recruitment, vetting, and training (see for example, Marland 2020, 38).

In contrast to the logic of consequences, which is anchored in acknowledgment of explicit and direct consequences, the logic of appropriateness appears as an internalized fear of the party. This fear is more diffuse and evokes a generalized sense of negativity associated with disobedience that stems from inappropriate behaviour. Put differently, internalized fear manifests without conscious weighing of expected consequences. Brent Rathgeber (2014, 112) recounts his understanding of party caucus discipline: "the team polices itself. Team members will occasionally feel the need to encourage players who have been tempted to stray from the pack to get back in line. More often, however, such action is unnecessary; the members exercise self-discipline entirely of their own volition." The logical reasoning connected to internalized fear of the party is nearly unconscious and self-reinforcing.

Research participants who refrained from undisciplined behaviour despite a stated ability and attitudinal predisposition to engage in it were asked to reflect on their reasoning. Some appeared to indicate a subconscious fear of their party. An NDP candidate (2015, Alberta) explains why they had refrained from voicing their negative opinion of a senior party official: "[d]eep down there's sometimes a voice from [the party] telling me not to do or say this thing or that thing … [if] there's conflict between what I want to do and what [the party wants], I would default to the party position." Similarly, a Liberal candidate (2015, Alberta) explains that "If you don't follow an instruction from the party, the risk is very low that you'll suffer any consequences … [but] a risk is still a risk so I probably won't do it. At the end of the day, I would default to doing what the party wants almost every time."

Party Culture, Shared Values, and Appropriateness

According to strategists, their parties seek to generate candidate roles that embrace discipline and solidarity. As a Liberal strategist explains, "from the time of expressing interest [in running for office], to the campaign and beyond, there is a habituation or socialization into the role. The candidate is at the centre because they have a unique responsibility to represent the party and the leader and it's very different than anything else even if they've been a campaign manager." In terms of candidate development, an NDP strategist explains that "training is a sort of holistic process to prepare candidates with clear and realistic expectations as much as we can." The party aims to teach "candidates to pull their weight, follow instructions … once the campaign starts you should know what to expect day to day … how to deal with unforeseen problems and when to ask the party for help." In this respect, campaign training equips local actors with a logic of appropriateness to underpin their behaviour. For example, candidates must sign declarations attesting to their loyalty and suitability for the party (Marland 2020, 41). Conservative strategist Hamish Marshall further emphasizes the link between the difficulty of maintaining party authority during the campaign period, and the importance of establishing party norms beforehand, in declaring that parties can exert minimal control over 338 candidates during the campaign period. For this reason, parties seek to prevent unpredictable candidates and campaign managers from reaching the campaign stage.

These desires are not unique to political parties. Most large organizations create similar pressures towards discipline, cohesion, and productivity (Lawler and Bacharach 1983; Vigoda 2001). In so doing, they construct operational logics that do not exist outside of the organization (Weick 1995). Understanding the major disincentives to deviating from the preferred candidate roles helps to reveal candidates' underlying motivations and reasoning. The seminal work of March and Simon ([1958] 1993) highlights incentives that are needed to maintain compliance or loyalty from participants in an organization. They include economic inducements related to career advancement as well as social satisfaction, shared values, and satisfaction with the organization itself. These inducements are certainly applicable to the candidate role. But party organizations have an added intensity to their public-facing dimensions: substantial media coverage, public policy implications, and face-to-face interactions with political audiences.

Roles are also reinforced through symbolic cues. Weick (1995, 65) argues that organizations feature carefully chosen language and symbols that allow members to make sense of their organizational identities. Within a party, such symbolic cues reinforce the candidate role, as belonging entails identification with the party's major symbols, such as revered party figures or policy commitments. These sensibilities are reinforced through socialization and everyday practice.

Crucially, those who disturb them experience the discomfort of performing inappropriate behaviour. Some research participants explained that violating party norms disturbed their sensibilities. For example, a Conservative candidate (2015, Alberta) explains that if they deviate from a party position, "[the party] probably won't know, but I would know and that may or may not be a problem for me in the future. But it would bother me all the same." Along these same lines, a Liberal candidate (2015, Quebec) suggests that "there's a little party voice in your head at the end [that] would hold most people in check, including me," and an NDP candidate (2015, Alberta) agrees that "no one is holding a gun to my head but I want to do the right thing, meaning for the party."

E-31 Campaign Brief

With 31 days left campaign, it's clear that only NDP will defeat Stephen Harper.

We have the momentum across Canada. Rallies from Nova Scotia to BC are spilling out the door, as record numbers of Canadians come to hear Tom Mulcair talk about our plan to bring change to Ottawa.

The more Canadians hear about $15/day childcare, a $15/hour lederal minimum wage, and a plan to create good, middle class jobs, they more excited they are about change in Ottawa, and the more they are putting their trust in Tom Mulcair to defeat Stephen Harper.

TOM TODAY

Tom is announcing our next major expansion of Canada's healthcare system; universal, national pharmacare

THE WEEK AHEAD:

This week is all about health care. That means better care for you and your family. Better care for seniors, more nurses, doctors, more clinics and more affordable prescription drugs.

MESSAGES OF THE DAY:

Tom Mulcair announced today his plan to work with provinces to make prescription drugs more affordable, by supporting universal prescription drug coverage and controlling drug costs through bulk purchasing

The NDP's offer is built on a long standing commitment to the well-being of families; a commitment that led Tommy Douglas to establish universal Medicare.

Our health care priorities will lower the price Canadians have to pay for their prescriptions

---

Figure 6.1 NDP Internal Campaign Memo, 2015 Election

Moreover, a Conservative candidate (2019, Quebec) states that, "I know what's expected [from the party] and I understand why … I could do something else I suppose and it's not that I am afraid of a punishment, it's just the right thing to do."

This behavioural logic is also reinforced by shared values, which are a fundamental component of any organizational culture (Dempsey 2015). It's especially true for political parties, as candidates typically share ideological convictions and beliefs with them. During campaigns, parties' internal communications evoke values that initially made campaign workers and volunteers align with their parties. Figure 6.1 illustrates this effect, as NDP talking points remind candidates of key policy priorities and their continuity with the party's legacy through exalted figure and former leader Tommy Douglas. As a Liberal strategist explains, "we want to give [local campaign] talking points but also to keep the team invested and to remind them why [they] are doing this." While these shared values may perpetuate campaign discipline, a commitment to the same values can cause disunity, if local actors perceive that the party is deviating from its core purpose or is deeply mistaken in its efforts to advance them.

Among research participants, the logic of appropriateness is more frequently responsible for constituency campaign discipline than the logic of consequence. This is seen in the greater number of local actors who contend they have the ability to engage in undisciplined behaviour, but do not perceive such behaviour to be warranted or desirable. In other words, they have little interest in undisciplined behaviour, even if they could engage in it without difficulty. Despite their lack of constraint, they show little appetite for contravening their parties, as undisciplined behaviour offends a sense of appropriateness. As an NDP candidate (2019, Ontario) explains, "I could probably go my own way on some of these things, even if the party doesn't want me to. But I'm not convinced that's the best approach ... [it has] nothing to do with burning bridges, I'd say it's more tactical from the campaign ... and maybe at the end of the day ... more often than not we rise and fall together." Local actors are not especially confident that their parties can prevent undisciplined behaviour. But this does not mean they are insulated from party influence.

Habituated Decision-Making

Local compliance is also motivated by a logic of habit that leads local actors to instinctively self-regulate in a manner that aligns with party preferences. This impetus for self-discipline is related to the logic of appropriateness but entails reliance on cognitive shorthands or reflexive behaviour, rather than conscious decision-making processes (Hodgkinson and Sadler-Smith 2018; Jones 2020, 244). As with logics of appropriateness, a pre-existing organizational culture may condition behaviour by defining the universe of conceivable actions. But as Porter (2018, 13) explains, habit constrains behaviour because it is "a type of path dependency, the process whereby prior historical developments limit the scope of choices set before decisionmakers, reproducing behavior even in the absence of the conditions where it began."

It is difficult to critically deconstruct habituated decision-making. When questioning local campaign practices and asking candidates or campaign managers to explain decisions, some replied that they could not explain why they behaved a certain way, but felt it was simply the correct or only option, and they had not considered their reasoning.

For example, in describing the process of asking for party approval for campaign literature, a local candidate (2019, Ontario) explained that "when thinking about it I don't see the value [in the procedure] ... I don't think they care ... But I'm still automatically doing it."

Unlike with logics of appropriateness, logics of habit may coincide with attitudinal openness to undisciplined behaviour. Some local actors offer habituated decision-making as an explanation for why they endorsed but did not engage in undisciplined behaviour. Several candidates had trouble explaining their lack of undisciplined behaviour. For example, a 2019 candidate in Quebec states that "I'm actually not even sure why I went along with [a policy that I disagreed with]." Similarly, a Liberal candidate (2019, Ontario) wonders, "why would I do anything else? I'm here for a reason and it's not to cause any issues for the party regardless of what I might think." These candidates do not view their reflexive self-disciplinary tendencies as resulting from party coercion. For example, another Liberal candidate (2019, Ontario) puts a positive spin on instinctive decision-making: "I wouldn't say I'm forced, I would say we're conditioned to do our roles, and I fully accept that." Similar thoughts were expressed when candidates were questioned on the instinctive dismissal of their personal preferences in favour of party expectations.

Habituated decision-making can also foster party cohesion because it sometimes requires less effort to maintain discipline than to engage in undisciplined behaviour. In other words, inertia and apathy can lead local actors to reject undisciplined behaviour. For example, as a Liberal candidate (2015, Alberta) conveys, "I have no problem with [undisciplined behaviour], but I can't be bothered." Similarly, an NDP candidate (2019, Quebec) explains, "I would actually like to do more of my own thing but it's easier to do the scripts ... I like the idea of criticizing my own party when it's deserved but I just don't have the time and energy right now." In each case, local actors default to party norms even when they are open to other behaviours. Ultimately, with logics of appropriateness and habit, candidates internalize their external regulations from the central party. Their disciplined behaviour results from an ingrained organizational role that constrains the universe of conceivable actions.

Kantian Optimization

According to findings displayed in Table 6.1, a small number of candidates indicate that they have the capacity to engage in undisciplined behaviour but hold unfavourable attitudes towards it. For example, 77 per cent indicate that local campaigns have the ability to distribute unvetted campaign materials, while only 70 per cent endorse this behaviour. Similarly, 64 per cent of candidates in the sample believe that local campaigns can privately critique their party leadership, but 55 per cent think they should do this. This gap between ability and attitude highlights the existence of candidates who are uncomfortable with undisciplined behaviour despite its feasibility. In some cases, these candidates indicate that they prefer to only take actions they wish to see practiced by all local campaigns. These candidates practice self-discipline because they fear the consequences if *all* local campaigns behaved in an undisciplined manner. In other words, they display the behaviours that they would like to see universalized.[7]

A 2015 Liberal candidate in Alberta helps to illustrate this logic: "I may want to do something without permission and make something move more quickly, but if everyone did that, I actually think it would be chaotic ... how would [that] help [my campaign]?" When questioned on their reluctance to engage in undisciplined behaviour, a Conservative candidate (2015, Quebec) explains, "I could go around telling voters that I don't agree with the party when it suits me, but just because you can do something doesn't mean you should do it ... if everyone was doing that, what kind of campaign would that be? What kind of party would that be? We would have no core message, no consistent values ... it would hurt [all campaigns] across the country."

Multiple candidates questioned the implications of undisciplined behaviour for other campaigns and the party. According to a 2019 NDP candidate in Quebec, "We're behaving the way that I hope everyone, that all campaigns are behaving, that I think we should behave." Similarly, former NDP MP Matthew Dubé (Beloeil–Chambly) explains his appreciation for campaign discipline:

> let's say we had a strong position on respecting Quebec on a particular issue and we had an MP or candidate in [British Columbia] expressing a view contradictory to that. It's a guarantee that I would be frustrated about that because it would reflect poorly on me ... People would say well if that's what the NDP thinks ... even though we know ... [Dubé] is going to stand up for us, this is his party and the standard that he's bearing.

Likewise, a 2019 Conservative candidate in Quebec explains that "we're refraining from [undisciplined behaviour] because we don't believe that's how any campaign should behave, ours included, and if we did ... I'm not sure that would be a very good result for the party." The candidate suggests that by extension "we would all be in trouble."

These ideas are consistent with John Roemer's research on Kantian optimization. Roemer (2015, 46) explains the impetus of this behaviour:

> Each agent evaluates not the profile that would result if only he deviated, but rather the profile of actions that would result if all deviated in similar fashion. Kant's categorical imperative says: take those and only those actions that are universalizable, meaning that the world would be better (according to one's own preferences) were one's behavior universalized.

This logic applies to candidates who behave as they wish others would behave; in other words, if all local campaigns were to deviate from the central party it would negatively affect the party, and by extension, the local campaign. Thus, the campaign decides to remain disciplined.

Kantian logic has been applied to organizational ethics (Arnold and Harris 2012; Clegg, Kornberger, and Rhodes 2007) and behavioural economics (Van Long 2017) but not to political campaign behaviour.[8] Roemer offers a more direct path to cooperative behaviour than Elinor Ostrom (1990), who famously contends that the tragedy of the commons can be solved through external sanctions that prevent free riding. Parties create sanctions for local actors who seek to benefit from party strengths and resources while potentially undermining the party or acting in a more self-interested manner when it is convenient. But if local agents behave as Kantian optimizers, this cooperative behaviour can occur even in the absence of external sanctions.

Roemer specifies that Kantian optimization is cooperative but not altruistic. While altruistic behaviour is motivated by selfless concern for others, cooperation can be motivated by self-interest. Roemer contends (2015, 46): "we do not cooperate because we care about *others*, but because we recognize we are *all in the same boat*, and cooperation will advance each individual interest. Of course, *if* altruism exists, it may also motivate cooperation, but I wish to emphasize that cooperation does not require altruism." Thus, despite the cooperative outcomes it entails, Kantian optimization is a fundamentally self-interested mode of behaviour. Agents do not necessarily behave as Kantian optimizers for the benefit of anyone other than themselves. Indeed, they refrain from uncooperative behaviour because of the negative effects they would personally experience, were everyone to engage in it. In other words, Kantian optimization conceives of self-interest in terms of universal rather than individualized behaviour. It is a type of self-interest that yields a cooperative equilibrium without a sanctions regime. Subjects model the behaviour they seek from others because this would be best for them. They prefer not to deviate from party doctrine even if they have an incentive to do so, because of a belief they are better off if everyone else maintains this behaviour. This applies to candidates who express concern for their own campaigns' political prospects, were all campaigns to behave in an undisciplined manner. As a Liberal candidate (2015, Alberta) suggests, "If [constituency campaigns] ignore the party ... without discipline there would be campaign chaos ... which would mean that no one would get what they want. At the end of the day we might be sinking ourselves."

In Roemer's view, agents can realize they may be slightly better off by defecting or free riding, but also realize that if everyone behaved similarly, they would be significantly worse off. They refrain from deviant behaviour for their own benefit. At times, candidates appear to consider the benefits and risks associated with undisciplined behaviour, ultimately concluding that risks to all outweigh potential benefits to themselves. As an NDP candidate (2015, Quebec) explains, "I might get a small boost if I [contradict the party] ... but if everyone did that all the time, it would be a disaster." Similarly, a Conservative candidate (2019, Quebec) explains their decision to renounce their desired canvassing tactic: "I want this, but it probably won't make a real difference to how many votes I get ... If everyone wanted to [use their own techniques], I think the party couldn't do its job and that would trickle back down as all sorts of issues."

Some candidates clearly think and behave as Kantian optimizers and choose to exhibit the behaviours that if universalized would be best for them. That said, based on interview and observational data, relatively few candidates engage in Kantian optimization. One reason for this could be that Kantian optimizers tend to overestimate the influence their behaviour has on others, in the case of local campaigns. Local decisions may not be detectable beyond their immediate vicinity, at least during the campaign period. Thus, whether or not they engage in undisciplined behaviour may have minimal bearing on others. Moreover, according to Roemer (2015, 46), the absence of Kantian optimization may stem from the challenge of cultivating foundations of trust and solidarity that are necessary to sustain it. Indeed, this behaviour relies on trust that others will behave similarly. Therefore, candidates who are Kantian optimizers may demonstrate above average trust in their fellow candidates.

Local Campaign Agency

In certain cases, the aforementioned behavioural logics of action cannot account for local campaign behaviour. In these instances, local agency is the foundation of decision-making. Put differently, local campaign behaviour is at times reducible to local agency and irreducible beyond agency. Although foundational agency is more often observable in cases of undisciplined behaviour, it can also be detected in decisions to uphold party cohesion.[9] In the latter case, the best explanation for local campaign discipline is the decision-making of local candidates and campaign managers.

Despite direct or indirect party influences, local actors often make choices of their own volition; in these cases, axiomatic rules or general behavioural tendencies cannot be established. Based on interview and observational data, the following markers showed that, taken together, individual agency was a decisive factor in campaign decision-making: some decisions were not explained by other behavioural pathways, an individual was ultimately responsible for the decision, their choice was contingent with many possible outcomes, and the substitution of another person would conceivably have altered the decision. In some cases, local agency, exercised by the candidate or campaign manager, results in self-discipline and compliance with the party. For example, a 2019 candidate explained that they had previously instructed supporters who had maximized their allowable riding-level contribution to stop donating money to the national party, since that money was not being transferred back down at a level that was acceptable to them. But they subsequently reverted to the party procedure for a reason unrelated to the campaign or to partisan politics. Similarly, a 2019 Conservative candidate who altered their messaging on a contentious political issue to fall in line with party orthodoxy explains, "I decided today to play by the rules … I was feeling a little more rebellious [yesterday] because I read [a story] … that was upsetting." Further, a 2019 NDP campaign manager explains that "There's [a] couple that I've been [allowing] to do [paper] canvassing … but it won't go properly on the app. Today I might switch them over." They ultimately decided not to switch these volunteers to electronic canvassing until the day before the election. In each case, local actors came to these decisions without party awareness or coercion and engaged in analysis-based decision-making. Their decisions demonstrated self-discipline and the party's preferred choice, given viable alternatives.

In some cases, decisions are drawn out and deliberate, and in others, they are nearly instinctive. In opposing an NDP national campaign commitment, 2015 candidate Daniel Beals (Kingston and the Islands) recalls, "the interesting thing about it is I did it on purpose. I came out hard about it … [by] putting that stake into the ground, as a candidate … I wanted to force this on the party." Conversely, another NDP candidate (2019, Ontario) explains grappling with their response to a party position that clashed with their personal convictions: "This is something that I thought about a lot. I decided against [voicing opposition] because I didn't think there was much to gain. But right when I started the [all candidates'] forum I changed my mind ... [then] I changed it again and softened that opinion." And when questioned on their canvassing messages, a Conservative candidate (2015, Ontario) explains, "Most times my own preference was not to deviate from [the party] ... so I didn't. I don't think there would have been an issue with it though ... I decided on instinct a lot of the time, what I would say [to voters]."

These cases suggest that local behaviour is not merely structurally determined in the campaign context. This echoes research conducted by Koop, Bastedo, and Blidook (2018, 13) that confronts scholarly tendencies to minimize the agency of MPs as local representatives, while aggrandizing institutional structures that shape their behaviour. The authors contend that, despite the strictures of party discipline, MPs should be viewed as "individuals with substantial agency to make choices about what types of representatives they will be." In the case of local campaign actors, decision-making can be unpredictable and contingent, based on individual preferences, and the substitution of a different person in one's place could result in a different outcome.

The Implications of Constituency Campaign Self-Discipline

Local campaign discipline is shaped by the logics of consequence, appropriateness, and habit, as well as Kantian optimization. This begs the question of which logics are most influential for constituency campaigns. Unfortunately, ascribing specific frequencies to each behavioural pathway is unfeasible, as they are not mutually exclusive and may be displayed multiple times every day within each constituency campaign. Moreover, a candidate and campaign manager may embrace duelling behavioural logics, with mixed results for constituency campaign discipline.[10] Nonetheless, based on interview and observational data, it is possible to draw general conclusions regarding the prevalence of the four logical pathways. Some logics appear to be more useful than others in terms of their applicability to many local actors. Notably, the logic of consequence appears to be excessively structural. Although incentive structures reliably guide action, it is clear from interview and observational data that party norms and obligations are not typically viewed through logics of anticipated consequences. And despite the rapid pace and demands of an election campaign, local actors in this research sample seldom act reflexively and out of habit. In fact, the dynamic nature of a campaign may discourage the type of routinized activity that is conducive to habituated decision-making and behaviour. There are similarly few candidates who think and behave as Kantian optimizers, which leaves the logic of appropriateness as the most frequent behavioural logic structuring campaign discipline. Many candidates and campaign managers perceive campaign discipline as a rightful component of their role. This perception is reinforced through socialization and a party culture that draws from members' shared values. It also bears noting that some choices to exercise self-discipline can only be explained in terms of individual agency.[11]

Evidence suggests that local campaigns may favour certain logics but are also prone to move between them. Therefore, these logical frameworks constitute dynamic categorizations rather than fixed modes of behaviour. To be sure, candidates and campaign managers do not appear to move constantly between these four pathways, since local campaign behaviour is heavily anchored in a campaign management style, as well as local political conditions and logistical demands. Moreover, the appearance of campaign discipline and cohesion may be overdetermined. This is consistent with research on legislative unity in party voting. As Andeweg and Thomassen (2011, 669) explain, disciplined voting in the Dutch Parliament is overdetermined because the pathways to this outcome are "complementary to each other rather than redundant, that it is a case of 'different horses for different courses.'"

While organizational culture may provide a structural context, a finer-grained understanding of campaign behaviour must account for the local environment, logistical realities, and contingent individual preferences. This chapter has distinguished four behavioural logics that capture the mechanics of local campaign self-discipline. Taken together, they help to explain the mechanisms underlying the exercise of local campaign self-discipline. Each pathway is rooted within the context of a party's institutional culture and expected candidate roles. These are notably similar for all three parties, in that there are no major differences in the norms and expectations for local campaigns expressed by party strategists or within their campaign guidelines. Evidently, parties feature different symbolic and ideological foundations, but these do not appear to affect how local campaign actors are expected to fulfil their roles. An important reason for the similarities in organizational cultures is expressed by a Liberal Party strategist:

[the parties] essentially have access to the same knowledge base and very similar technologies, goals, and outlooks for how to run a campaign operation ... there's some variation but we generally know the optimal ... conventional way to run a national campaign ... you sometimes might think [another party can] have a secret weapon. In reality, they just have greater capacity to do what all the parties know we have to do. Of course, we don't always have the resources we'd like to.

Similarly, a Conservative strategist confides that "we know for the most part what the other parties are doing, we have ways of finding that out ... and it's part of what different staff, consultants and so forth do ... to know the other guys." A Liberal strategist suggests that these similarities may even permeate national borders since they aim to adopt best practices from parties in other countries. For instance, the Liberalist platform was developed by a former Obama campaign employee (Patten 2017, 54).

Understanding why local campaigns choose or choose not to practice self-discipline reveals how and when their behaviour is directed by party structures. Of those campaigns that ultimately refrain from undisciplined behaviour, outright fear of the central party is a relatively minor explanation. This is consistent with evidence of the limitations of central party authority in maintaining discipline. Many local actors have options or inclinations to engage in undisciplined behaviour but choose not to. This indicates the importance of self-discipline rather than party authority in conditioning their behaviour. Candidates are able to make decisions simply because they choose to do so, and party influences do not overwhelm local agency.

Chapter 7

Conclusion

Canada's federal elections take place within 338 individual constituencies. Accordingly, they entail collaboration between party headquarters and local campaigns. Scholarship suggests that campaign discipline is essential to this relationship, as constituency campaigns are expected to carefully follow party instructions. But constituency actors face competing pressures to accommodate local political conditions and impulses. In sum, they often struggle to accommodate local forces under the disciplinary oversight of a central party. This concluding chapter examines implications drawn from key issues and concepts explored in this book. What do these findings signify for our understanding of Canadian elections, parties, and representation?

Interrogating the Franchise Model

Carty's (2002, 2004) influential accounts of stratarchical party organization emphasize multiple centres of authority, underpinned by a power-sharing bargain between national and local levels. This franchise dynamic is under strain, particularly as the central party interferes in the candidate selection process (e.g., Cross 2018). Recent Liberal Party promises to end these practices have not materialized (Carty 2015). And technological changes have placed increased power in the hands of central party officials. Evidence from this book suggests these trends have not yet resulted in the hyper-disciplined constituency campaigns anticipated by some, nor have they negated the relevance of local actors. This is shown in the nature of undisciplined campaign behaviour and the necessity of constituency campaign self-discipline in maintaining party cohesion. Party authority is regularly limited by practical realities of the campaign environment, including local ambitions. Party oversight, particularly through intra-party communications, is constrained, and thus in some ways overstated. As Carty and Eagles declared in 2005 (175), the ground campaign continues to be fundamentally shaped by local attitudes and decisions. The model's persistence underscores the relevance of local actors in understanding federal campaign dynamics, our view of which tends to magnify the significance of national forces.

Alongside the franchise model, scholars sometimes describe election campaigns in military terms. For example, Flanagan (2010, 156) states that "rhetoric makes up the weaponry of a political campaign." This language of order and hierarchy aligns with notions of campaign centralization. On-the-ground events clash with these military metaphors and ideas about the local execution of party orders. Local decision-making is unpredictable and contingent. Structural explanations of local behaviour provide an incomplete picture as local actors remain meaningfully autonomous and able to realize their preferences. And local actors themselves offer other metaphors, suggesting their party is more like a sports team, a hospital, or a chaotic restaurant kitchen. For these reasons, constituency campaigns merit greater attention, especially when they are sites of political innovation or resistance to their own parties.

Despite the enduring relevance of the franchise analogy, this study highlights potential limitations. Unlike corporate franchises, political franchises contend with election campaigns, which entail intense but short-term relations between local and national levels and a heightened demand for discipline. Corporate franchises are predicated on consistency and recognizability, as they offer a familiar and often identical product across space. Political franchises are characterized by programmatic flexibility with substantial reinvention and tailoring to local tastes. This suggests that local candidates behave more as party-affiliated entrepreneurs than as franchisees or local managers (Busenitz and Barney 1997). The endurance of the franchise model further suggests that Canada has not yet shifted to a different form of party organization, such as hierarchical parties or party federation (Bolleyer 2012).

In 1963, Meisel wrote that Canada's federal parties "are among the relatively few genuinely national forces" (370). It is clear that the major federal parties continue to play an important role in terms of local and regional representation (Bakvis and Tanguay 2020). Given the weakness of Canadian institutions for intrastate federalism,[1] these interests are poorly represented in national politics (e.g., Simeon [1972] 2006). Local campaigns provide an avenue for the articulation of issues and voices beyond the focus-grouped agendas of party leaders and their coteries (e.g., Blidook 2012). To an extent, they push back against a single-minded focus on political expediency. If greater attention were paid to local campaigns, this would conceivably elevate genuine local and regional concerns. Conversely, if constituency campaigns began to merely reflect central party desires and act as appendages of the central office, this would signify a further weakening of local inputs within national politics.

Message Dissonance and Political Accountability

Franchise parties allow candidates to tailor political messages to their constituencies (e.g., Cross and Young 2015). This raises the possibility that some local actors deviate from their parties and present conflicting positions to electors. As Stephenson et al. (2019, 76–8) suggest, local campaigns deliver different messages in different regions of the country. In their view, based on evidence from candidate surveys, this is largely a matter of emphasizing different political issues. But evidence in this book shows that local actors sometimes deliver messages that contradict the national campaign or other local campaigns. This is especially true with voter canvassing, which is subject to minimal public scrutiny. Message dissonance may stem from the relatively low media and public attention paid to constituency campaigns (Carty and Eagles 2000, 2005), as well as the non-transparent nature of informal campaign activities such as canvassing. Whether or not these tensions are known by parties, this poses an accountability problem when citizens are unaware of an array of political claims underpinning campaigns. And if electors receive conflicting messages, these ambiguities can confuse citizens and hinder their ability to make the correct choice in voting consistently with their preferences (Gidengil et al. 2004). If constituency campaigns merit greater stature, then they also require greater scrutiny.

The potential for message dissonance aligns with Carty's (2002, 727) view of a franchise system that "ensures that in many constituencies the two campaigns will coexist in this uneven and unbalanced way. It is hardly a process designed to produce clear or intelligible collective decision making, or coherent teams of decision makers." Carty further suggests (745) that "[w]hen the discipline demanded ... becomes an unacceptably high franchise fee, exit (to another association, party or out of politics) becomes a more viable option than voice, and a more tolerable option than loyalty." Rather than exiting, some dissatisfied partisans may remain with their parties but obfuscate or misrepresent party positions, even if this is done carelessly rather than intentionally.[2]

Understanding Parties and Candidates

Most studies about how politics affects citizens incorporate political parties in some respect. Our assumptions about a multitude of related issues and processes stem from our understanding of parties, as their influence is widely felt throughout political life. While parties are often key actors in these stories, without ground-level knowledge of their operations, we risk misunderstanding essential qualities. By extension, accurately understanding political parties generates improved knowledge of how democratic and well-functioning our political system is. Parties shape how inclusive and responsive to various interests electoral politics can be. If we are wrong about what parties are doing during election campaigns, we risk making fundamental mistakes in reasoning about their substantive impact. Advancing our understanding of how parties behave enriches discussions of our democratic institutions (Koop, Bastedo, and Blidook 2018, 13). For example, an important and poorly understood aspect of parties is their internal communications. Further research on local actors would advance our understanding of Canadian parties, which themselves affect all major aspects of democratic life.

Savoie (2019, 168) summarizes five major functions of Canadian parties: "they offer candidates for elected office; engage citizens in politics; facilitate communications between Parliament, government, and citizens; educate citizens on policy; and make Parliamentary government work." Constituency campaigns and national-local party relations are relevant to each of these functions. Local campaigns perform essential ground-level work of mobilizing volunteers, connecting with electors, and advancing political agendas. As Cross (2016b, 604) argues, "many questions relating to Canadian politics can only be fully understood when we include in our analyses consideration of local party life."

Along these lines, the experiences of political candidates merit further study. Politics and government fundamentally consist of determining the binding rules we must live under as a society. Political candidates are fundamental to this process, helping to shape these binding rules and to engage the general public, yet their experiences are poorly understood. Candidates make considerable sacrifices to enter the ground level of electoral politics. Most will expend significant time, organizational effort, and financial resources, or surrender other professional opportunities. It is worth better understanding what this experience concretely entails for the thousands of candidates who present themselves each federal election. If the candidate experience becomes untenable for most citizens and their willingness to run for office further deteriorates, then the quality of elected officials, their capacity to represent constituents, and public policy outcomes will suffer as a result. Most candidates are heartened by the dedication of their volunteers and grateful for the opportunity to intimately encounter their communities. But romanticizing the experience leads to disappointment. Many candidates are dissatisfied with their parties, frustrated with a lack of campaign resources, and even discouraged by the behaviour of their constituents. Given these frustrations, this chapter concludes with suggestions for improving relations between local and national party organizations.

Remedial Insights

During initial discussions with local and national campaign actors, most claimed they were appreciative of their counterparts at the other levels of party organization. However, these sentiments changed as more details emerged during interviews and campaign observation. National-local party relationships can be far from harmonious. Research participants use colourful language to describe problems they have encountered with a stubborn local campaign or ineffective party advice. Generally speaking, the central party often feels that local campaigns have an unwarranted sense of their uniqueness. Party officials deal with large-scale trends and polling data; they may consequently view local knowledge as inferior or quaint. Their overloaded campaign radar sometimes leaves little patience for local concerns. Conversely, local actors may feel the central party gives overly generic directions and is willing to sacrifice their well-being for other priorities. The centre can also be viewed as inattentive or close-minded to local concerns.

To address such concerns, parties might begin by establishing and enforcing clearer expectations for local actors. In the 2015 and 2019 elections, local actors from all parties often misunderstood or were unfamiliar with party protocols, particularly regarding intra-party communications. To this end, a more concise standardized accountability contract would help to delineate campaign roles and responsibilities. To emphasize the importance of these expectations, parties could enforce them more assertively and proactively, avoid preferential treatment of some local actors, and reduce the amount of information directed towards constituency campaigns.

Partisan social circles are small but perceptions of preferential treatment for some local actors are demoralizing to others. Parties could take more proactive steps to prevent this. In the case of intra-party communications, the campaign relationship would benefit from reducing the use of informal communications channels. More generally, effective communication requires prioritizing the most essential information (Welch and Jackson 2007). While the party is adamant about protecting its limited time and resources, this logic could be extended to local campaigns. Parties can aim to reduce unnecessary communications with fewer, shorter, and more narrowly targeted messages.

There are also potential benefits from granting local actors greater latitude to speak for themselves. Parties might consider allowing more substantive unscripted local interactions with electors and the media. As a 2019 Conservative campaign manager suggests, "respect goes both ways and candidates want to be treated like adults." The central party fears the derailment of their strategy with negative media coverage of local actors (Marland 2021). Yet candidate controversies are likely to increase in frequency while decreasing in perceived severity as newer cohorts of politicians who have lived most of their lives online desensitize the public. Similarly, local actors who seek greater autonomy could simply try exercising their existing autonomy more often. Indeed, the central party is often unable to or uninterested in regulating local behaviour. A more radical step towards local empowerment would be for all major parties to institutionalize a requirement for formal EDA executive approval for candidate nominations, in addition to party leader approval. This would protect the local role in candidate selection and demonstrate the centre's trust and goodwill towards grassroots activists. As one local campaign manager and activist declared, "if we can't even choose the candidates, most of us feel ... what's the point?"

These steps may result in greater local buy-in to party objectives.[3] According to Verbos et al. (2007, 28), organizational cohesion benefits from mutual respect, transparency, and a shared purpose, in the form of "enhanced motivation, strong desire to remain affiliated with an organization, and greater willingness to engage in cooperative and prosocial behavior on its behalf." Ultimately, efforts to improve the health of intra-party relations would enhance the well-being of Canadian democracy more generally. Finally, party strategists sometimes lament a lack of strong local candidates willing to step forward and campaign effectively with minimal party supervision. But they might also recognize that their party's domineering reputations can prevent such candidates from running in the first place.

These topics and questions also present opportunities for further study. Some lines of inquiry may be limited by the confidential nature of internal party operations (see for example, Marland 2020). For instance to what extent is the central party aware of undisciplined behaviour, and when are internal discussions on the removal of a candidate or campaign manager triggered? Despite the notable frequency of undisciplined behaviour, the central party is rarely affected by it in terms of negative media attention. If the frequency of undisciplined behaviour were to increase, would parties act to repress it, or accept it as a latent feature of campaigns? In addition, a natural question that follows from this research is whether undisciplined behaviour correlates with stronger electoral performance for local candidates. Unfortunately, this is difficult to investigate, as more popular candidates may be more prone to undisciplined behaviour, rather than undisciplined behaviour bolstering the popularity of local candidates.

To conclude, this book explains how the central party does and does not influence constituency campaigns. A reassessment of Carty's seminal franchise model helps to reveal organizational proclivities, behavioural tendencies, and political incentives within multi-tiered parties. The book has aimed to offer a fine-grained examination of the mechanisms underlying local decision-making within a federal campaign organization. Undisciplined behaviour is greater than anticipated by existing research and is derived from insubordination, innovation, and incompetence within constituency campaigns. Despite this, constituency campaigns often behave consistently with central party preferences. Crucially, their discipline typically stems from self-discipline, rather than central party authority. While party structures are important influences in explaining self-discipline, party authority is circumscribed and not straightforward. For Canada's major parties, the central office's lack of effective coercive communications authority is complemented by a latent ability to inspire discipline through particular behavioural logics of action. Notably, some campaigns internalize party norms and self-police their behaviour according to a logic of appropriateness.

In significant and compelling ways, local campaign behaviour continues to be fundamentally determined by local actors. The local administration of central party procedures is replete with conflicting objectives, communications failures, and unforced errors. These tendencies may anticipate future difficulties for franchise-style parties. They also offer avenues for sustaining unique local party organizations. Opportunities exist for local representation, political engagement, and decision-making, which may even endure beyond the campaign period, if individuals choose to use them.

Methods

Interviews

Interviews with candidates who contested the 2015 election took place between July 2018 and July 2019. I sought to interview former candidates from different geographic regions and with varying levels of political experience, as well as a roughly even number of politicians from the three major parties. Flyvbjerg (2006, 230) labels this approach "information-oriented selection," referring to case selection on the basis of "expectations about their information content." In my selection criteria, geography refers both to regional differences and variation based on district population density. The salience of regional differences (e.g., Henderson 2004) may result in regionally differentiated interpretations of local-national party relations. For example, candidates in Ontario may feel more inclined to defer to party headquarters, given linkages with a party apparatus based in Ottawa and Toronto and geographic proximity and density that render southern Ontario constituencies easier for the party to monitor. Geography also refers to the distinction between urban, suburban, small city, and rural ridings. Carty and Eagles (2005) demonstrate that candidates outside of urban areas have relatively higher profiles in their constituencies, which also feature a more pronounced focus on local and regional political issues. Moreover, non-urban candidates can cultivate a stronger personal vote (Cross and Young 2015). Accordingly, I anticipate they may be less inclined than urban candidates to follow party directives and maintain campaign discipline.

Political experience is the second dimension that affected my interview selection criteria. I anticipated that experience in federal politics could entail different approaches to national-local party relations, as inexperienced candidates might be less comfortable challenging party norms. Lastly, I also considered partisan differences, since the three major parties may have different organizational expectations for local campaigns and different approaches to local-national party relations borne out of ideological or practical concerns.

Interviews typically lasted between forty and sixty minutes. Access and resources were the two major constraints in arranging them. In terms of gaining access to interview subjects, I anticipated a fairly low response rate from former candidates and planned to send many more interview requests than my target number of one hundred interviews.[1] Moreover, since a large number of former candidates are currently elected MPs, I first had to make contact with political staff, who act as gatekeepers in granting, denying, or delaying access (Goodyear-Grant 2013, 164; Marland and Esselment 2018b, 33). This further emphasized the need to send a large volume of requests, in anticipation of non-replies and refusals. According to Marland and Esselment (2018a, 697), it is difficult to obtain political interviews primarily due to the time constraints and cautious tendencies of potential interview subjects:

> elected representatives are saturated with requests ... The political casual-ties from wayward remarks that resulted in a negative news story or took a nasty viral turn are too numerous to count. Caution extends to grant-ing interviews with researchers ... Researchers must be mindful that their own social media use may have implications for persuading politicians and gatekeepers to grant an interview.

I sought to mitigate these risks by sending concise messages, empha-sizing confidentiality protections, and removing any indications of political leanings from my own online presence. I also made persistent, polite follow-up requests, up to three times, if no response was initially received or if a respondent asked for further information and subse-quently did not respond.

The limited online presence of certain former candidates was an additional challenge. Unlike elected MPs with parliamentary and party websites, the contact information of unsuccessful candidates can be difficult to locate. When Google searches and corporate directories were unhelpful, I found success by contacting local riding associations, which are typically listed online, and asking for the email address of the most recent candidate. If this option was unsuccessful, I attempted to contact interview subjects through social media (Marland and Essel-ment 2018a). While this was not a preferred mode of contact, many for-mer candidates maintained active Facebook pages, and brief messages were occasionally sent to request their email address or phone number, through which a more detailed request could be communicated.[2] If these approaches were unsuccessful, I moved on to a different candidate.

Research access to party strategists is especially challenging due to their motivations to guard politically sensitive information (Marland and Esselment 2018a, 2018b). This was reflected in a lower initial response rate of 22 per cent, or seven out of thirty-one contacts.[3] I relied on referrals from interviewees to gain access to three additional senior party strategists. Strategists who no longer held senior party positions were generally more receptive to interview requests. Three major party strategists agreed to be identified by name: Karl Bélanger and Brad Lavigne of the NDP, and Hamish Marshall of the Conservatives.

The second major limitation I faced was the time and resources required to conduct a large number of interviews. This difficulty was compounded by my decision to conduct in-person interviews in participants' home ridings[4] rather than telephone interviews. When feasible, in-person interviews can be preferable to telephone interviews, as they tend to generate higher quality data (Holbrook, Green, and Krosnick 2003; Seitz 2016; Shuy 2002).[5] They permit greater nuance in tone and body language and facilitate a stronger rapport with the interviewee, which is especially important when discussing controversial or sensitive topics such as campaign discipline, local autonomy, and party cohesion.[6] Building trust was essential, given the nature of these interviews and the candour they require (Mikecz 2012). Conversely, telephone interviews tend to produce more guarded answers. Additionally, in-person meetings allowed former candidates to provide concrete examples of campaign documents, which enriched these discussions, provided visual verification of certain statements, and provided access to primary source documents that would be otherwise inaccessible. Lastly, travelling to actual constituencies revealed local political perspectives in a manner and context not captured when discussing by phone or videoconference from many kilometres away. For the most part, I purposely timed interviews to take place at times when the House of Commons was not in session, as I preferred to meet sitting MPs in their constituencies rather than Ottawa. In the end, interviews took place in a wide variety of settings: constituency offices, coffee shops, private residences, and a variety of workplaces.

I selected participants from constituencies in three provinces: Alberta, Ontario, and Quebec. This geographic scope was restricted by in-person travel limitations as a single researcher. All Alberta interviews were conducted in August and September 2018. Quebec and Ontario interviews were conducted between September 2018 and July 2019. Ontario and Quebec are included for demographic and logistical reasons: they are the two largest provinces, comprising over 60 per cent of the Canadian population, and are geographically feasible for a single researcher to undertake. While these three provinces provide a baseline of considerable geographic and sociocultural diversity, the fact that seven provinces are excluded from the study is an important limitation.[7] This exclusion stemmed from the logistical challenge of in-person interviews conducted across a large territory with limited resources.

I initiated six waves of interview requests by email in order to achieve a sufficient response rate and a logistically feasible spread of interviews over time. I combined purposive and random sampling in the iterative selection process for interviewees (DiCicco-Bloom and Crabtree 2006). Logistical concerns and sufficient representation by party, region, and political experience informed my target population and sample design. This strategy for participant recruitment is consistent with those researchers seeking a representative sample of politicians (Walgrave and Joly 2018). I began the process by selecting randomly from a list of all constituencies in Ontario, Quebec, and Alberta, except for far northern constituencies, which were excluded for logistical reasons,[8] and I sampled separately from each province. Each time that I chose a constituency, I emailed former candidates from all three major parties. This was done intentionally in order to maximize efficiency of travel and potentially interview multiple candidates in each constituency. As I began assembling a sample of accepted interviews, I continually rebalanced to ensure I maintained the desired variation based on party, political experience, and riding type.

All participants were recruited by email from the randomly generated list of candidates.[9] I sent a total of 291 interview requests and obtained a successful response rate of 32 per cent, or ninety candidates,[10] from a diversity of regions, parties, and levels of political experience.[11] Participants were sent identical emails, in English, French, or both languages, with a brief greeting, explanation of the project, and their desired involvement. I also offered the option of taking notes instead of recording interviews and roughly two-thirds of participants agreed to have their interviews recorded.

For party elites, I did not have the luxury of a sampling strategy and had to pursue every possible avenue of access.[12] In keeping with Rossman and Rallis (2017, 135), interview requests were sent as cold email introductions after conducting Google searches for relevant contact information, with one exception where an academic connection helped to initiate contact. After locating sufficient contact information for a total of twenty-four senior party officials, eight interviews were ultimately conducted.

Interview subjects were not told in advance that I intended to study how local campaign discipline is maintained. However, I described the research as an application of Carty's franchise model and the relationship dynamic between local campaigns and the central party. In addition, I did not provide interview questions in advance, in order to prevent participants from crafting prepared responses. I decided to conduct semi-structured interviews, but to also include some closed-ended questions. As Blidook and Koop (2019, 8) contend, the advantage of semi-structured interviews is that they result "in data that is reasonably comparable, but which can also accommodate unexpected emphases and concerns that could not be accommodated within the confines of a structured interview format." Schmidt (2004) explains that semi-structured interviews are generally designed to avoid leading questions, keep open potentially unforeseen lines of inquiry, and allow participants to freely extrapolate on relevant topics and themes. While I relied on a list of questions, I recognized that unanticipated responses would shape the direction of the interview. Each semi-structured interview with former candidates featured thirteen open questions broadly concerned with local-national party relations (see Appendix C). The questions were general enough to permit flexibility and digression, and thus elicited a variety of responses. Party strategist interviews featured a different list of open questions (see Appendix D). I often asked follow-up questions to these open questions or departed from the question focus if this appeared to offer promising insights (Wang and Yan 2012, 195). I frequently obtained illuminating information and responses from these unplanned digressions.

For interviews with former federal candidates, I also asked closed-ended questions, which present response options and force subjects to choose from those options (Wang and Yan 2012, 239). The closed-ended questions permitted either yes/no responses or Likert scale responses, such as "strongly agree" or "agree" (see Appendix C). They involved the topics of intra-party campaign communications, campaign centralization, and undisciplined behaviour. I also regularly sought clarification on the meaning of certain responses, given the categories I knew I would later place them in (Kvale 2008, 58). The combination of open- and closed-ended responses permitted a balance between deeper qualitative interpretations with more quantitative-oriented analyses.

Participant Observation

Field observation was conducted during the 2019 election campaign. In August 2019, I sent out one hundred emails to local campaigns for the three largest parties that were located within roughly five hundred kilometres of my home research institution in Kingston, Ontario. Thirty-one local campaigns initially responded, twenty-one agreed in principle to participate, and ten of these were ultimately selected.[13]

Spradley (1980, 58) outlines the key components of participant observation, according to which researchers must perform a dual purpose:

> you will want to participate and to watch yourself and others at the same time. Make yourself explicitly aware of things that others take for granted. It will be important to take mental pictures with a wide-angle lens, looking beyond your immediate focus of activity. You will experience the feeling of being both an insider and outsider simultaneously. As you participate in routine activities, you will need to engage in introspection to more fully understand your experiences.

Regrettably, participant observation and other ethnographic approaches are rarely employed in political science (Gillespie and Michelson 2011). Obtaining access and building trust with participating research subjects, who can be hesitant to expose their workings to outsiders, is a major obstacle. In the case of campaign research, timing is also a crucial obstacle, since research can only occur during an election period, which may be years away.

Others find this method valuable for learning about local campaign behaviour and national-local party relations. Sayers's (1999) research, examined in Chapter 2 of this book, argues that varying nomination processes result in conceptually distinct candidate types and local campaign styles. His findings are based on campaign observation in seven BC constituencies during the 1988 federal election. Koop's (2011) study of grassroots Liberal activists includes research on the level of organizational integration between national and provincial Liberal partisans and resources during a campaign period. And Belfry Munroe and Munroe (2018) argue that local campaigns differ in how they perceive, generate, and strategically deploy voter data, based on their partisanship and campaign resources. Their analyses rely on participant observation of three local campaigns in the same Vancouver-area constituency. Each study is enthusiastic about the benefits of participant observation, in terms of its ability to generate rich and nuanced data (Belfry Munroe and Munroe 2018, 140; Koop 2011, 33; Sayers 1999, 13). Each of these studies influenced the approach to participant observation employed here, particularly in terms of building trust, determining how to behave as a researcher in the campaign setting, and realizing the need to complement observational data with interviews.

In terms of the nature and logistics of this campaign observation, Spradley's (1980, 5) work proved useful in identifying five different types of participant observation based on the degree of researcher involvement: non-participation, passive, moderate, active, and complete. For the purposes of my research, I eliminated the first two options, which risked making volunteers feel uncomfortable[14] and closing off opportunities to experience certain aspects of constituency campaign behaviour, such as accompanying candidates during canvassing activities. Moreover, I preferred not to adopt active or complete participation, since I did not seek to immerse myself in a particular role, but rather to gain general understanding of local campaign behaviour, particularly in terms of local-national party relations, which are not restricted to a single task or role.[15] In entering a local campaign with a defined volunteer role, the completion of associated duties could interfere with the observation of elements of local-national party relations. Accordingly, I determined that moderate participation provided an ideal balance between the participation and observation elements of this method (DeWalt, DeWalt, and Wayland 1998; Koop, Bastedo, and Blidook 2018, 25).

I was also influenced by Uldam and McCurdy's (2013) emphasis on the overt/covert and insider/outsider dimensions of participant observation. As the authors explain, the former refers to "informing subjects they are being studied, or overt research, versus studying the community in secret, or covert research," while the latter distinguishes "the positions of insider participant where the researcher is a member or has links with the community being studied versus outsider participant observation who does not" (942). I felt that an insider approach would be more likely to put other campaign subjects at ease, and minimize the "Hawthorne effect," where the presence of a researcher causes subjects to alter their behaviour. At the same time, I feared that covert participation would either entail an unethical and unmanageable amount of deception or confine me to an overly narrow role. Accordingly, I settled on the approach of a semi-covert insider, and this is what I pitched to receptive constituency campaign managers. My researcher identity provided to all subjects, except for the campaign manager and candidate, was that of a research student, arriving to contribute to and study the campaign, and helping out the campaign manager as needed. I intended to achieve insider status by untruthfully claiming to know the candidate on a personal level. These basic details were agreed upon with the campaign manager and candidate beforehand. In this capacity, I engaged in activities such as data entry and canvassing, but I maintained a distance from these actions by maintaining the mandate of a student researcher I sought not to appear to observe others. For instance, while listening and observing in the vicinity of the campaign office, I opened a document on my computer and appeared to be entering data and sending emails. I kept a detailed record of my observations as well as more subjective impressions, reflecting afterwards on the importance of what I had observed (Blidook and Koop 2019, 6; Spradley 1980).

In August 2019, with an impending federal campaign, I began contacting local campaign offices from the three largest parties with requests to observe their activities. The target population for campaign observation was significantly constrained by the time required to visit multiple campaigns during a relatively short election period. Therefore, I created a list of ridings within roughly five hundred kilometres of my home research institution in Kingston, Ontario. This produced a list of ninety-four ridings in Ontario and Quebec which I randomized and then I began sending emails to local candidates or general campaign email addresses if the former were not available. I sent out one hundred emails, describing my potential observation as unobtrusive, discreet, and nonpartisan.[16] Observation in ten local campaign offices began at the official start of the campaign period on 11 September 2019 and continued until election day on 21 October. During this forty-one-day period, thirty days were spent observing constituency campaigns. I observed for roughly nine hours per day, either with a single constituency campaign or splitting this time between two nearby campaigns.

Selection bias and generalizability are key limitations of this method. Campaigns that accept the presence of a researcher may be systematically different from those that do not. I asked each local campaign manager why they had accepted my observation request. The most common response was their eagerness to support Canadian politics research. Other reasons given were idiosyncratic, such as having a positive experience with Queen's University, my home institution, which suggests they were not influenced by the specific topics of the study. Although some local campaigns might have accepted research observation because they were confident in their scrupulous campaign operation, I learned through observation that the opposite was true for others, who were proud to display their defiance or independence from party headquarters. Ideally, these differing approaches are self-cancelling.

A second potential limitation is the validity or authenticity of the behaviours I observed. The "Hawthorne effect" refers to the presence of a researcher causing subjects to alter their behaviour. I sought to minimize this by ensuring that my identity as a researcher was known only to core campaign staff. Many core campaign staff had an apparent interest in Canadian politics research and no apparent intention of misrepresenting their activities. Moreover, as Koop, Bastedo, and Blidook (2018, 30) contend, if subjects trust the research observer, there is minimal reason to change their behaviour. It would also be difficult for participants to consistently remember to modify their behaviour given the relatively lengthy observation periods and hectic context of an election campaign. Based on the observation of surprising and sometimes unflattering events, some of which cannot be ethically disclosed, it seems unlikely that subjects were meaningfully altering their behaviour.

Campaign Materials

In terms of internal party documents, local campaign guidelines and party talking points were the main items of interest. Most participants did not have access to these documents at the time of our meeting or were unwilling to share them. In two cases, I was able to view and publish internal party documents by agreeing not to reveal who had provided them. In three other cases, I viewed internal party documents by agreeing not to publish them or discuss their source. When available, these materials complement and validate information provided from other sources.

Partisan campaign literature can also be difficult to obtain after an election campaign has ended. In the summer of 2018, I contacted 112 EDAs from the three major parties and asked for copies of materials from the 2015 campaign period. Many EDAs declined the request or did not respond, however, approximately twenty-five shared their past campaign literature. These requests were generally sent to different constituencies than those associated with local candidates interviewed for this research, with a small amount of overlap. In order to seek additional materials, pieces of literature, and greater geographic coverage, I also conducted internet searches, largely focused on former candidates' Twitter and Facebook pages. Altogether, I obtained ninety-six pieces of print or electronic campaign literature from thirty-two different constituencies in Ontario, Quebec, and Alberta.

Ethics Clearance Letters

June 22, 2018

Mr. Jacob Robbins-Kanter
Department of Political Studies,
Queen's University
68 University Avenue
Mackintosh-Corry Hall, Room C321
Kingston, ON, K7L 3N9

GREB Ref #: GPLST-141-18; TRAQ # 6023783
Title: "GPLST-141-18 The Franchise Model Reframed: Asymmetry, Autonomy, and Local Responsiveness in Canadian Federal Parties"

Dear Mr. Robbins-Kanter:

The General Research Ethics Board (GREB), by means of a delegated board review, has cleared your proposal entitled **"GPLST-141-18 The Franchise Model Reframed: Asymmetry, Autonomy, and Local Responsiveness in Canadian Federal Parties"** for ethical compliance with the Tri-Council Guidelines (TCPS 2 (2014)) and Queen's ethics policies. In accordance with the Tri-Council Guidelines (Article 6.14) and Standard Operating Procedures (405.001), your project has been cleared for one year. You are reminded of your obligation to submit an annual renewal form prior to the annual renewal due date (access this form at http://www.queensu.ca/traq/signon.html/; click on "Events"; under "Create New Event" click on "General Research

Ethics Board Annual Renewal/Closure Form for Cleared Studies").
Please note that when your research project is completed, you need
to submit an Annual Renewal/Closure Form in Romeo/traq indicating that the project is "completed" so that the file can be closed. This
should be submitted at the time of completion; there is no need to wait
until the annual renewal due date.

You are reminded of your obligation to advise the GREB of any
adverse event(s) that occur during this one-year period (access this
form at http://www.queensu.ca/traq/signon.html/; click on "Events";
under "Create New Event" click on "General Research Ethics Board
Adverse Event Form"). An adverse event includes, but is not limited to,
a complaint, a change, or unexpected event that alters the level of risk
for the researcher or participants or situation that requires a substantial
change in approach to a participant(s). You are also advised that all
adverse events must be reported to the GREB within 48 hours.

You are also reminded that all changes that might affect human
participants must be cleared by the GREB. For example, you must
report changes to the level of risk, applicant characteristics, and implementation of new procedures. To submit an amendment form, access
the application at http://www.queensu.ca/traq/signon.html; click
on "Events"; under "Create New Event" click on "General Research
Ethics Board Request for the Amendment of Approved Studies." Once
submitted, these changes will automatically be sent to the Ethics Coordinator, Ms. Gail Irving, at University Research Services for further
review and clearance by the GREB or Chair, GREB.

On behalf of the General Research Ethics Board, I wish you continued success in your research.

Sincerely,

Dean Tripp, Ph.D.
Chair
General Research Ethics Board

c: Dr. Elizabeth Goodyear-Grant and Dr. Jonathan Rose, Supervisors
      Dr. Grant Amyot, Chair, Unit REB
      Dept. Admin.

September 06, 2019

Mr. Jacob Robbins-Kanter
Department of Political Studies,
Queen's University
Mackintosh-Corry Hall, Room C321
68 University Avenue
Kingston, ON, K7L 3N9

GREB Ref #: GPLST-156-19; TRAQ # 6027316
Title: "GPLST-156-19 The Franchise Model Reframed: Asymmetry, Autonomy, and Local Responsiveness in Canadian Federal Parties"

Dear Mr. Robbins-Kanter:

The General Research Ethics Board (GREB), by means of a delegated board review, has cleared your proposal entitled **"GPLST-156-19 The Franchise Model Reframed: Asymmetry, Autonomy, and Local Responsiveness in Canadian Federal Parties"** for ethical compliance with the Tri-Council Guidelines (TCPS 2 (2014)) and Queen's ethics policies. In accordance with the Tri-Council Guidelines (Article 6.14) and Standard Operating Procedures (405.001), your project has been cleared for one year. You are reminded of your obligation to submit an annual renewal form prior to the annual renewal due date (access this form at http://www.queensu.ca/traq/signon.html/; click on "Events"; under "Create New Event" click on "General Research Ethics Board Annual Renewal/Closure Form for Cleared Studies"). Please note that when your research project is completed, you need to submit an Annual Renewal/Closure Form in Romeo/traq indicating that the project is "completed" so that the file can be closed. This should be submitted at the time of completion; there is no need to wait until the annual renewal due date.

You are reminded of your obligation to advise the GREB of any adverse event(s) that occur during this one-year period (access this form at http://www.queensu.ca/traq/signon.html/; click on "Events"; under "Create New Event" click on "General Research Ethics Board Adverse Event Form"). An adverse event includes, but is not limited to, a complaint, a change, or unexpected event that alters the level of risk for the researcher or participants or situation that requires a substantial change in approach to a participant(s). You are also advised that all adverse events must be reported to the GREB within 48 hours.

You are also reminded that all changes that might affect human participants must be cleared by the GREB. For example, you must report changes to the level of risk, applicant characteristics, and implementation of new procedures. To submit an amendment form, access the application at http://www.queensu.ca/traq/signon.html; click on "Events"; under "Create New Event" click on "General Research Ethics Board Request for the Amendment of Approved Studies." Once submitted, these changes will automatically be sent to the Ethics Coordinator, Ms. Gail Irving, at University Research Services for further review and clearance by the GREB or Chair, GREB.

On behalf of the General Research Ethics Board, I wish you continued success in your research.

Sincerely,

Chair, General Research Ethics Board (GREB)
Professor Dean A. Tripp, PhD
Departments of Psychology, Anesthesiology & Urology, Queen's University

c: Dr. Elizabeth Goodyear-Grant and Dr. Jonathan Rose, Supervisors
      Dr. Oded Haklai, Chair, Unit REB
      Michelle Knapp-Hermer, Dept. Admin.

Candidate Interview Questions

1. In your opinion, is the franchise model a useful or accurate way to think about Canadian political parties?
2. On the topic of campaign centralization, how involved was the central party in your campaign?
3. On the topic of party communications, how did your [local] campaign stay in touch or communicate with the central party?
4. To what extent was intra-party communications important to your campaign? What did you hope to accomplish from these interactions?
5. When speaking to voters, what was the balance of party talking points versus your personal views?
6. Did the party [headquarters] have a tailored message that fit with your riding? Did you tailor messages your own?
7. Is there anything that your party [headquarters] did poorly during the campaign? In terms of policy, strategy, or otherwise?
8. Is it a problem for local candidates to deviate from party messaging? Why or why not?
9. Did you ever feel obligated to support a party policy or position that you personally did not agree with?
10. Do you think that the party punishes local campaigns that don't follow their instructions?
11. Who was involved in the creation of your campaign literature?
11b. If applicable, how did you develop non-official language materials and campaign messaging?
12. Did your campaign do anything creative or unusual? Please elaborate.
13. Is there anything on these topics you would like to add that I haven't thought to ask you about?

*Note: closed-ended question data are available from the author.

Party Strategist Interview Questions

1. In your opinion, is the franchise model a useful or accurate way to think about Canadian political parties?
2. What sort of campaign training did the party offer for candidates and campaign managers in 2015 [2019]?
3. What are the major roles of the party's regional offices?
4. During a federal election, what would you say are the most important things that local campaigns must do?
5. Is there anything that local campaigns can do that would cause concern for the central party?
5b. Based on past experience, what activities or behaviour would you want local campaigns to avoid?
6. How does the central party ensure discipline and cohesion across 338 constituency campaigns?
7. How does the party gather information on the activities of local campaigns?
8. To what extent is it problematic if local campaigns are more concerned with their own election than the party as a whole?
9. What can the party do to sanction an uncooperative local campaign? Do you have any experience dealing with problematic campaigns or candidates?
10. Does the central party always pay greater attention to target ridings? What other factors attract party attention to a particular local campaign?
11. Do you think the central party should consider allowing greater latitude for local candidates to address local issues? Why or why not?
12. Should the central party consider allowing greater latitude for local candidates to express their personal beliefs? Why or why not?
13. Is there anything on these topics you would like to add that I haven't thought to ask you about?

Notes

1. Introduction

1 See also Mair and Katz (2002); Katz (2002).
2 On political brands, see Marland (2016). The author notes that political branding serves to evoke tangible and intangible associations that visually and conceptually differentiate political offerings from competitors, in similar fashion to corporate branding.
3 Political marketing generally refers to using business marketing techniques to inform party policy, strategy, and communications, with the goal of identifying and responding to demands of the electoral marketplace (Cwalina, Falkowski, and Newman 2011, 17; Lees-Marshment 2014; Marland, Giasson, and Esselment 2017, 231; Marland, Giasson, and Lees-Marshment 2012b, 262).
4 Research by Alex Marland and colleagues is a major exception to this tendency (see for example, Marland 2020; Marland and Snagovsky 2023).

2. Local-National Party Relations

1 For example, a president, treasurer, secretary, and so on.
2 To be sure, there is often overlap between constituency associations and campaigns. Most constituency associations maintain an election planning committee and association members often take on various campaign positions.
3 Belfry Munroe and Munroe (2018, 136) identify three research strains on local campaigns: their use of campaign resources, their relationship to the central party, and the candidate nomination process.
4 Question wording may further complicate the analysis of potential candidate effects. Blais et al. (2003) and Sevi, Mendoza, and Blais (2022) derive their analysis from the CES question, "was there a candidate in your

riding you particularly liked?" The authors classify those who respond in the negative as indifferent to the local candidate, suggesting that "just over half of Canadian voters did not really care about their local candidates" (Blais et al. 2003, 660). The authors only proceed with analysis of candidate impact on vote choice for those who respond in the affirmative. However, it is plausible that voters with no strong feelings about their local candidates were nonetheless influenced by them.

5 Since this is a relatively large proportion of the electorate, the authors caution against dismissing the significance of local candidate effects.

6 Local campaigns may also affect party performances over time, in ways that are not captured when citizens are asked to explain their vote choice. Perceptions can be influenced by the activities of local party organizations, regardless of voters' stated familiarity with local candidates and issues.

7 As of 2024, local party organizations reside within one of 338 federal constituencies.

8 Grassroots members can vote on policy resolutions at national policy conventions and leadership conventions. But the trend towards universal membership voting has diminished the power of EDAs in these venues.

9 In subsequent chapters, I introduce undisciplined behaviour as an alternative to exit or fighting for leadership change

10 For example, Carty views candidate selection as a core element of the local role, but parties now routinely intervene in this process (Pruysers and Cross 2018).

11 Carty indicates that corporate franchises must also adapt to local tastes (2002, 731), for example when McDonald's offers a lobster roll in Nova Scotia. Yet such practices are supererogatory to the operation and success of corporate franchises, which instead rely upon marketing an unvarying product upon which consumers depend (Davies et al. 2011).

12 For example, the Liberal Party has used a program called Liberalist since 2015.

13 These accounts are largely derived from campaign practitioners who adopt the central party's perspective (e.g., Brodie 2018; Flanagan 2007; Kinsella 2007; Laschinger 2016; Lavigne 2013; Sorbara 2019). Two exceptions are Thompson (2016) and Richler's (2016) firsthand accounts of their experiences as local candidates for the Liberals and NDP, respectively.

14 Some practitioners reject this view of hyper-concentrated power and emphasize constraints on the Prime Minister's Office. See for example, Brodie 2018; Goldenberg 2009.

15 Once writs of election are issued, incumbents are technically no longer the MP for their riding.

16 One limitation of Carty's franchise model is the absence of consideration for regional party branches. Regional offices perform crucial intermediate functions in linking the national office to particular regions, providing

guidance, resources, and exercising decision-making authority on behalf of the centre. Their role is addressed in Chapter 5 of the book.

17 More recent changes in the regional distribution of party support, political attitudes, and demographics have led some scholars to conclude that the country is significantly less regionalized than in previous decades (Gidengil et al. 2012, 22; Koop and Bittner 2013, 316; Marland and Wesley 2017, 387; Pruysers 2014a; Pruysers, Sayers, and Czarnecki 2020; Thorlakson and Keating, 2018, 139). Some contend that regional brokerage, which once constituted a key component of Canadian party politics, is receding in favour of micro-targeting voters based on other demographic categories such as ethnocultural background and occupation (e.g., Marland and Giasson 2017). These trends should arguably exert centripetal pressures and strengthen central party authority.

18 Corporate franchises often face challenges in maintaining organizational cohesion and commitment to shared goals, rather than particularistic goals (Davis 2004). In fact, franchises are more likely to fail than independent businesses (Watson and Everett 1996). In this respect, feelings of organizational alienation may compound the political detachment of constituency campaigns if they are combined with regional alienation. For example, some constituency-level actors interviewed for this project felt that the central party exhibits an Ontario or Quebec bias.

19 While centralized personalism refers to an emphasis on party leaders and their personalities.

3. Constituency Campaign Discipline

1 The singular pronoun "they" is used for confidentiality purposes throughout this book.

2 Patten (2017, 57) contends that Liberal Party headquarters' approach of focusing on the most promising tiers was credited with winning certain close constituency races for the party in 2015.

3 This interaction highlights two further issues in local-national party relations that are explored in Chapter 5 of this book. First, ridings are subject to uneven scrutiny from party headquarters. While the central party may prefer to visit ridings in person, this is more easily done in Toronto-area ridings, as compared to rural ridings or smaller provinces where resources are spread thin. Second, personal or professional networks constitute important but uneven linkages between select local campaigns and party offices. In this case, there was a pre-existing professional relationship between the party official and campaign manager. Chapter 5 focuses on the ability of intra-party communications to monitor and manage constituency campaigns.

4 Please see Appendix A for a complete description of research methods.

5 See Trier-Bieniek (2012) for an opposing view.

6 The physical presence of an interviewer creates greater rapport and facilitates communication of emotions and other important visual cues, the absence of which can inhibit the discussion of sensitive information (Moum 1998; Pridemore, Damphousse, and Moore 2005; Rubin and Rubin 2011; Sturges and Hanrahan 2004).

7 Ethics clearance for interviews was granted by the General Research Ethics Board (GREB) at Queen's University on 22 June 2018. Ethics clearance was granted for a second application for local campaign observation on 6 September 2019 (see Appendix A). The research conforms with Tri-Council Guidelines (TCPS 2 (2014)) and Queen's University ethics policies for research with human participants: https://ethics.gc.ca/eng/about_us -propos_de_nous.html.

8 Two constituency campaigns kept private back rooms in their offices that I was not allowed to enter, but the others did not.

9 It has also proven useful in other countries for studying the behaviour of politicians and civil servants (Bevir and Rhodes 2003; Gaddie 2004; Nielsen 2012; Wodak 2009).

10 These arguments stand in contrast to quantitative research that illustrates general tendencies across a large population of cases. While providing analytical breadth and generalizability, the aggregation process may sacrifice analytical depth and the study of causal mechanisms that serve as underlying, finer-grained explanations of the social world. As Koop, Bastedo, and Blidook summarize of their 2018 study: "the depth of description in this work would not be possible in the absence of participant observation" (34).

11 Sayers quotes Barton (1968).

12 This number is always lower than the number of votes required to win, since each candidate's total votes obtained in a constituency will always exceed the number of confirmed supporters that they are able to identify. To illustrate, even a constituency campaign with a formidable voter identification operation would not account for additional votes received from defectors from other parties, new residents to the constituency, and first-time voters.

13 As explained by local campaign managers, a social media war can develop for two primary reasons: first, if a campaign encourages its sympathizers to post continuous negative comments on opponents' social media pages, and second, when campaigns browse their opponents' social media posts to find organizations they have met with and subsequently contact these organizations to request their own meetings. For example, if the Ukrainian-Canadian Association has recently met with a Liberal candidate,

the Conservative campaign could then use this information to request a meeting of their own. To prevent these time-consuming and potentially unflattering outcomes, local campaigns generally aim to avoid escalation and maintain a state of detente in their social media.

A sign war generally refers to aggressive sign placement in areas that strategically frustrate opponents and may escalate in a tit-for-tat manner. In more extreme cases this can include damaging opponents' signs or requesting opponents' signs for people who did not order them, which is illegal but difficult to enforce.

14 Constituency campaigns sometimes have multiple campaign managers. For a technical explanation of the official agent's role, see Elections Canada 2023. The actual role of the official agent may vary from minimal practical involvement to a de facto co-campaign manager.

15 One campaign that I observed in 2019 even featured a catering coordinator to feed staff and volunteers.

16 Carty and Eagles (2005, 76) assert that "party insider" or "stop-gap" candidates usually depend on long-time party loyalists for volunteer labour. Conversely, high-profile or local notable candidates tend to draw teams of volunteers from their personal and professional networks. These terms are derived from Sayers's (1999) fourfold candidate typology, consisting of local notable, high-profile, party insider, or stopgap candidates.

17 In other words, they hoped to win their own seat, but for their party to lose. In their view, this would hopefully result in a new party leader and a majority government win in the next election.

18 The candidate, campaign managers, including temporary or de facto campaign managers, and core staff with responsibility for canvassing, finances, communications, or volunteers.

19 Unacceptable behaviours are not always specified in these campaign manuals. But they are often clear by implication.

20 The indicators represent an amalgamation of the initial eight indicators with party strategist input.

21 Responses were collected during interviews with local candidates who stood for election in 2015 ($n=87$).

22 This evidence consisted of communications with local party members, details of which cannot be disclosed for confidentiality purposes.

23 Cross-tabulations could also jeopardize confidentiality – for example, by identifying a Liberal candidate in Alberta who won their election.

24 In fact, within-province tensions often emerged during interviews. A 2015 Liberal candidate in Southwestern Ontario recalls "I sometimes felt hung out to dry because it was all about the GTA [Greater Toronto Area]." And an NDP candidate in the GTA suggests that "the party was completely

tone deaf to Toronto ... it was a write-off compared to ... Quebec and Southwestern Ontario ... [But] I ran as a champion of Toronto." Conservative MP Brad Butt also stated that his re-election chances were harmed by his party's neglect of the GTA during the campaign.

25 At times, insubordinate behaviour appears to stem from alienation or detachment from the central party. But as shown in Table 3.4, there are no major differences in undisciplined behaviour between Alberta, Ontario, and Quebec candidates, and this is largely due to within-province variation.

26 In multiple interviews, party strategists mentioned that constituency campaigns should "be smart" in their behaviour, but the implied meaning intended by such suggestions appeared to be that campaigns should follow the stated or assumed wishes of the central party.

27 Decades ago, the proliferation of television exerted a nationalizing effect on political advertising, as citizens who once received disparate radio messages across the country now viewed nationwide broadcasts through major networks (Carty 1992; Stephenson et al. 2019, 6). Conversely, digital advertising may entail denationalizing tendencies, as these advertisements are viewed by small slices of voters, often geographically targeted, and are comparatively difficult to scrutinize or even trace back to specific party actors (Bennett 2019; Patten 2017, 60).

28 See, for example, Carty 2004; Carty and Cross 2006.

29 Rather than the more conventional interpretation that the party's unpopular embrace of extending public funding for religious schools cost them the election.

4. Voter Canvassing and Campaign Literature

1 To recall, these indicators are: Ignore party instructions; Distribute unvetted material; Critique party leadership (privately); Contradict party's position; Cooperate with opposing party; Critique party leadership (publicly).

2 Technically speaking, a *voter* is someone who has voted while an *elector* is someone eligible to vote. But in common parlance, the term *voter* often refers to anyone qualified to vote. For simplicity's sake, these terms are used interchangeably throughout this chapter.

3 Research indicates the growing frequency of voter contact via mass text messages, but this impersonal form of communication does not constitute live unmediated interaction (e.g., Dale and Strauss 2009; Green and Gerber 2019; Marland 2020, 151).

4 That said, experts disagree on the effectiveness of phone canvassing. Nickerson (2006) finds that phone canvassing, if sufficiently personal and done with care, can increase turnout at similar levels to door canvassing.

5 Field organizers provide local campaigns with target goals for voter contact and identification.

6 For phone canvassing, local campaigns receive similar voter contact targets, and data can be directly uploaded into campaign software where it is visible to regional and national party officials. Some canvassers are told to stick to a script that has been developed by the party, while others are told to adjust the script in order to feel more comfortable and produce more natural-sounding interactions with voters.

7 The practice clearly stems from regional differences in political preferences (see, for example Héroux-Legault 2016). In 2015, interview subjects mentioned the Conservative government's proposal to ban the wearing of the niqab at citizenship ceremonies, the controversial antiterror legislation Bill C-51, and proposed pipeline construction, as issues of internal party divergence. These issues varied substantially in popularity by region. In 2019, message dissonance was observed surrounding the Quebec government's proposed secularism law Bill 21, Justin Trudeau's blackface makeup scandal, and Andrew Scheer's perceived social conservatism (Lebeuf 2019).

8 Conservative and NDP candidates typically rate their own political viewpoints as respectively further to the right and left than their parties (Stephenson et al. 2019, 78–9).

9 It is less clear whether local campaign message dissonance during canvassing constitutes undisciplined behaviour, specifically, if parties are wilfully blind to it. When a 2019 Liberal campaign manager was questioned about comments made by canvassers that seemed to contradict official party positions, they stated: "the party is well aware ... if you win they'll be happy." By implication, some within the party may tolerate or even encourage this practice. Whereas NDP strategist Karl Bélanger does not support this view: "politics is a team sport. To use the franchise language, McDonald's will never say we don't offer the Big Mac here because our customers don't like it."

10 Another informal rule of thumb mentioned by some candidates is that a citizen must encounter a candidate's name, party, and image several times before it makes any impression. As a Conservative candidate (2015, Alberta) explains, "When you're bombarded with so many messages in general, it takes several times to break through." A former NDP MP suggests that "seven times is how many it takes before they can recall the local candidate ... we need to get them again until it's entered their brain." And a Liberal campaign manager (2019, Ontario) explains that flyers are part of an overall strategy to occupy space in voter's minds: "it's about touches, you win elections by touching people over and over again."

11 All materials are double-sided. These sizes encompass the most commonly used size formats for the three major parties.

12 Intangible brand components such as emotional cues are not included, as these are more subjective and difficult to compare across materials.

13 "Proven Leadership for a Stronger Economy" was also a widely used slogan and is coded as a primary national slogan.

14 Slogans are derived from Perron 2015 and MacLeod 2015.

15 The size or prominence of the name and picture are not considered, as there was not enough variation in either to justify an additional coding option.

16 Some Quebec Liberal candidates referred to this aesthetic as "Time Magazine style" due to the resemblance to the popular magazine's colour backdrop.

17 The Liberals' historic strength in Quebec may also help them to more easily tailor campaign content to the Quebec market.

18 These three campaigns were quite different in their levels of competitiveness and available resources. Scott's campaign in former party leader Jack Layton's riding of Toronto–Danforth was one of the strongest NDP campaigns in the country (Sachgau 2015), while Naidoo and Brooke ran in relatively uncompetitive races.

19 Undisciplined behaviour is less visible in the final products of campaign literature than in the authorization and distribution stages. These results anticipate the lower-than-anticipated implementation of undisciplined behaviour, reported in Chapter 6 of this book, given the positive attitudes towards it and practical abilities to engage in it.

20 Anderson and Coletto (2015) convey the higher public favourability scores for Mulcair and Trudeau, relative to Harper. See also Stephenson et al. 2019, 68.

21 More generally, Kuzminski found central party responses to be problematically slow: "I did my own press releases, I did my own … interviews and I just told them to watch for them later because … by the time I got talking points on the subject it was past the time for me to submit for publication to paper or radio or television interview."

22 Not seeking party authorization is undisciplined behaviour by definition.

23 As opposed to corporate franchises, which feature substantially less variation between franchises and corporate headquarters.

5. Internal Party Communications

1 Candidate controversies can attract significant negative media attention, regardless of the competitiveness or prominence of the candidate. Gibson (2019) documents several of these controversies that occurred early in the 2019 federal election.

2 The party's ability to prevent undisciplined behaviour is addressed in greater detail in Chapters 5 and 6.

3 See also Strömbäck and Kiousis 2014.

4 Exceptions include Koop 2011; Richler 2016; Thompson 2016.

5 Strategists were asked to describe their communications with local campaigns, as well as the extent to which they prioritized gathering feedback from local campaigns and whether they recalled a specific instance where this feedback led them to change strategies or reverse a prior decision. Candidates also filled out an eight-question survey on intra-party communications integration, answered using a four-point Likert scale (strongly disagree, disagree, agree, strongly agree).

6 These scores are determined from the eight questions with Likert-scale response options in conjunction with interview data. Each campaign is classified as zero to ten. A score of zero means that a campaign responded "strongly disagree" to all eight items and confirmed this insularity through interview responses. Scores are indexed to responses on the Likert scale, with follow-up clarifications sometimes obtained in interviews. A one entails the same responses as a zero, but with a mix of disagree and strongly disagree. A two entails one "agree" or "strongly agree" along with seven "disagree" or "strongly disagree." A three entails two "agree" or "strongly agree" and six "disagree" or "strongly disagree." A four entails three "agree" or "strongly agree" and five "disagree" or "strongly disagree," and so forth.

7 District competitiveness is determined by subtracting the candidates' ultimate vote share, either in 2015 or 2019, from that of the next closest challenger (Cheng and Tavits 2011).

8 This score is based on the constituency-level margin of victory in the previous federal election, either in 2011 or 2015. For example, in the constituency of Northwest Territories in 2015, there was an eighteen-point differential between the victorious Michael McLeod (48 per cent) and the second-place finisher, Dennis Bevington (30 per cent).

9 Party assistance includes communications with regional offices. I anticipated that Quebec campaigns would be more likely to rely on regional offices as a result of language and cultural factors.

10 They also report that an MP from an opposing party was tasked with finding negative personal and professional information on several candidates in the region.

11 Several constituency campaigns spoke of volunteers covertly recruited from opposing parties to gather information, but this was the only reported instance of what was labelled by the candidate as a central party mole.

12 Organizational theory demonstrates that one-way communications often fail to elicit compliance. In corporate communications, headquarters often face difficulties in achieving franchisee support or "buy-ins" to corporate-

led initiatives. Davis (2004) argues that gaining compliance requires meaningful explanation and justification. These may be time-consuming luxuries during a campaign period.

13 In practice, local campaigns do not actually use these labels, referring instead to a variety of positions such as field manager, Toronto manager, regional supervisor, etc.

6. Local Campaign Self-Discipline

1 That said, some observers highlight weaknesses in Conservative campaign strategy, such as ineffective messaging on leader Andrew Scheer's socially conservative views and failure to capitalize on Liberal Party scandals (see for example, Boisclair 2019; Lebeuf 2019).

2 Those who respond "Yes" to behavioural indicators in column three are undisciplined candidates, whose behaviour is explained in Chapter 3 (see Table 3.3). Their behaviour is not examined in this chapter, as it seeks to explain disciplined behaviour.

3 Existing research and commentary links career incentives and strict discipline for elected politicians (e.g., Delacourt 2020; Godbout 2020). Since it appears that campaign discipline is less severe than caucus discipline, factors distinct to elected officials should account for the heightened discipline in legislatures. In other words, the deference shown by elected politicians is qualitatively distinct from campaign discipline. The comparatively weaker pull of party discipline during a campaign period helps to pinpoint career incentives and group dynamics that engender conformity as important factors for caucus discipline (see, for example Chong, Simms, and Stewart 2017, 4; Loat and MacMillan 2014; Rathgeber 2014, 104). Conversely, this book focuses on party discipline in a campaign setting, and the extent to which local actors behave consistently with party preferences.

4 Related work includes research on political ambition, as well as the behaviour of legislators. Such work tends to focus either on decisions to enter politics and career trajectories (e.g., Fox and Lawless 2005), or the motivations and incentives that exist for elected officials, particularly from their parties, constituents, and interest groups (e.g., Fouirnaies and Hall 2022). This research does not apply to those who have already chosen to enter politics, and who operate in a campaign context, rather than from an established position as an elected official or party official. Despite a wide-ranging voting behaviour literature, this research is focused on the political behaviours of ordinary citizens rather than political candidates themselves.

5 Similarly, some politicians are reluctant to speak with researchers because they fear retribution from their parties (Marland 2020, 28).

6 That said, the relatively small numbers could signify a limitation with the sample of local candidates. Those who agreed to interviews or campaign observation may be less fearful of the central party, while those who are more fearful may reject interview requests from academics or journalists. Regardless, the prevalence of this motivation is less significant than its identification as a pathway to constituency campaign self-discipline.

7 This logic exemplifies the categorical imperative, which calls to, "act only according to that maxim whereby you can at the same time will that it should become a universal law" (Kant [1785] 1994, 30).

8 Kantian optimization has been applied to environmental policy as a framework to study climate change mitigation strategies (Carattini, Levin, and Tavoni 2019; Schwerhoff et al. 2018). Grafton, Kompas, and Van Long (2017) find that environmental quality improves as the proportion of Kantian optimizers increases. The question then arises of how to stimulate Kantian behavioural logic. In terms of election campaigns, parties may face temptations to behave unethically to gain electoral advantage (Goodwin-Gill 1998). Kantian optimization could conceivably help to analyse and even mitigate these risks by explaining mechanisms that produce non-altruistic cooperative behaviour.

9 Broadly speaking, candidates who embrace undisciplined behaviour are more agential than those who do not. Those who reject undisciplined behaviour are more influenced by the logics of consequence, appropriateness, and habit.

10 The leadership dynamics within local campaigns also merit greater scrutiny. In particular, the relationship between candidates and campaign managers represents a potential area for future research. Unlike the central party apparatus, which is led by a national campaign manager, it is often unclear whether the local candidate or campaign manager is the leading or ultimate authority figure.

11 In terms of predictors of behaviour logics, I also considered four conditional variables when assessing patterns of constituency campaign discipline: party, region, riding type, and candidate experience. Region refers to Ontario, Quebec, or Alberta constituencies. Riding type refers to urban, suburban, small city, or rural. Candidate experience distinguishes incumbent MPs and those who have contested at least two prior elections from novice candidates. However, these four variables have no reliable effects on the nature and prevalence of the four behavioural logics. There is one minor exception: NDP candidates appeared to be slightly less driven by fear of consequences and the logic of habit. They were also disproportionately likely to be Kantian optimizers.

7. Conclusion

1 Intrastate federalism refers to representation for the constituent units within the federal government (Smiley and Watts 1985). Canada fares poorly in this regard, as seen for example in its politically weak upper house, lack of provincial input in Supreme Court appointments, and diminished power of regional cabinet ministers (Bakvis 1991).
2 Party switching is rare in Canadian federal politics; see for example, Sevi, Yoshinaka, and Blais 2018.
3 Similarly, organizational theory (e.g., Davis 2004) suggests that corporate headquarters can gain the support of their franchises through improved and sustained justification of their decision-making.

Appendix A. Methods

1 I selected one hundred interviews as a target that would be large enough for sample diversity and generalizability to assess differences within the group, but small enough to remain feasible for a single researcher and facilitate in-depth analyses of each interview (Kvale 2008, 48–9).
2 In all initial contact attempts, I provided minimal details on the project, in order to avoid priming responses before initiating an interview. I directed questions to the standard information letter and consent form that was provided to each interviewee. In some cases, I had to explain that interview questions could not be provided in advance, in order to maintain interview consistency.
3 Seven party officials initially replied, two party officials agreed to interviews but ultimately did not follow through and participate.
4 In all cases this proposal was accepted, although five MPs later changed their preference to a Parliament Hill interview. In four separate cases, interview subjects cancelled their in-person interviews and asked to reschedule as telephone interviews. All interviews were conducted prior to the COVID-19 pandemic.
5 See Trier-Bieniek (2012) for an opposing view.
6 For example, Pridemore, Damphousse, and Moore (2005) find greater willingness to admit to substance abuse for in-person interviews of welfare recipients. The physical presence of an interviewer creates greater rapport and facilitates communication of emotions and other important visual cues, the absence of which can inhibit the discussion of sensitive information (Moum 1998; Rubin and Rubin 2011; Sturges and Hanrahan 2004).
7 I initially aimed to include Alberta in order to examine how regional differences in campaigning compare to linguistic differences. Alberta and

Ontario are two culturally dissimilar English-speaking regions, while Quebec is French-speaking. But these linguistic and cultural differences were de-emphasized as the study progressed. They were less important than anticipated and it was more difficult to access certain French-language source materials.

8 The total number of constituencies from which the sample was derived was Ontario: ninety-four; Quebec: sixty-two; Alberta: twenty-two.

9 I did not rely on referral sampling, except for party strategist interviews.

10 A total of 34 per cent, or ninety-nine candidates, initially responded but only 30 per cent, or eighty-seven candidates, resulted in a successful interview. This response rate is consistent with Marland and Esselment's (2018a) response metric for elite interview requests with journalists, academics, and politicians.

11 Regardless of their status as current or former elected officials, all are referred to as "candidates" in this text.

12 See Brinkmann (2013, 58).

13 I sought to include a relatively equal number of local campaigns from the three major parties. I also considered the feasibility of moving between different constituencies in short periods of time.

14 For example, if they became suspicious of my presence or felt they were under scrutiny.

15 This approach differs from that of Belfry Munroe and Munroe (2018), whose research included entering local campaigns as volunteers.

16 In most cases, the campaign manager requested a phone or in-person interview prior to granting permission to observe their campaign.

Works Cited

Anderson, Bruce, and David Coletto. 2015. "Election 2015: May, Trudeau, and Mulcair Images Improve, Harper Negatives Rise." *Abacus Data*, 19 August 2015. https://abacusdata.ca/election-2015-may-trudeau-and-mulcair-images-improve-harper-negatives-rise/.

Andeweg, Rudy B., and Jacques Thomassen. 2011. "Pathways to Party Unity: Sanctions, Loyalty, Homogeneity and Division of Labour in the Dutch Parliament." *Party Politics* 17 (5): 655–72. https://doi.org/10.1177/1354068810377188.

Ansolabehere, Stephen, and Eitan Hersh. 2017. "Validation: What Big Data Reveal About Survey Misreporting and the Real Electorate." *Political Analysis* 20 (4): 437–59. https://doi.org/10.1093/pan/mps023.

Arnold, Denis Gordon, and Jared D. Harris. 2012. *Kantian Business Ethics: Critical Perspectives.* Cheltenham, UK: Edward Elgar.

Bakvis, Herman. 1991. *Regional Ministers: Power and Influence in the Canadian Cabinet.* Toronto: University of Toronto Press.

Bakvis, Herman, and Brian Tanguay. 2020. "Federalism, Political Parties, and the Burden of National Unity: Still Making Federalism Do the Heavy Lifting?" In *Canadian Federalism: Performance, Effectiveness, and Legitimacy*, 4th ed., edited by Herman Bakvis and Grace Skogstad, 138–64. Toronto: University of Toronto Press.

Balmas, Meital, Gideon Rahat, Tamir Sheafer, and Shaul R. Shenhav. 2012. "Two Routes to Personalized Politics: Centralized and Decentralized Personalization." *Party Politics* 20 (1): 37–51. https://doi.org/10.1177/1354068811436037.

Barton, Alan H. 1968. "Bringing Society Back In: Survey Research and Macro-Methodology." *The American Behavioral Scientist* 12 (2): 1–12.

Basen, Ira. 2009. "A Schlemiel Is the Elephant in the Room: The Framing of Stéphane Dion." *Canadian Journal of Communication* 34 (2): 297–305. https://doi.org/10.22230/cjc.2009v34n2a2215.

Belfry Munroe, Kaija, and H.D. Munroe. 2018. "Constituency Campaigning in the Age of Data." *Canadian Journal of Political Science* 51 (1): 135–54. https://doi.org/10.1017/S0008423917001135.

Bell, David V.J., and Frederick J. Fletcher. 1991. *Reaching the Voter: Constituency Campaigning in Canada*. Toronto: Dundurn.

Bennett, Colin J. 2019. "Data-Driven Elections in Canada: What We Might Expect in the 2019 Federal Election Campaign?" Special issue, *Journal of Parliamentary and Political Law* 2019:277–90.

Bevir, Mark, and Rod A.W. Rhodes. 2003. *Interpreting British Governance*. London: Routledge.

Bittner, Amanda. 2011. *Platform or Personality? The Role of Party Leaders in Elections*. Oxford: Oxford University Press.

Bittner, Amanda, and Royce Koop, eds. 2013.*Parties, Elections, and the Future of Canadian Politics*. Vancouver: University of British Columbia Press

Black, Jerome H. 1984. "Revisiting the Effects of Canvassing on Voting Behaviour." *Canadian Journal of Political Science* 17 (2): 351–74. https://doi.org/10.1017/S0008423900031322.

Blais, André, and Marc André Bodet. 2006. "How Do Voters Form Expectations About the Parties' Chances of Winning the Election?" *Social Science Quarterly* 87, no. 3 (September): 477–93. https://doi.org/10.1111/j.1540-6237.2006.00392.x.

Blais, André, and Jean-François Daoust. 2017. "What Do Voters Do When They Like a Local Candidate from Another Party?" *Canadian Journal of Political Science* 50 (4): 1103–9. https://doi.org/10.1017/S0008423917000609.

Blais, André, Elisabeth Gidengil, Agnieszka Dobrzynska, Neil Nevitte, and Richard Nadeau. 2003. "Does the Local Candidate Matter? Candidate Effects in the Canadian Election of 2000." *Canadian Journal of Political Science* 36 (3): 657–64. https://doi.org/10.1017/S0008423903778810.

Blais, André, and Ignacio Lago. 2009. "A General Measure of District Competitiveness." *Electoral Studies* 28, no. 1 (March): 94–100.

Blidook, Kelly. 2012. *Constituency Influence in Parliament: Countering the Centre*. Vancouver: University of British Columbia Press.

Blidook, Kelly and Royce Koop. 2019. "Observing Representation: Participant Observation with Elected Officials." In *SAGE Research Methods Cases Part 2*, edited by Luigi Curini and Robert Franzese. London: SAGE.

Bodet, Marc André. 2013. "Strongholds and Battlegrounds: Measuring Party Support Stability in Canada." *Canadian Journal of Political Science* 46 (3): 575–96. https://doi.org/10.1017/S000842391300067X.

Bøggild, Troels, and Helene Helboe Pedersen. 2018. "Campaigning on Behalf of the Party? Party Constraints on Candidate Campaign Personalisation." *European Journal of Political Research* 57, no. 4 (November): 883–99.

Boisclair, Valérie. 2019. "Andrew Scheer reconnaît qu'il est 'personnellement pro-vie.'" *Radio Canada*, 3 October 2019. https://ici.radio-canada.ca/nouvelle/1329309/avortement-debat-parti-conservateur-chef-andrew-scheer.

Bolleyer, Nicole. 2012. "New Party Organization in Western Europe: Of Party Hierarchies, Stratarchies and Federations." *Party Politics* 18 (3): 315–36. https://doi.org/10.1177/1354068810382939.

Brinkmann, Svend. 2013. *Qualitative Interviewing*. Oxford: Oxford University Press.

Brodie, Ian. 2018. *At the Centre of Government: The Prime Minister and the Limits on Political Power*. Montreal: McGill-Queen's University Press.

Brown, Steven D., Andrea M.L. Perrella, and Barry J. Kay. 2010. "Revisiting Local Campaign Effects: An Experiment Involving Literature Mail Drops in the 2007 Ontario Election." *Canadian Journal of Political Science* 43 (1): 49–67.

Busenitz, Lowell W., and Jay B. Barney. 1997. "Differences between Entrepreneurs and Managers in Large Organizations: Biases and Heuristics in Strategic Decision-Making." *Journal of Business Venturing* 12, no. 1 (January): 9–30. https://doi.org/10.1016/S0883-9026(96)00003-1.

Carattini, Stefano, Simon Levin, and Alessandro Tavoni. 2019. "Cooperation in the Climate Commons." *Review of Environmental Economics and Policy* 13, no. 2 (Summer): 227–47.

Carey, John M. 2007. "Competing Principals, Political Institutions, and Party Unity in Legislative Voting." *American Journal of Political Science* 51, no. 1 (January): 92–107. https://doi.org/10.1111/j.1540-5907.2007.00239.x.

Carty, R. Kenneth. 1991. *Canadian Political Parties in the Constituencies*. Toronto: Dundurn.

Carty, R. Kenneth. 1992. *Canadian Political Party Systems: A Reader*. Peterborough, ON: Broadview.

Carty, R. Kenneth. 2002. "The Politics of Tecumseh Corners: Canadian Political Parties as Franchise Organizations." *Canadian Journal of Political Science* 35 (4): 723–45. https://doi.org/10.1017/S0008423902778402.

Carty, R. Kenneth. 2004. "Parties as Franchise Systems: The Stratarchical Organizational Imperative." *Party Politics* 10 (1): 5–24. https://doi.org/10.1177/1354068804039118.

Carty, R. Kenneth. 2015. *Big Tent Politics: The Liberal Party's Long Mastery of Canada's Public Life*. Vancouver: University of British Columbia Press.

Carty, R. Kenneth, and William Cross. 2006. "Can Stratarchically Organized Parties be Democratic? The Canadian Case." *Journal of Elections, Public Opinion and Parties* 16 (2): 93–114. https://doi.org/10.1080/13689880600715912.

Carty, R. Kenneth, and William Cross. 2010. "Political Parties and the Practice of Brokerage Politics." In *The Oxford Handbook of Canadian Politics*, edited by John C. Courtney and David E. Smith, 191–207. New York: Oxford University Press.

Carty, R. Kenneth, William Cross, and Lisa Young. 2000. *Rebuilding Canadian Party Politics*. Vancouver: University of British Columbia Press.

Carty, R. Kenneth, and Munroe Eagles. 2000. "Is There a Local Dimension to Modern Election Campaigns? Party Activists' Perceptions of the Media and Electoral Coverage of Canadian Constituency Politics." *Political Communication* 17 (3): 279–94. https://doi.org/10.1080/105846000414287.

Carty, R. Kenneth, and Munroe Eagles. 2005. *Politics Is Local: National Politics at the Grassroots*. Toronto: Oxford University Press.

Carty, R. Kenneth, and Lisa Young. 2012. "The Local Underpinnings of Electoral Competition in Canada, 1979–2008." *Canadian Political Science Review* 6 (2–3): 227–36. https://doi.org/10.24124/c677/2012306.

Castonguay, Alec. 2011. "Thomas Mulcair: l'homme fort d'Outremont," *L'actualité*, 19 May 2011. https://lactualite.com/politique/thomas-mulcair -lhomme-fort-doutremont/.

Cheng, Christine, and Margit Tavits. 2011. "Informal Influences in Selecting Female Political Candidates." *Political Research Quarterly* 64, no. 2 (June): 460–71. https://doi.org/10.1177/1065912909349631.

Chiru, Mihail. 2018. "Exploring the Role of Decentralized Personalization for Legislative Behaviour and Constituency Representation." In Cross, Katz, Pruysers 2018, 143–61. London: ECPR.

Chong, Michael, Scott Simms, and Kennedy Stewart, eds. 2017. *Turning Parliament Inside Out: Practical Ideas for Reforming Canada's Democracy*. Madeira Park, BC: Douglas and McIntyre.

Clarkson, Stephen. 2014. *The Big Red Machine: How the Liberal Party Dominates Canadian Politics*. Vancouver: University of British Columbia Press.

Clegg, Stewart, Martin Kornberger, and Carl Rhodes. 2007. "Business Ethics as Practice." *British Journal of Management* 18, no. 2 (June): 107–22. https://doi .org/10.1111/j.1467-8551.2006.00493.x.

Coletto, David. 2010. "A Matter of Quality? Candidates in Canadian Constituency Elections." PhD diss., University of Calgary.

Coletto, David, Harold J. Jansen, and Lisa Young. 2011. "Stratarchical Party Organization and Party Finance in Canada." *Canadian Journal of Political Science* 44 (1): 111–36. https://doi.org/10.1017/S0008423910001034.

Cormack, Patricia. 2012. "Double Double: Branding, Tim Hortons, and the Public Sphere." In Marland, Giasson, and Lees-Marshment 2012b, 209–23.

Cosgrove, Kenneth M. 2007. *Branded Conservatives: How the Brand Brought the Right from the Fringes to the Center of American Politics*. New York: Peter Lang.

Cosgrove, Kenneth M. 2012. "Political Branding in the Modern Age: Effective Strategies, Tools and Techniques." In *Routledge Handbook of Political Marketing*, edited by Jennifer Lees-Marshment, 107–23. New York: Routledge.

Craft, Jonathan. 2017. *Backrooms and Beyond: Partisan Advisers and the Politics of Policy Work in Canada*. Toronto: University of Toronto Press.

Cross, William. 2002. "The Increasing Importance of Region to Canadian Election Campaigns." In *Regionalism and Party Politics in Canada*, edited by Lisa Young and Keith Archer. Toronto: Oxford University Press.

Cross, William. 2004. *Political Parties*. Vancouver: University of British Columbia Press.

Cross, William. 2006. "Candidate Nomination in Canada's Political Parties." In *The Canadian General Election of 2006*, edited by Jon H. Pammett and Christopher Dornan, 171–95. Toronto: Dundurn Publishing.

Cross, William. 2016. "The Importance of Local Party Activity in Understanding Canadian Politics: Winning from the Ground Up in the 2015 Federal Election." *Canadian Journal of Political Science* 49 (4): 601–20. https://doi.org/10.1017/S0008423916000962.

Cross, William. 2018. "Understanding Power-Sharing Within Political Parties: Stratarchy as Mutual Interdependence between the Party in the Centre and the Party on the Ground." *Government and Opposition* 53 (2): 205–30. https://doi.org/10.1017/gov.2016.22.

Cross, William, Rob Currie-Wood, and Scott Pruysers. 2020. "Money Talks: Decentralized Personalism and the Sources of Campaign Funding." *Political Geography* 82 (October): 102242.

Cross, William, Richard S. Katz, and Scott Pruysers, eds. 2018. *The Personalization of Democratic Politics and the Challenge for Political Parties*. London: ECPR.

Cross, William, Jonathan Malloy, Tamara A. Small, and Laura B. Stephenson. 2015. *Fighting for Votes: Parties, the Media, and Voters in an Ontario Election*. Vancouver: University of British Columbia Press.

Cross, William, and Scott Pruysers. 2019. "Sore Losers? The Costs of Intra-party Democracy." Party Politics 25 (4): 483–94.

Cross, William, Scott Pruysers, and Rob Currie-Wood. 2022. *The Political Party in Canada*. Vancouver: University of British Columbia Press.

Cross, William, and Lisa Young. 2013. "Candidate Recruitment in Canada: The Role of Political Parties." In Bittner and Koop 2013, 24–45.

Cross, William, and Lisa Young. 2015. "Personalization of Campaigns in an SMP System: The Canadian Case." *Electoral Studies* 39 (September): 306–15. https://doi.org/10.1016/j.electstud.2014.04.007.

Currie-Wood, Rob. 2020. "The National Growth of a Regional Party: Evidence of Linkages between Constituency Associations in the Conservative Party of Canada." *Canadian Journal of Political Science* 53 (3): 618–37. https://doi.org/10.1017/S0008423920000360.

Cutler, Fred. 2002. "Local Economies, Local Policy Impacts and Federal Electoral Behaviour in Canada." *Canadian Journal of Political Science* 35 (2): 347–82. https://doi.org/10.1017/S000842390277827X.

Cwalina, Wojciech, Andrzej Falkowski, and Bruce I. Newman. 2011. *Political Marketing: Theoretical and Strategic Foundations*. London: Routledge.

Dale, Allison, and Aaron Strauss. 2009. "Don't Forget to Vote: Text Message Reminders as a Mobilization Tool." *American Journal of Political Science* 53, no. 4 (October): 787–804. https://doi.org/10.1111/j.1540-5907.2009.00401.x.

Datts, Mario, and Katharina Gerl. 2023. "Intra-Party Communication in the Digital Era – An Empirical Case Study of Party Delegates from the German Greens." *German Politics* 33 (1): 155–77. https://doi.org/10.1080/09644008 .2023.2168649.

Davies, Mark A.P., Walfried Lassar, Chris Manolis, Melvin Prince, and Robert D. Winsor. 2011. "A Model of Trust and Compliance in Franchise Relationships." *Journal of Business Venturing* 26, no. 3 (May): 321–40. https://doi.org/10.1016/j.jbusvent.2009.09.005.

Davis, Paul J. 2004. "Effective Communication Strategies in a Franchise Organization." *Corporate Communications: An International Journal* 9 (4): 276–82.

Delacourt, Susan. 2016. *Shopping for Votes: How Politicians Choose Us and We Choose Them*, 2nd ed. Toronto: Douglas & McIntyre.

Delacourt, Susan. 2020. "Attention, New MPs: Don't Be Robots." *Toronto Star*, 22 January. https://www.thestar.com/politics/political-opinion/attention-new -mps-don-t-be-robots/article_06db7063-89cc-518f-aa6d-0fb71368e22a.html.

Dempsey, James. 2015. "Moral Responsibility, Shared Values, and Corporate Culture." *Business Ethics Quarterly* 25 (3): 319–40. https://doi.org/10.1017 /beq.2015.31.

DeWalt, Kathleen M., Billie R. DeWalt, and Coral B. Wayland. 1998. "Participant Observation." In *Handbook of Methods in Cultural Anthropology*, edited by H. Russell Bernard and Clarence C. Gravlee, 251–92. Walnut Creek, CA: AltaMira Press.

DiCicco-Bloom, Barbara, and Benjamin F. Crabtree. 2006. "The Qualitative Research Interview." *Medical Education* 40, no. 4 (April): 314–21. https://doi .org/10.1111/j.1365-2929.2006.02418.x. Medline:16573666.

Docherty, David C. 2005. *Legislatures*. Vancouver: University of British Columbia Press.

Eagles, Munroe, and Annika Hagley. 2010. "Constituency Campaigning in Canada." In MacIvor 2010, 109–34.

Elections Canada. 2023. "Transcript of Video on Becoming an Official Agent." 31 October 2023. https://www.elections.ca/content.aspx?section=pol&dir=tra /fin/can/co18&document=trans&lang=e.

Esselment, Anna. 2012. "Market Orientation in a Minority Government." In Marland, Giasson, and Lees-Marshment 2012b, 123–38.

Esselment, Anna, and Paul Wilson. 2017. "Campaigning from the Centre." In Marland, Giasson, and Esselment 2017, 222–40.

Esser, Frank, and Jesper Strömbäck. 2012. "Comparing Election Campaign Communication." In *Handbook of Comparative Communication Research*, edited by Frank Esser and Thomas Hanitzsch, 289–307. New York: Routledge.

Farney, James, and Royce Koop. 2017. "The Conservative Party in Opposition and in Government." In *The Blueprint: Conservative Parties and Their Impact on Canadian Politics*, edited by J.P. Lewis and Joanna Everitt, 25–45. Toronto: University of Toronto Press.

Farney, James, and Royce Koop. 2018. "Auditing Party Democracy: The Case of Canadian Party Constituency Associations." *Comparative and Commonwealth Politics* 56 (1): 84–102. https://doi.org/10.1080/14662043.2017.1371939.

Fenno, Richard F. 1990. *Watching Politicians: Essays on Participant Observation*. Berkeley, CA: Institute of Governmental Studies Press.

Fenno, Richard F. 1998. *Senators on the Campaign Trail: The Politics of Representation*. Norman: University of Oklahoma Press.

Fielding, Nigel G. 2012. "Triangulation and Mixed Methods Designs: Data Integration with New Research Technologies." *Journal of Mixed Methods Research* 6 (2): 124–36. https://doi.org/10.1177/1558689812437101.

Flanagan, Tom. 2007. *Harper's Team: Behind the Scenes in the Conservative Rise to Power*. Montreal: McGill-Queen's University Press.

Flanagan, Tom. 2010. "Campaign Strategy: Triage and the Concentration of Resources." In MacIvor 2010, 155–72.

Flanagan, Tom. 2013. "Something Blue: The Harper Conservatives as Garrison Party." In *Conservatism in Canada*, edited by James H. Farney and David Rayside, 79–94. Toronto: University of Toronto Press.

Flanagan, Tom. 2014. *Winning Power: Canadian Campaigning in the Twenty-First Century*. Montreal: McGill-Queens University Press.

Flyvbjerg, Bent. 2006. "Five Misunderstandings About Case-Study Research." *Qualitative Inquiry* 12 (2): 219–45. https://doi.org/10.1177/1077800405284363.

Fouirnaies, Alexander, and Andrew B. Hall. 2022. "How Do Electoral Incentives Affect Legislator Behavior? Evidence from US State Legislatures." *American Political Science Review* 116 (2): 662–76.

Fox, Colm A. 2018. "Is All Politics Local? Determinants of Local and National Election Campaigns." *Comparative Political Studies* 51 (14): 1899–934. https://doi.org/10.1177/0010414018774354.

Fox, Richard L., and Jennifer L. Lawless. 2005. "To Run or Not to Run for Office: Explaining Nascent Political Ambition." *American Journal of Political Science* 49, no. 3 (July): 642–59.

Gaddie, Ronald K. 2004. *Born to Run: Origins of the Political Career*. Lanham, MD: Rowman & Littlefield.

Gerber, Alan S., and Donald P. Green. 2000. "The Effects of Canvassing, Telephone Calls, and Direct Mail on Voter Turnout: A Field Experiment." *American Political Science Review* 94 (3): 653–63. https://doi.org/10.2307/2585837.

Gerber, Alan S., Donald P. Green, and Matthew N. Green. 2003. "Partisan Mail and Voter Turnout: Results from Randomized Field Experiments." *Electoral Studies* 22, no. 4 (December): 563–79. https://doi.org/10.1016/S0261-3794(02)00029-X.

Gerber, Linda M. 2006. "The Visible Minority, Immigrant, and Bilingual Composition of Ridings and Party Support in the Canadian Federal Election of 2004." *Canadian Ethnic Studies Journal* 38, no. 1 (Spring): 65–82.

Gibson, Victoria. 2019. "Who's No Longer in the Running? The Candidates Who've Resigned or Been Turfed so Far." *iPolitics*, 18 September 2018. https://www.ipolitics.ca/news/whos-no-longer-in-the-running-the-candidates-whove-resigned-or-been-turfed-so-far.

Gidengil, Elisabeth, André Blais, Richard Nadeau, and Neil Nevitte. 1999. "Making Sense of Regional Voting in the 1997 Canadian Federal Election: Liberal and Reform Support Outside Quebec." *Canadian Journal of Political Science* 32 (2): 247–72. https://doi.org/10.1017/S0008423900010489.

Gidengil, Elisabeth, André Blais, Neil Nevitte, and Richard Nadeau. 2004. *Citizens*. Vancouver: University of British Columbia Press.

Gidengil, Elisabeth, Neil Nevitte, André Blais, Joanna Everitt, and Patrick Fournier. 2012. *Dominance and Decline: Making Sense of Recent Canadian Elections*. Toronto: University of Toronto Press.

Gillespie, Andra, and Melissa R. Michelson. 2011. "Participant Observation and the Political Scientist: Possibilities, Priorities, and Practicalities." *PS: Political Science & Politics* 44 (2): 261–5. https://doi.org/10.1017/S1049096511000096.

Gillies, Jamie, Vincent Raynauld, and André Turcotte. 2023.*Political Marketing in the 2021 Canadian Federal Election*. Cham, Switzerland: Palgrave Macmillan.

Gillies, Jamie, and Angela Wisniewski. 2023. "Clowns to the Left of Me, Jokers to the Right: Branding Challenges in the 2021 Conservative Party Campaign." In Gillies, Raynauld, and Turcotte 2023, 25–39.

Godbout, Jean-François. 2020. *Lost on Division: Party Unity in the Canadian Parliament*. Toronto: University of Toronto Press.

Goldenberg, Eddie. 2009. *The Way It Works: Inside Ottawa*. Ottawa: Douglas Gibson Books.

Goodwin-Gill, Guy. 1998. *Codes of Conduct for Elections*. Geneva: Inter-Parliamentary Union.

Goodyear-Grant, Elizabeth. 2013. *Gendered News: Media Coverage and Electoral Politics in Canada*. Vancouver: University of British Columbia Press.

Grafton, R. Quentin, Tom Kompas, and Ngo Van Long. 2017. "A Brave New World? Kantian–Nashian Interaction and the Dynamics of Global Climate Change Mitigation." *European Economic Review* 99 (October): 31–42.

Green, Donald P., and Alan S. Gerber. 2001. "Getting out the youth vote: Results from randomized field experiments." Report to the Pew Charitable Trusts, Institution for Social and Policy Studies.

Green, Donald P., and Alan S. Gerber. 2019. *Get Out the Vote: How to Increase Voter Turnout*, 4th ed. Washington, DC: Brookings Institution Press.

Green, Donald P., Alan S. Gerber, and David W. Nickerson. 2003. "Getting Out the Vote in Local Elections: Results from Six Door-to-Door Canvassing Experiments." *Journal of Politics* 65, no. 4 (November): 1083–96. https://doi.org/10.1111/1468-2508.t01-1-00126.

Guzmán, Francisco, and Vicenta Sierra. 2009. "A Political Candidate's Brand Image Scale: Are Political Candidates Brands?" *Journal of Brand Management* 17: 207–17. https://doi.org/10.1057/bm.2009.19.

Hallahan, Kirk, Derina Holtzhausen, Betteke van Ruler, Dejan Verčič, and Krishnamurthy Sriramesh. 2007. "Defining Strategic Communication." *International Journal of Strategic Communication* 1 (1): 3–35. https://doi.org/10.1080/15531180701285244.

Henderson, Ailsa. 2004. "Regional Political Cultures in Canada." *Canadian Journal of Political Science* 37 (3): 595–615.

Héroux-Legault, Maxime. 2016. "Substate Variations in Political Values in Canada." *Regional & Federal Studies* 26 (2): 171–97. https://doi.org/10.1080/13597566.2016.1161612.

Hodgkinson, Gerard P., and Eugene Sadler-Smith. 2018. "The Dynamics of Intuition and Analysis in Managerial and Organizational Decision Making." *Academy of Management Perspectives* 32 (4): 473–92. https://doi.org/10.5465/amp.2016.0140.

Holbrook, Allyson L., Melanie C. Green, and Jon A. Krosnick. 2003. "Telephone versus Face-to-Face Interviewing of National Probability Samples with Long Questionnaires: Comparisons of Respondent Satisficing and Social Desirability Response Bias." *Public Opinion Quarterly* 67, no. 1 (March): 79–125. https://doi.org/10.1086/346010.

Jeffrey, Brooke. 2017. "The Liberal Party of Canada: Rebuilding, Resurgence, and Return to Power." In *Canadian Parties in Transition: Recent Trends and New Paths to Research*, 4th ed., edited by Alain G. Gagnon and Brian Tanguay, 127–45. Toronto: University of Toronto Press.

Jones, Robert G. 2020. *The Applied Psychology of Sustainability*. New York: Routledge.

Kaid, Lynda Lee. 2012. "Political Advertising as Political Marketing: A Retro-Forward Perspective." *Journal of Political Marketing* 11 (1–2): 29–53. https://doi.org/10.1080/15377857.2012.642731.

Kam, Christopher J. 2009. *Party Discipline and Parliamentary Politics*. Cambridge: Cambridge University Press.

Kam, Christopher J. 2014. "Party Discipline." In *The Oxford Handbook of Legislative Studies*, edited by Shane Martin, Thomas Saalfeld, Kaare Strøm, 399–417. Oxford: Oxford University Press.

Kant, Emmanuel. (1785) 1994. *Ethical Philosophy*, 2nd ed. Translated by James Ellington. Indianapolis: Hackett.

Kara, Helen. 2015. *Creative Research Methods in the Social Sciences: A Practical Guide*. Bristol, UK: Policy Press.

Katz, Richard S. 2002. "The Internal Life of Parties." In *Political Parties in the New Europe: Political and Analytical Challenges*, edited by Kurt Richard Luther and Ferdinand Müller-Rommel, 87–118. New York: Oxford University Press.

Katz, Richard S., and Peter Mair. 1993. "The Evolution of Party Organizations in Europe: The Three Faces of Party Organization." *American Review of Politics* 14 (Winter): 593–617. https://doi.org/10.15763/issn.2374-7781.1993.14.0.593-617.

Kawulich, Barbara B. 2005. "Participant Observation as a Data Collection Method." *Forum: Qualitative Social Research* 6 (2): Art. 43. https://doi.org/10.17169/fqs-6.2.466.

Kendall, Chad, and Marie Rekkas. 2012. "Incumbency Advantages in the Canadian Parliament." *Canadian Journal of Economics* 45, no. 4 (November): 1560–85. https://doi.org/10.1111/j.1540-5982.2012.01739.x.

King, Karen N. 2002. "The Art of Impression Management: Self-Presentation in Local-Level Campaign Literature." *The Social Science Journal* 39 (1): 31–41. https://doi.org/10.1016/S0362-3319(01)00177-X.

Kinsella, Warren. 2007. *The War Room: Political Strategies for Business, NGOs, and Anyone Who Wants to Win*. Toronto: Dundurn.

Koop, Royce. 2011. *Grassroots Liberals: Organizing for Local and National Politics*. Vancouver: University of British Columbia Press.

Koop, Royce. 2015. "Constituency Campaigning in the 2015 Federal Election." In *Canadian Election Analysis 2015: Communication, Strategy, and Democracy*, edited by Alex Marland and Thierry Giasson, 42–3. Vancouver: University of British Columbia Press.

Koop, Royce, Heather Bastedo, and Kelly Blidook. 2018. *Representation in Action: Canadian MPs in the Constituencies*. Vancouver: University of British Columbia Press.

Koop, Royce, and Amanda Bittner. 2011. "Parachuted into Parliament: Candidate Nomination, Appointed Candidates, and Legislative Roles in Canada." *Journal of Elections, Public Opinion and Parties* 21 (4): 431–52. https://doi.org/10.1080/17457289.2011.609297.

Koop, Royce, and Amanda Bittner. 2013. "Parties and Elections After 2011: The Fifth Canadian Party System?" In Bittner and Koop 2013.

Krosnick, Jon A. 1999. "Survey Research." *Annual Review of Psychology* 50:537–67.

Kvale, Steinar. 2008. *Doing Interviews*. London: SAGE.

Laschinger, John. 2016. *Campaign Confessions: Tales from the War Rooms of Politics*. Toronto: Dundurn.

Lavigne, Brad. 2013. *Building the Orange Wave: The Inside Story Behind the Historic Rise of Jack Layton and the NDP*. Toronto: Douglas and McIntyre.

Lawler, Edward J., and Samuel Bacharach. 1983. "Political Action and Alignments in Organizations." In *Research in the Sociology of Organizations, Vol. 2*, edited by Samuel Bacharach, 83–107. Greenwich, CT: JAI Press.

Lebeuf, Sophie-Hélène. 2019. " Avortement: confusion et flou chez les conservateurs," *Radio Canada*, 27 August 2019. https://ici.radio-canada .ca/nouvelle/1276846/avortement-andrew-scheer-alain-rayes-parti -conservateur-lieutenant-quebec.

Lees-Marshment, Jennifer. 2014. *Political Marketing: Principles and Applications*, 2nd ed. London: Routledge.

Lees-Marshment, Jennifer. 2021. "The New (Old) Trudeau in 2019: The Challenges and Potential for Branding Prime Ministers in Government." In *Political Marketing in the 2019 Canadian Election*, edited by Jamie Gillies, Vincent Raynauld, and André Turcotte, 11–26. London: Palgrave Macmillan.

Lees-Marshment, Jennifer, and Salma Malik. 2023. "Political Branding in a Crisis and the Shifting Strategies of the Trudeau 2021 Campaign." In Gillies, Raynauld, and Turcotte 2023, 9–23.

Lilleker, Darren G. 2005. "Local Campaign Management: Winning Votes or Wasting Resources?" *Journal of Marketing Management* 21 (9–10): 979–1003. https://doi.org/10.1362/026725705775194166.

Lilleker, Darren G. 2006. *Key Concepts in Political Communication*. London: SAGE.

Liu, Yan, Krista J. Li, Haipeng (Allan) Chen, and Subramanian Balachander. 2017. "The Effects of Products' Aesthetic Design on Demand and Marketing-Mix Effectiveness: The Role of Segment Prototypicality and Brand Consistency." *Journal of Marketing* 81 (1): 83–102. https://doi .org/10.1509/jm.15.0315.

Loat, Allison, and Michael MacMillan. 2014. *Tragedy in the Commons: Former Members of Parliament Speak Out About Canada's Failing Democracy*. Toronto: Random House.

Loosveldt, Geert, and Vicky Storms. 2008. "Measuring Public Opinions About Surveys." *International Journal of Public Opinion Research* 20, no. 1 (Spring): 74–89. https://doi.org/10.1093/ijpor/edn006.

MacIvor, Heather, ed. 2010.*Election*. Toronto: Emond Montgomery.

Mair, Peter. 1994. "Party Organizations: From Civil Society to the State." In *How Parties Organize: Change and Adaptation in Party Organizations in Western Democracies*, edited by Richard S. Katz and Peter Mair, 1–22. London: SAGE.

Mair, Peter, and Richard S. Katz. 2002. "The Ascendancy of the Party in Public Office: Party Organizational Change in Twentieth-Century Democracies." In *Political Parties: Old Concepts and New Challenges*, edited by Richard Gunther, José Ramón Montero, and Juan J. Linz, 113–36. Oxford: Oxford University Press.

Malloy, Jonathan. 2003. "High Discipline, Low Cohesion? The Uncertain Patterns of Canadian Parliamentary Party Groups." *The Journal of Legislative Studies* 9 (4): 116–29. https://doi.org/10.1080/1357233042000306290.

March, James G., Erhard Friedberg, and David Arellano. 2011. "Institutions and Organizations: Differences and Linkages from Organization Theory" *Gestión y política pública* 20 (2): 235–46.

March, James G., and Johan P. Olsen. 1989. *Rediscovering Institutions: The Organizational Basis of Politics*. New York: Free Press.

March, James G., and Johan P. Olsen. 1998. "The Institutional Dynamics of International Political Orders." *International Organization* 52 (4): 943–69. https://doi.org/10.1162/002081898550699.

March, James G., and Johan P. Olsen. 2011. "The Logic of Appropriateness." In *The Oxford Handbook of Political Science*, edited by Robert E. Goodin, 478–97. Oxford: Oxford University Press.

March, James G., and Herbert Simon. (1958) 1993. *Organizations*. New York: Wiley.

March, James G., and Herbert A. Simon. 1993. "Organizations Revisited." *Industrial and Corporate Change* 2 (3): 299–316. https://doi.org/10.1093/icc/2.3.299.

Marland, Alex. 2016. *Brand Command: Canadian Politics and Democracy in the Age of Message Control*. Vancouver: University of British Columbia Press.

Marland, Alex. 2020. *Whipped: Party Discipline in Canada*. Vancouver: University of British Columbia Press.

Marland, Alex. 2021. "Vetting of Election Candidates by Political Parties: Centralization of Candidate Selection in Canada." *American Review of Canadian Studies* 51 (4): 573–91. https://doi.org/10.1080/02722011.2021.1986558.

Marland, Alex, and Anna Lennox Esselment. 2018a. "Negotiating with Gatekeepers to Get Interviews with Politicians: Qualitative Research Recruitment in a Digital Media Environment." *Qualitative Research* 19 (6): 685–702. https://doi.org/10.1177/1468794118803022.

Marland, Alex, and Anna Lennox Esselment. 2018b. "Tips and Tactics for Securing Interviews with Political Elites." In *Political Elites in Canada: Power and Influence in Instantaneous Times*, edited by Alex Marland, Thierry Giasson, and Andrea Lawlor, 29–50. Vancouver: University of British Columbia Press.

Marland, Alex, Anna Lennox Esselment, and Thierry Giasson. 2017. "Welcome to Non-Stop Campaigning." In Marland, Giasson, and Esselment 2017, 3–27.

Marland, Alex, and Thierry Giasson. 2017. "From Brokerage to Boutique Politics: Political Marketing and the Changing Nature of Party Politics in Canada." In *Canadian Parties in Transition: Recent Trends and New Paths to Research*, 4th ed., edited by Alain G. Gagnon and Brian Tanguay, 343–63. Toronto: University of Toronto Press.

Marland, Alex, and Thierry Giasson. 2022. *Inside the Local Campaign: Constituency Elections in Canada*. Vancouver: University of British Columbia Press Press.

Marland, Alex, Thierry Giasson, and Anna Lennox Esselment, eds. 2017. *Permanent Campaigning in Canada*. Vancouver: University of British Columbia Press.

Marland, Alex, Thierry Giasson, and Jennifer Lees-Marshment. 2012a. "Introducing Political Marketing." In Marland, Giasson, and Lees-Marshment 2012, 3–21.

Marland, Alex, Thierry Giasson, and Jennifer Lees-Marshment, eds. 2012b. *Political Marketing in Canada*. Vancouver: University of British Columbia Press.

Marland, Alex, Thierry Giasson, and Tamara A. Small, eds. 2014. *Political Communication in Canada: Meet the Press and Tweet the Rest*. Vancouver: University of British Columbia Press.

Marland Alex, and Fedor Snagovsky. 2023. "Representation and Partisanship: What Determines the Topics That Members of Parliament Prioritize in Communications with Their Constituents?" *Canadian Journal of Political Science* 56 (4): 848–70. https://doi.org/10.1017/S0008423923000641.

Marland, Alex, and Angelia Wagner. 2020. "Scripted Messengers: How Party Discipline and Branding Turn Election Candidates and Legislators into Brand Ambassadors." *Journal of Political Marketing* 19 (1–2): 54–73. https://doi.org/10.1080/15377857.2019.1658022.

Marland, Alex, and Jared Wesley. 2017. "Surveying the Canadian State: Evolution of Canadian Political Science, Politics, and Government Since 1967." *Canadian Journal of Political Science* 50 (1): 377–93. https://doi.org/10.1017/S000842391600113X.

McGrane, David. 2019. *The New NDP: Moderation, Modernization, and Political Marketing*. Vancouver: University of British Columbia Press.

McLean, James S. 2012. *Inside the NDP War Room: Competing for Credibility in a Federal Election*. Montreal: McGill-Queen's University Press.

Meisel, John. 1963. "The Stalled Omnibus: Canadian Parties in the 1960s." *Social Science Research* 30, no. 3 (Autumn): 367–90.

Merolla, Jennifer L., Laura B. Stephenson, and Elizabeth J. Zechmeister. 2008. "Can Canadians Take a Hint? The (In)Effectiveness of Party Labels as Information Shortcuts in Canada." *Canadian Journal of Political Science* 41, no. 3 (September): 673–96.

Mikecz, Robert. 2012. "Interviewing Elites: Addressing Methodological Issues." *Qualitative Inquiry* 18 (6): 482–93. https://doi.org/10.1177/1077800412442818.

Miller, Roy E., and William M. Richey. 1980. "The Effects of a Campaign Brochure 'Drop' in a County-Level Race for State's Attorney." *Annals of the International Communication Association* 4, no. 1 (December): 483–95. https://doi.org/10.1080/23808985.1980.11923820.

Milligan, Kevin, and Marie Rekkas. 2008. "Campaign Spending Limits, Incumbent Spending, and Election Outcomes." *Canadian Journal of Economics* 41 (4): 1351–74. https://doi.org/10.1111/j.1540-5982.2008.00507.x.

Morden, Michael. 2020. *Real House Lives: Former Members of Parliament on How to Reclaim Democratic Leadership*. Victoria, BC: Friesen Press.

Moum, Torbjørn. 1998. "Mode of Administration and Interviewer Effects in Self-Reported Symptoms of Anxiety and Depression." *Social Indicators Research* 45:279–318. https://doi.org/10.1023/A:1006958100504.

Nickerson, David W. 2006. "Volunteer Phone Calls Can Increase Turnout: Evidence from Eight Field Experiments." *American Politics Research* 34 (3): 271–92. https://doi.org/10.1177/1532673X05275923.

Nielsen, Rasmus Kleis. 2012. *Ground Wars: Personalized Communication in Political Campaigns*. Princeton, NJ: Princeton University Press.

Noël, Christian, and Louis Blouin. 2019. "Justin Trudeau en 'blackface': une controverse, deux solitudes?" *Radio Canada*, 19 September 2019. https://ici .radio-canada.ca/nouvelle/1308899/justin-trudeau-brownface-blackface -controverse-solitudes-reactions-ontario-quebec.

Omar, Maktoba, Robert L. Williams, and David Lingelbach. 2009. "Global Brand Market-Entry Strategy to Manage Corporate Reputation." *Journal of Product and Brand Management* 18 (3):177–87. https://doi.org/10.1108 /10610420910957807.

Ostrom, Elinor. 1990. *Governing the Commons: The Evolution of Institutions for Collective Action*. Cambridge: Cambridge University Press.

Ostrom, Elinor. 1998. "A Behavioral Approach to the Rational Choice Theory of Collective Action" *American Political Science Review* 92 (1): 1–22. https:// doi.org/10.2307/2585925.

Patten, Steve. 2017. "Databases, Microtargeting, and the Permanent Campaign: A Threat to Democracy?" In Marland, Giasson and Esselment 2017, 47–66.

Perron, Louis-Samuel. 2015. "Les slogans électoraux décortiqués." *La presse*, 31 August 2015. Accessed 2019.

Pich, Christopher, Dianne Dean, and Khanyapuss Punjaisri. 2016. "Political Brand Identity: An Examination of the Complexities of Conservative Brand and Internal Market Engagement During the 2010 UK General Election Campaign." *Journal of Marketing Communications* 22 (1): 100–17. https://doi .org/10.1080/13527266.2013.864321.

Pimlott, Herbert. 2011. "'Eternal Ephemera' or the Durability of 'Disposable Literature': The Power and Persistence of Print in an Electronic World." *Media, Culture & Society* 33 (4): 515–30. https://doi.org/10.1177 /0163443711398690.

Plummer, Joseph T. 1984–5. "How Personality Makes a Difference." *Journal of Advertising Research* 24 (6): 27–31.

Porter, Patrick. 2018. "Why America's Grand Strategy Has Not Changed: Power, Habit, and the US Foreign Policy Establishment." *International Security* 42 (4): 9–46. https://doi.org/10.1162/isec_a_00311.

Pow, James T. 2018. "Amateurs versus Professionals: Explaining the Political (in)Experience of Canadian Members of Parliament." *Parliamentary Affairs* 71, no. 3 (July): 633–55. https://doi.org/10.1093/pa/gsx082.

Pridemore, William Alex, Kelly R. Damphousse, and Rebecca K. Moore. 2005. "Obtaining Sensitive Information from a Wary Population: A Comparison of Telephone and Face-to-Face Surveys of Welfare Recipients in the United States." *Social Science & Medicine* 61, no. 5 (September): 976–84. https://doi.org/10.1016/j.socscimed.2005.01.006. Medline:15955399.

Pruysers, Scott. 2014a. "Canadian Party Politics in the 2000s: A Re-examination of the Regionalization Thesis." *Canadian Political Science Review* 8 (1): 27–42. https://doi.org/10.24124/c677/2014500.

Pruysers, Scott. 2014b. "Reconsidering Vertical Integration: An Examination of National Political Parties and Their Counterparts in Ontario." *Canadian Journal of Political Science* 47 (2): 237–58. https://doi.org/10.1017/S0008423914000407.

Pruysers, Scott, and Julie Blais. 2018. "A Little Encouragement Goes a (not so) Long Way: An Experiment to Increase Political Ambition." *Journal of Women, Politics & Policy* 39 (3): 384–95. https://doi.org/10.1080/1554477X.2018.1475793.

Pruysers, Scott, and William Cross. 2016. "Candidate Selection in Canada: Local Autonomy, Centralization, and Competing Democratic Norms." *American Behavioral Scientist* 60 (7): 781–98. https://doi.org/10.1177/0002764216632820.

Pruysers, Scott, and William Cross. 2018. "Personalism and Election Campaigning: National and Local Dynamics." In Cross, Katz, Pruysers 2018, 57–78.

Pruysers, Scott, Anthony Sayers, and Lucas Czarnecki. 2020. "Nationalization and Regionalization in the Canadian Party System, 1867–2015." *Canadian Journal of Political Science* 53 (1): 151–69. https://doi.org/10.1017/S0008423919000957.

Rathgeber, Brent. 2014. *Irresponsible Government: The Decline of Parliamentary Democracy in Canada.* Toronto: Dundurn.

Reeves, Peter. 2013. "Local Political Marketing in the Context of the Conservative Party." *Journal of Nonprofit & Public Sector Marketing* 25 (2): 127–63. https://doi.org/10.1080/10495142.2013.760990.

Richler, Noah. 2016. *The Candidate: Fear and Loathing on the Campaign Trail.* Toronto: Doubleday.

Robbins-Kanter, Jacob. 2022a. "Undisciplined Constituency Campaign Behaviour in Canadian Federal Elections," *Canadian Journal of Political Science* 55(2): 444–66. https://doi.org/10.1017/S0008423922000282.

Robbins-Kanter, Jacob. 2022b. "Voter Canvassing." In Marland and Giasson 2022, 226–44.

Robson, Paul J.A., and Dennis Tourish. 2005. "Managing Internal Communication: An Organizational Case Study." *Corporate Communications: An International Journal* 10 (3): 213–22. https://doi.org/10.1108/13563280510614474.

Roemer, John E. 2015. "Kantian Optimization: A Microfoundation for Cooperation." *Journal of Public Economics* 127 (July): 45–57. https://doi.org/10.1016/j.jpubeco.2014.03.011.

Rossman, Gretchen B., and Sharon F. Rallis. 2017. *An Introduction to Qualitative Research: Learning in the Field*, 4th ed. London: SAGE.

Roy, Jason, and Christopher Alcantara. 2015. "The Candidate Effect: Does the Local Candidate Matter?" *Journal of Elections, Public Opinion and Parties* 25 (2): 195–214. https://doi.org/10.1080/17457289.2014.925461.

Rubin, Herbert J., and Irene S. Rubin. 2011. *Qualitative Interviewing: The Art of Hearing Data*. Thousand Oaks, CA: SAGE.

Sachgau, Oliver, 2015. "Liberal Takes Toronto-Danforth from NDP," *Toronto Star*, 20 October 2015. https://www.thestar.com/politics/federal-elections/liberal-takes-toronto-danforth-from-ndp/article_d2018b51-fb88-5aee-ab0e-f5f4e46a3574.html.

Savoie, Donald J. 2019. *Democracy in Canada: The Disintegration of Our Institutions*. Montreal: McGill-Queen's University Press.

Sayers, Anthony M. 1999. *Parties, Candidates, and Constituency Campaigns in Canadian Elections*. Vancouver: University of British Columbia Press.

Scammell, Margaret. 2015. "Politics and Image: The Conceptual Value of Branding." *Journal of Political Marketing* 14 (1–2): 7–18. https://doi.org/10.1080/15377857.2014.990829.

Schmidt, Christiane. 2004. "The Analysis of Semi-Structured Interviews." In *A Companion to Qualitative Research*, edited by Uwe Flick, Ernst von Kardoff, and Ines Steinke, 253–59. London: SAGE.

Schwerhoff, Gregor, Ulrike Kornek, Kai Lessmann, and Michael Pahle. 2018. "Leadership in Climate Change Mitigation: Consequences and Incentives." *Journal of Economic Surveys* 32, no. 2 (April): 491–517. https://doi.org/10.1111/joes.12203.

Searing, Donald. 1994. *Westminster's World: Understanding Political Roles*. Cambridge, MA: Harvard University Press.

Seitz, Sally. 2016. "Pixilated Partnerships, Overcoming Obstacles in Qualitative Interviews via Skype: A Research Note." *Qualitative Research* 16 (2): 229–35. https://doi.org/10.1177/1468794115577011.

Sevi, Semra, Marco Mendoza Aviña, and André Blais. 2022. "Reassessing Local Candidate Effects." *Canadian Journal of Political Science* 55 (2): 480–5. https://doi.org/10.1017/S000842392200004X.

Sevi, Semra, Antoine Yoshinaka, and André Blais. 2018. "Legislative Party Switching and the Changing Nature of the Canadian Party System, 1867–2015." *Canadian Journal of Political Science* 51 (3): 665–95. https://doi.org/10.1017/S0008423918000203.

Shuy, Roger W. 2002. "In-Person versus Telephone Interviewing." in *Handbook of Interview Research: Context and Method*, edited by Jaber F. Gubrium and James A. Holstien, 537–56. Thousand Oaks, CA: SAGE.

Sieberer, Ulrich. 2006. "Party Unity in Parliamentary Democracies: A Comparative Analysis." *The Journal of Legislative Studies* 12 (2): 150–78. https://doi.org/10.1080/13572330600739413.

Simeon, Richard. (1972) 2006. *Federal-Provincial Diplomacy: The Making of Recent Policy in Canada*. Toronto: University of Toronto Press.

Smiley, Donald V., and Ronald L. Watts. 1985. *Intrastate Federalism in Canada*. Toronto: University of Toronto Press.

Smith, David E. 2007. *The People's House of Commons: Theories of Democracy in Contention*. Toronto: University of Toronto Press.

Smith, Gareth, and Alan French. 2009. "The Political Brand: A Consumer Perspective." *Marketing Theory* 9 (2): 209–26. https://doi.org/10.1177/1470593109103068.

Sorbara, Patricia. 2019. *Let 'Em Howl: Lessons from a Life in Backroom Politics*. Gibsons, BC: Nightwood Editions.

Soroka, Stuart, Marc André Bodet, Lori Young, and Blake Andrew. 2009. "Campaign News and Vote Intentions." *Journal of Elections, Public Opinion and Parties* 19(4): 359–76. https://doi.org/10.1080/17457280903275030.

Spradley, James P. 1980. *Participant Observation*. Long Grove, IL: Waveland Press.

Stephenson, Laura Beth, Andrea Lawlor, William P. Cross, André Blais, and Elisabeth Gidengil. 2019. *Provincial Battles, National Prize? Elections in a Federal State*. Montreal: McGill-Queen's Press.

Stevens, Benjamin Allen, Md Mujahedul Islam, Roosmarijn de Geus, Jonah Goldberg, John R. McAndrews, Alex Mierke-Zatwarnicki, Peter John Loewen, and Daniel Rubenson. 2019. "Local Candidate Effects in Canadian Elections." *Canadian Journal of Political Science* 52 (1): 83–96. https://doi.org/10.1017/S0008423918000367.

Stockemer, Daniel, and Aksel Sundstrom. 2023. "The Gender Gap in Voter Turnout: An Artefact of Men's Over-Reporting in Survey Research? *The British Journal of Politics and International Relations* 25 (1): 21–41. https://doi.org/10.1177/13691481211036850.

Strömbäck, Jesper. 2007. "Political Marketing and Professionalized Campaigning: A Conceptual Analysis." *Journal of Political Marketing* 6 (2–3): 49–67. https://doi.org/10.1300/J199v06n02_04.

Strömbäck, Jesper, and Spiro Kiousis. 2014. "Strategic Political Communication in Election Campaigns." In *Political Communication*, edited by Carsten Reinemann, 109–28. Berlin: De Gruyter Mouton.

Sturges, Judith E., and Kathleen J. Hanrahan. 2004. "Comparing Telephone and Face-to-Face Qualitative Interviewing: A Research Note." *Qualitative Research* 4 (1): 107–18. https://doi.org/10.1177/1468794104041110.

Tavits, Margit. 2009. "The Making of Mavericks: Local Loyalties and Party Defection." *Comparative Political Studies* 42 (6): 793–815. https://doi.org/10.1177/0010414008329900.

Tessier, Charles, and Alexandre Blanchet. 2018. "Ballot Order in Cueless Elections: A Comparison of Municipal and Provincial Elections in Québec." *Canadian Journal of Political Science* 51 (1): 83–102. https://doi.org/10.1017/S0008423917000701.

Thompson, Allan. 2016. "Mounting a Local Campaign." In *The Canadian Federal Election of 2015*, edited by Jon Pammett and Christopher Dornan. Toronto: Dundurn.

Thorlakson, Lori, and Michael Keating. 2018. "Party Systems and Party Competition." In *Constitutional Politics and the Territorial Question in Canada and the United Kingdom: Federalism and Devolution Compared*, edited by Michael Keating and Guy Laforest, 135–58. New York: Palgrave.

Trier-Bieniek, Adrienne. 2012. "Framing the Telephone Interview as a Participant-centred Tool for Qualitative Research: A Methodological Discussion." *Qualitative Research* 12 (6): 630–44.

Uldam, Julie, and Patrick McCurdy. 2013. "Studying Social Movements: Challenges and Opportunities for Participant Observation." *Sociology Compass* 7, no. 11 (November): 941–51. https://doi.org/10.1111/soc4.12081.

Van Long, Ngo. 2017. "Mixed-Strategy Kant-Nash Equilibrium and Private Contributions to a Public Good." In *The Theory of Externalities and Public Goods*, edited by Wolfgang Buchholz and Dirk Rübbelke, 107–26. Cham, Switzerland: Springer.

Vastel, Marie. 2019. "Singh et Scheer embêtés par la Loi sur la laïcité." *Le Devoir*, 9 October 2019. https://www.ledevoir.com/plan-de-site/semaine/2019/10/2.

Veloutsou, Cleopatra, and Luiz Moutinho. 2009. "Brand Relationships Through Brand Reputation and Brand Tribalism." *Journal of Business Research* 62, no. 3 (2009): 314–22. https://doi.org/10.1016/j.jbusres.2008.05.010.

Verbos, Amy Klemm, Joseph A. Gerard, Paul R. Forshey, Charles S. Harding, and Janice S. Miller. 2007. "The Positive Ethical Organization: Enacting a Living Code of Ethics and Ethical Organizational Identity." *Journal of Business Ethics* 76:17–33. https://doi.org/10.1007/s10551-006-9275-2.

Vigoda, Eran. 2001. "Reactions to Organizational Politics: A Cross-Cultural Examination in Israel and Britain." *Human Relations* 54 (11): 1483–518. https://doi.org/10.1177/00187267015411004.

Walgrave, Stefaan, and Jeroen K. Joly. 2018. "Surveying Individual Political Elites: A Comparative Three-Country Study." *Quality & Quantity* 52:2221–37. https://doi.org/10.1007/s11135-017-0658-5.

Wang, Jinjun, and Ying Yan. 2012. "The Interview Question" In *The SAGE Handbook of Interview Research: The Complexity of the Craft*, edited by Jaber F. Gubrium, James A. Holstein, Amir B. Marvasti, and Karyn D. McKinney, 231–42. London: SAGE.

Warburton, Rebecca N., and William P. Warburton. 2004. "Canada Needs Better Data for Evidence-Based Policy: Inconsistencies between Administrative and Survey Data on Welfare Dependence and Education." *Canadian Public Policy* 30, no. 3 (September): 241–55. https://doi.org/10.2307/3552301.

Watson, John, and Jim E. Everett. 1996. "Do Small Businesses Have High Failure Rates?" *Journal of Small Business Management* 34, no. 4 October): 45–62.

Weber, J. Mark, Shirli Kopelman, and David M. Messick. 2004. "A Conceptual Review of Decision Making in Social Dilemmas: Applying a Logic of Appropriateness." *Personality and Social Psychology Review* 8 (3): 281–307. https://doi.org/10.1207/s15327957pspr0803_4. Medline:15454350.

Weick, Karl E. 1995. *Sensemaking in Organizations*, vol. 3. Thousand Oaks, CA: SAGE.

Welch, Mary, and Paul R. Jackson. 2007. "Rethinking Internal Communication: A Stakeholder Approach." *Corporate Communications: An International Journal* 12 (2): 177–98. https://doi.org/10.1108/13563280710744847.

Wesley, Jared, and Michael Moyes. 2014. "Selling Social Democracy: Branding the Political Left in Canada." In Marland, Giasson, and Small 2014, 74–91.

Westlake, Daniel. 2022. "Ready or Not? The Strength of NDP Riding Associations and the Rise and Fall of the NDP." *Canadian Journal of Political Science* 55 (2): 418–43. https://doi.org/10.1017/S0008423922000014.

Westwood, Sean J., Justin Grimmer, Matthew Tyler, and Clayton Nall. 2022. "Current Research Overstates American Support for Political Violence." *Proceedings of the National Academy of Sciences* 119 (12): e2116870119. https://doi.org/10.1073/pnas.2116870119.

White, Graham. 2012. "The 'Centre' of the Democratic Deficit: Power and Influence in Canadian Political Executives." In *Imperfect Democracies: The Democratic Deficit in Canada and the United States*, edited by Patti Tamara Lenard and Richard Simeon, 226–47. Vancouver: University of British Columbia Press.

Wodak, Ruth. 2009. *The Discourse of Politics in Action: Politics as Usual*. London: Palgrave Macmillan.

Yanow, Dvora, and Peregrine Schwartz-Shea. 2012. *Interpretation and Method: Empirical Research Methods and the Interpretive Turn*. New York: Routledge.

Yates, Stephanie. 2022 "National-Local Messaging." In Marland and Giasson 2022.

Zittel, Thomas. 2015. "Constituency Candidates in Comparative Perspective – How Personalized Are Constituency Campaigns, Why, and Does It Matter?" *Electoral Studies* 39 (September): 286–94. https://doi.org/10.1016/j.electstud.2014.04.005.

Zittel, Thomas, and Thomas Gschwend. 2008. "Individualised Constituency Campaigns in Mixed-Member Electoral Systems: Candidates in the 2005 German Elections." *West European Politics* 31 (5): 978–1003.

Index